Neo-Authoritarian Masculinity in Brazilian Crime Film

Reframing Media, Technology, and Culture in Latin/o America

NEO-AUTHORITARIAN MASCULINITY IN BRAZILIAN CRIME FILM

JEREMY LEHNEN

University of Florida Press

Gainesville

Publication of this work is made possible by a Sustaining the Humanities through the American Rescue Plan grant from the National Endowment for the Humanities.

First cloth printing, 2022
First paperback printing, 2025

30 29 28 27 26 25   6 5 4 3 2 1

Library of Congress Cataloging-in-Publication Data
Names: Lehnen, Jeremy, author.
Title: Neo-authoritarian masculinity in Brazilian crime film / Jeremy
   Lehnen.
Other titles: Reframing Media, Technology, and Culture in Latin/o America.
Description: Gainesville : University of Florida Press, 2022. | Series:
   Reframing media, technology, and culture in Latin/o America | Includes
   bibliographical references and index.
Identifiers: LCCN 2021031886 (print) | LCCN 2021031887 (ebook) | ISBN
   9781683402541 (hardback) | ISBN 9781683402787 (pdf) |
   ISBN 9781683405436 (pbk.)
Subjects: LCSH: Masculinity in motion pictures. | Authoritarianism in
   motion pictures. | Crime films—Brazil—History and criticism. | Motion
   pictures—Social aspects—Brazil. | BISAC: PERFORMING ARTS / Film /
   Genres / Crime | SOCIAL SCIENCE / Media Studies
Classification: LCC PN1995.9.M34 L44 2022 (print) | LCC PN1995.9.M34
   (ebook) | DDC 791.43/653—dc23
LC record available at https://lccn.loc.gov/2021031886
LC ebook record available at https://lccn.loc.gov/2021031887

University of Florida Press
2046 NE Waldo Road
Suite 2100
Gainesville, FL 32609
http://upress.ufl.edu

UF PRESS

UNIVERSITY
OF FLORIDA

GPSR EU Authorized Representative: Mare Nostrum Group B.V., Mauritskade 21D, 1091
GC Amsterdam, The Netherlands, gpsr@mare-nostrum.co.uk

Leila, you make all things possible.

CONTENTS

FIGURES

ACKNOWLEDGMENTS

This book would never have been possible without a robust community of friends, scholars, and artists who have accompanied me along the way, pushing me to think, inviting me to participate, and supporting me in ways that are the backbone of this project, my research, my life. I would like to thank my mother, Therrie, without whom I would not have survived to write this. To the rest of my family (Wendy, Clint, Casey, and Natalie): I may be the first to write a book, but the story of our lives is what made this possible. I would like to thank Arno Carlos Lehnen for the countless films and texts he has searched for and sent to me. I would like to extend my heartfelt gratitude to Maricarmen Zorrilla Medianero and family (La Niña Maricarmen, Francis, Carlos, Salva, Andrés). They welcomed me into their hearts so many years ago and changed the trajectory of my life. I would also like to thank Walter Putnam, a mentor and friend who has guided me through the academic maze with his calm spirit, critical sense, deep humanity, and generous friendship. I thank Laura Bass and Claude Goldstein, whose friendship and warmth have grounded us and made Providence our home.

I also want to acknowledge my robust community at Brown that has welcomed us with open arms and their unending support: James Green, Janet Blume, Patrícia Sobral, Luiz Valente, Suzanne Stewart-Steinberg. I would also like to give a shout-out to the UNM community for their years of support and friendship: Ronda Brulotte, Amy Brandzel, Liz Hutchison, Diana Rebolledo, Eleuterio Santiago-Diaz. In addition, I want to recognize the web of Brazilianists with whom we weave our work: Kathryn Bishop-Sánchez, Rebecca Atencio, Emanuelle Oliveira, Anderson da Mata, Ricky Santos, Marguerite Harrison, Rex Nielson, Severino de Albuquerque, Regina Dalcastagnè and the Grupo Estudos de Literatura Brasileira Contemporânea, Steve Manteigão Butterman, Jaime Ginsburg, and Benito Schmidt. Finally, I also want to thank the many friends I have met along the way: Todd Ruecker, Fran de Alba, Fábio Cerneviva, Alberto Prieto-Calixto, Cathy Jrade, Marion Whalen, and to thank those in memoriam with whom I wish I could share this moment, Fernando Arenas, David William Foster, Betty Wolf, Tara Yeck, and Bill Hume. I would like to thank my editor, Stephanye Hunter, for her patience and guidance, as well as my manuscript's anonymous reviewers, whose incisive comments significantly strengthened this study.

I can only end by expressing my deeply felt thanks to my spouse and soul mate, Leila, without whom none of this would ever have been possible. Your sharp tongue, barbed wit, thirst to learn, ever-inquisitive gaze, unending support, and love have guided me to where I am and inspire me for where we will go.

Introduction

Neo-Authoritarian Masculinity in the New Millennium

Since early 2014, when I sat down to write a draft proposal for this book, much has changed in Brazil and Latin America. At that time, I held hope in the wave of female presidents coming to power in the Americas: Michelle Bachelet in Chile (2006–2010 and 2014–2017), Cristina Fernández de Kirchner in Argentina (2007–2015), and Dilma Rousseff in Brazil (2011–2016).[1] They were part of a surge of women assuming powerful positions in Latin America in the political, economic, and social spheres.

Concurrently, the LGBTQIA+ movement was making significant social and legal advances in the Americas. In Brazil, São Paulo's Gay Pride Parade had grown from 1997 to such a degree that since 2006 it has retained the title for the world's largest gay pride parade.[2] In 2011 the Supreme Court of Brazil recognized stable homoaffective unions as "family entities and decreed that they should enjoy the same rights as stable heteroaffective unions." In 2013 Brazil's National Council of Justice adopted resolution 175, which denies authorities the ability to "refuse a license, civil wedding celebrations, or conversion of a stable union into a marriage of the same sex." These shifts were all part of what Larry Rohter termed the Latin American "pink tide," a wave of social democracy and the resurgence of a new Left, all holding significant promise for a profound shift in gender and power relations across South America.[3]

In Brazil the resurgence of the Left has its roots in the 1985 transition to democratic rule. The political regime change ushered in an expansion of citizen's rights, initially with the passing of the 1988 Citizen Constitution and the subsequent consolidation of democratic rule in the country. Political scientists Peter Kingstone and Timothy Power, in the introduction to their edited volume of 2000, *Democratic Brazil*, hold that formal democracy had been cemented in Brazil by 2000 but had not advanced in a substantive manner. This disjuncture between formal and substantive rights is important. Closer examination reveals that although the 1988 Constitution succeeded in creating the legal framework for implementing a system of formal rights, Brazil has continued to operate according to an entrenched system of differentiated rights. Ideally, the constitutional rights promise individual liberty and project the possibility of a renewed public ambit (Dagnino 549–51). However, this expansion was premised on a free and open public arena.

Following the transition, public space in Brazil increasingly became less secure and more lawless. As a result, there was an overall reduction in public sociability, especially between individuals of different socioeconomic groups (Caldeira and Holston 695). This stalled progress affected the lived realities of Brazilians, particularly those from the lower classes who were exposed to a more violent public arena. Concomitantly, many individuals from the upper echelons of society abandoned the public domain in favor of private spaces such as guarded high-rise condominiums, gated communities, private transportation, and secured shopping malls. This segregation created a situation in which individuals of diverse socioeconomic strata were experiencing democracy differently, what Holston and Caldeira both have termed a "disjunctive democracy" (Caldeira 339; Holston *Insurgent Citizenship*, 309–14).

Within democratic systems, there are three primary areas of rights: political, civil, and social (Marshall).[4] Respectively, they are synonymous with membership in the polity, access to juridical procedures and process (claims to and protection of one's rights), and the right to economic security and social welfare. Brazil is a political democracy that theoretically guarantees all citizens these rights. Social science literature generally agrees that political rights were consolidated in Brazil by 2000. While social rights were legitimated, they were not applied equally (Kingstone and Power *Democratic Brazil*). Regarding civil rights, the democratic transition did not usher in a period of profound respect for these entitlements or for the law (Caldeira 339). Instead, violations of civil rights rose through both civilian and state violence.

In 2008, Kingstone and Power's follow-up tome *Democratic Brazil Revisited* was published. In contrast to their first edited volume on the state of democracy in Brazil, *Revisited* affirms that Brazil had shown a marked expansion of substantive democratic breadth and depth between 2000 and 2008. The extension of democracy in Brazil had pulled new constituencies—women, Afro-Brazilians, Indigenous groups, and peripheral communities—into the struggle for recognition of formal and now substantive rights. The consolidation of political rights through formal democratic reforms permitted these groups to focus their efforts on the expansion of social and civil rights. Such efforts imply increased competition for the benefits that accompany the expansion of rights and the "democratization of expectations" (Buarque de Hollanda 179). Society's elites saw the emergence of these new constituencies and their claims to expanded rights and power as threatening the privileges they traditionally held almost exclusively. Here I am not referring solely to access to material goods, notably since the distribution of wealth in Brazil remained unequal despite the progress made in these other formal arenas. Instead, new groups began to challenge society's ideological structures. For example, concepts of rights, justice, equality, and even democracy itself became terrains of contestation and competition (Holston "Citizenship in Disjunctive Democracies," 82–83).

The challenges that emerged at the turn of the century in Brazil are visible in the explosion of contestatory voices and spaces within Brazilian society, particularly in the areas of education and culture. The first quota system in university admissions guaranteeing racial and ethnic minorities positions within higher education started at the Universidade do Estado do Rio de Janeiro (State University of Rio de Janeiro) in 2001, the Universidade do Estado da Bahia (State University of Bahia) in 2002, the Universidade de Brasília (University of Brasília) in 2004, and nationally in 2012. In 2003, law 10.639 passed and then morphed in 2008 into law 11.645, guaranteeing Afro-Brazilians the right to recognition through self-identification as part of national culture. This legislation led to the inclusion of Afro-Brazilian culture as part of the mandatory national public-school curriculum. These measures reflect the ongoing struggles of minorities to be recognized as an integral part not only of Brazilian society but also of its culture. In the process, said minorities have challenged traditional assumptions of what constitutes national culture.

Another example would be representatives of *cultura marginal* (marginal culture) who began expanding their claims to increased recognition and acceptance within the cultural realm at the turn of the century. In music, in 1997, Racionais MC's released their foundational album *Sobrevivendo no inferno,* which was ranked as the 14th best Brazilian album of all times by *Rolling Stone* magazine in November 2007 (Preto). Rapper and political activist MV Bill released *Traficando informação* in 2000. The album included the infamous "Soldado do morro," a music video that embroiled the rapper in a legal battle with the city because he refused to hand over to police the names of the hooded, armed youth who appear in the video. In literature, Paulo Lins's *Cidade de Deus* in 1997 and Reginaldo Ferreira da Silva Ferréz's *Capão pecado* in 2000 were groundbreaking works that challenged literary standards of content and style.

In three *atos* (acts) in special issues of the magazine *Caros Amigos* dedicated to *literatura marginal* (2001, 2002, and 2004), Ferréz also reclaims the Portuguese term *marginal* from its pejorative status in Brazil's dominant society. *Marginal* in Brazil is used colloquially as a pejorative reference imbued with socioeconomic and racial implications along the lines of "thug" or "hoodlum."[5] *Saraus,* local cultural events that incorporate poetry, music, literary readings, and performances, have grown to prominence as sites of peripheral culture and social exchange. Sérgio Vaz founded the *sarau* Cooperifa in the bar Zé Batidão in the peripheral neighborhood of Jardim Guarujá in São Paulo in 2001, and it has grown to be one of the largest and most renowned in the country. More recently, slam poetry has taken to Brazilian streets, from the informal gatherings of youth at the Praça Roosevelt in São Paulo to the Slam das Minas in Ceilândia, Brasília, to literary festivals such as the Festa Literária das Periferias (FLUP) that Ecio Salles and Julio Ludemir idealized and began in Rio de Janeiro in 2012. The shifting political landscape spawned all of these movements and held out the promise of a widespread democratic movement across Brazil.

Returning to Kingstone and Power's first two volumes, the consolidation of formal democracy in Brazil at the turn of the century in part explains the precipitous growth of peripheral voices in the twenty-first century. Only after formal democracy was firmly established did a space open that permitted the expansion of rights and democratic ideals into fields beyond the strictly political realm. However, democracy is not unidimensional in the development of rights. The expansion of democratic rights has also occasioned a backlash (Holston *Insurgent Citizenship*). In contemporary Brazil, as peripheral artists were pushing the boundaries of rights in and through their production, other forces were driving back, ideologically promoting a status quo agenda aimed at undermining the advances of the pink wave. These works reflect what many scholars (da Matta; Chauí; Machado da Silva; Moritz Schwarcz) have identified as an authoritarian strand in Brazilian society, politics, and culture.

The sociologist Roberto da Matta, especially in his 1979 book *Carnavais, malandros e heróis,* has exposed this authoritarian thread that undergirds the everyday practices of Brazilian life. Da Matta points to authoritarian structures that guide fundamental personal interactions. He finds that common adages such as the question "Sabe com quem está falando?" ("Do you know who you are talking to?") exemplify the hierarchical system sociolinguistically at a micro level. Such sayings reify social relations that privilege an authoritarian position many times assumed by men and seen as foundational to their construction of masculinity and masculine relations. Da Matta also finds that at the macro level, national celebrations such as *carnaval* momentarily invert social hierarchies as temporary pressure valves that ultimately also serve to reaffirm the status quo of the social power structure.[6]

Marilena Chauí links these everyday practices to the country's colonial history, arguing that authoritarianism is not a political system that afflicts Brazilian society through the periodic imposition of dictatorial regimes but rather a social system that sporadically reveals itself through more evident manifestations within the political realm. The most prominent upheaval would be the 1964–1985 dictatorship (Chauí 94). From this assertion, Chauí plots the multiple forms authoritarianism takes in contemporary democratic Brazil: unequal access to rights, naturalized inequalities, private relations based on obedience, public relations of patronage, police repression, consumerism as a mark of distinction (in the sense of Bourdieu), unequal pay, poverty, and socioeconomic exclusion (Chauí 94–98).[7] Juremir Machado da Silva demonstrates how this authoritarian conjecture has historically relied on racialized discourses to propagate a conservative ideology to the white elites within the country. And Lilia Moritz Schwarcz unravels Brazil's dominant narrative that projects a façade of tolerance but is underscored by the country's legacy of slavery and heritage of exclusion and control evident in Brazilian authoritarianism.

Within the political realm, events of the second decade of the twenty-first century have very clearly exposed the authoritarian vein that runs through the nation. During Dilma's 2010 and 2014 election campaigns and the subsequent buildup to her impeachment proceedings, demonstrations by middle- and upper-class protesters called for the return of the military dictatorship. Their discourses nostalgically recalled an almost mythical time of peace and security. Preceding Michel Temer's assumption of the presidency on August 31, 2016, the authoritarian vein in the country began to flow more openly. Various current and retired military officers openly called for military intervention within the political sphere of the country. General Luiz Eduardo Rocha Paiva wrote an opinion piece published in the *Estadão/Estado de São Paulo* on October 5, 2017, seeking to justify such an intervention. Weeks earlier, on September 15, General Antônio Hamilton

Martins Mourão did not mince words when he attacked the political class and claimed that an intervention would be constitutional, in a speech he gave at the Loja Maçônica Grande Oriente (Masonic Grand Lodge) in Brasília. Five months later, Mourão retired from active duty, joined the conservative Partido Renovador Trabalhista Brasileiro (PRTB, Brazilian Labor Renewal Party), and ultimately assumed the nation's vice presidency. Mourão aligned himself with the politician and former military officer Jair Bolsonaro. Bolsonaro was elected president of Brazil on October 28, 2018, and assumed the presidency on January 1, 2019. During his campaign and after taking office, the far-right politician Bolsonaro has repeatedly expressed openly hostile political views toward the LGBTQIA+ community, women, and immigrants; he has promoted an end to affirmative action programs and fancies himself the Trump of the Tropics. In part, Bolsonaro is the culmination, over several decades, of the growing presence of the BBB congressional coalition, the Bancada da Bala, da Bíblia e do Boi (Bullet, Bible, and Bull coalition). These groups have assumed an ever more authoritarian stance.[8]

The bullet proponents in the BBB coalition held up public security as their flag, taking a hard-line approach to street crime and criminal violence particularly in the face of movements such as the 2005 referendum on the prohibition of the commercialization of arms sales and subsequent gun control movements. The Bible advocates in the coalition led demonstrations in which they laced their discourses with homophobic rhetoric opposed to LGBTQIA+ rights and the Supreme Court's pro-LGBTQIA+ decisions. The bull faction of the BBB coalition, a political bloc of rural landowners, has fought against any policies that limit agribusiness, protect the environment, or redistribute land rights to Indigenous or landless groups. To promote their political agendas, each of these groups has built platforms that rely on the authoritarian thread that Machado da Silva, Moritz Schwarcz, Chauí, and da Matta all argue is woven into the fabric of Brazilian society.

Concretely, following the impeachment of Dilma, Brazilian society experienced regressive political change that directly undermined the country's democratic principles. A few of these reactionary policies had profound effects on the C, D, and E classes of the population:[9]

- The Ministry of Education and Culture eliminated sections of the Base Nacional Comum Curricular (National Common Core Curriculum) that specified that students must respect others' sexual orientation. The ministry suppressed all references to the terms "gênero" (gender) and "orientação sexual" (sexual orientation) in the broader document. With these actions, the government effectively eliminated recognition of the LGBTQIA+ community and reimposed its members' closeting within primary education.

- LGBTQIA+ concerns were removed from the purview of the Ministry of Human Rights, and the entire Ministry of Human Rights was collapsed into the newly formed Ministry of Women, Family, and Human Rights headed by the conservative evangelical pastor Damares Alves.

- The Fundação Nacional do Índio (FUNAI, National Indian Foundation) was placed under the Ministry of Agriculture, effectively limiting FUNAI's ability to delineate Indigenous territories, which have been under siege in a general land grab by illegal groups. Indigenous leaders and communities have been directly affected by increasing levels of violence as land prospectors invade their territories with lethal force.

- New rules were put in place through the Ministry of Mining and Energy to loosen regulations that limit mining and extraction on Indigenous lands.

- Eased restrictions on gun ownership have been imposed through presidential decrees.

- Bolsonaro and his government have continuously promoted a tough-on-crime stance within the federal government that has essentially given state police carte blanche to employ lethal force. As a result, police killings in Brazil rose by 20% in 2018, according to the Instituto de Segurança Pública (Institute for Public Security) (cited in "World Report 2020" 83). And while crime rates dropped with the outbreak of Covid-19 in 2020, police killings continued to climb, according to Human Rights Watch ("World Report 2020").

These regressive policies challenge the foundations of democratic governance. Following almost two and a half years of Michel Temer's presidency, at the time of Bolsonaro's election, Brazil was one of the Latin American countries with the lowest rates of democratic support. Only 34% of the population supported a democratic system, and 41% were indifferent to the type of regime that runs the government, according to Latinobarómetro

(*Informe 2018*). Even more astoundingly, in less than ten years, Brazil went from 49% of the population being satisfied with democracy to only 9% in 2018 (*Informe 2018*). The writer Sacolinha confronts the decline of democracy through his public art project with the graffiti poem "Estado de exceção": "Ontem escrevi sobre pipa e bolinha de gude / Hoje, sobre uma democracia ameaçada / E amanhã? Será que terei mãos para escrever?" ("State of Exception": "Yesterday, I wrote about kites and marbles / Today, about a threatened democracy / And tomorrow? Will I have hands to write?").[10]

The (neo)authoritarian strand has also surged in the realm of culture, particularly since the turn of the millennium. It is particularly evident in the street-crime dramas focused on men that have proliferated in Brazilian cinema. In 2002, *Cidade de Deus* (*City of God*, directed by Fernando Meirelles and Kátia Lund) received resounding acclaim nationally and internationally. It was the first of five crime films centered on virile male protagonists to represent Brazil at the Academy Awards in the first decade of the twenty-first century. In subsequent years, similar feature films represented the country as Brazil's submissions to the Oscars: 2003, *Carandiru* (Héctor Babenco); 2008, *Última parada 174* (*Last Stop 174*, Bruno Barreto); 2009, *Salve geral* (*Time of Fear*, Sérgio Rezende); and 2011, *Tropa de Elite II: O inimigo agora é outro* (*Elite Squad: The Enemy Within*, José Padilha). These Oscar submissions show that crime films, especially those with virile male protagonists, were among Brazil's most significant export products during the first decade of the twenty-first century. Nationally, Padilha's *Tropa de Elite* held the record for the highest-grossing box-office hit in 2007 and the dubious record as the most successful bootleg copies to hit the streets of Brazil. *Tropa de Elite* garnered more than ten million national viewers in the three months after a bootleg copy was leaked to the pirate film market and before the actual official film release date, according to the Brazilian Instituto Brasileiro de Opinião Pública e Estatística (IBOPE, Institute of Public Opinion and Statistics). *Tropa de Elite II* ticket sales surpassed those of the original film, and in the year of its release, 2010, it held the record for the highest-grossing national box-office hit to date.[11] These examples underscore Brazilian film as part of a sociocultural landscape in which tales that intertwine male violence, crime, and homosocial relations have resonated with a broad audience, the same one that lived through the political and social changes of the previous two decades. When one surveys the corpus of Brazilian crime films from the early twenty-first century, what is notable is that they are projecting a particularly virile construction of neo-authoritarian men and masculinity onto the silver screen.

In this book I analyze paradigmatic Brazilian crime films through a cultural studies framework. I focus on the representation of gender, particularly masculinities, and gender's intersection with contemporary sociopolitical issues. More specifically, the lens of masculinity reveals how contemporary Brazilian street-crime films promote a sociopolitical agenda rooted in the (re)assertion of the neo-authoritarian male.

Methodologically, I privilege gender studies as well as qualitative sociological and political science literature, to position the cinematic works within their theoretical and material frames of reference. Close textual readings of film form tease out how form influences content and how both aspects of the visual works reference and dialogue with sociopolitical and historical circumstances. These tools permit the reader to understand how representations of masculinity in contemporary Brazilian crime films affect and contribute to hegemonic society's perception of who is responsible for crime, what risks crime poses to the everyday lives of individuals, and how society should respond to criminal violence.

Discussions of the effects of media violence (in this case, crime film), particularly in conjunction with masculinity, have traditionally led to comparisons between the frequency of violence on screen and the rate of its occurrence within society. These statistics are then used to condone or condemn representations of violence on screen (Anderson and Bushman; J. Funk et al.). Such debates are increasingly important when we consider the ever-growing presence of visual culture in our daily lives. As the screen becomes a central means of social representation and interaction, there has been a progressive substitution of experiential real-world encounters with mediated on-screen simulations (Baudrillard; Sartori; Friedberg). The image on screen has progressively become a governing medium of sociability that intercedes at a symbolic level into social relations and, as such, potentially influences sociopolitical agendas (Martín-Barbero). I endeavor to understand how contemporary Brazilian crime films dialogue with and participate in sociopolitical relations. Within these crime films are ideologically charged representations that fault the poor male for crime and emasculate the civilian middle-class male—particularly the middle-class intellectual—casting him as unable to respond to crime; the representations posit state security as the only force able to stem increasing crime rates through the expansion of neo-authoritarian policing. Exposing how masculinity is entwined and promoted within these frames of power allows an analysis of how gendered scripts are naturalized and contribute to sociopolitical power structures.

Social science literature of 2000–2008 delineates how democracy was consolidated in Brazil, as in *Democratic Brazil Revisited*, edited by Kingstone and Power. The strengthening of democracy implied an erosion of authoritarian power and the weakening of patriarchal culture. I understand the privileging of virile masculinity in twenty-first-century Brazilian crime films as a response to the strengthening of substantive democracy in the political, social, and cultural spheres in Brazil. These cinematic works react to a push toward the expansion of rights and the democratization of power; analysis of them shines light onto the shadows of the country's dictatorial legacy through its cultural production. This occurs through the cinematic positing of neo-authoritarian masculinity as an integral response to perceptions of criminal violence in twenty-first-century Brazil.

In contemporary Brazil, social and civil violence are ubiquitous in the public sphere. This violence is not new, but its frequency and framing have transformed; through this alteration, underlying ties to Brazil's dictatorial past have been obscured. Hence, despite democratization, the infringement on human rights continues to mark Brazilian society. These violations bear an uncanny resemblance to the abuses that the military dictatorship committed between 1964 and 1985. The victims have in part changed. Instead of the middle-class political dissidents along with social minorities such as Indigenous communities and Afro-Brazilians, the victims now are overwhelmingly poor, young, Afro-Brazilian men. Stratification in Brazilian society is so pronounced that the Instituto Brasileiro de Geografia e Estatística (IBGE, Brazilian Institute of Geography and Statistics) devised the five-tier ABCDE system to describe the span of socioeconomic classes. Human rights violations such as abuse by police, high numbers of prisoners held without trial, and the rapid growth of the prison population are often justified by the victims' precarious socioeconomic status as members of Brazil's C, D, and E classes, combined with racial and gender stereotypes.

This paradigm casts young, poor, black Brazilian males as the primary culprits for rising crime rates. By constructing them as criminals, dominant society undermines some of the gains that the expansion of rights should guarantee for this beleaguered segment of Brazilian society. Their exclusion from mainstream society is mirrored in their being denied political and social agency. Convicted criminals in Brazil do not have the right to vote; detainees who have not been convicted (*presos provisórios*), while officially having the right to vote, most of the time do not. The state has complicated the process of their provisional voting by raising the minimum threshold for the number of such registered provisional voters that is required before the state installs an "electoral zone" in a jail or prison. This designation effectively eliminates the possibility for those awaiting dispensation of their cases to vote in elections (D. Soares). The overarching construction of residents of peripheral communities as criminals also serves to revoke their social and civil rights in less official ways. Concretely, these tensions were displayed during the 2013–2014 *rolezinhos*, when marginalized youths formed flash mobs through social media such as Facebook and occupied some of the country's elite shopping centers. These acts of social confrontation were met with grave resistance from institutions and the elite classes. On multiple occasions, shopping malls were physically closed to keep the youths out (Brum), while the police retaliated against other groups with tear gas and rubber bullets to remove them from these spaces of privilege ("Polícia usa bombas de gás"). Those actions were displays of state power with clear (neo-)authoritarian undercurrents intended to control peripheral communities and allay the middle and upper classes' fears.

Can contemporary crime film be seen as participating in laying the groundwork for the (re)emergence of neo-authoritarian men and Brazil's authoritarian vein that sustains them? I contend that masculinity functions as a metonymic device to represent state power and promote the assertion of a neo-authoritarian paradigm within Brazilian society. In films such as *Quase Dois Irmãos* (*Almost Brothers*, Lúcia Murat, 2004) and *Tropa de Elite*, state power is affirmed through the representation of hegemonic masculinity, attributed to virile (state) agents. In these works, hegemonic masculinity defines itself through the binary structure of dominant masculinity, represented by the neo-authoritarian male characters who embody state power, and the male delinquent who personifies its antithesis, marginal masculinity. These two prototypes of masculinity are conjoined in a relation of confrontation but also of mutual dependence, one defining itself through its opposition to the other. The state assumes the role of guarantor of security and privilege for the middle and upper classes. It justifies its enactment of a neo-authoritarian masculine paradigm to stave off rising crime rates and the purported growing viciousness of the marginal male criminal who threatens the well-being of bourgeois society. Concomitantly, by criminalizing the lower-class male, these films symbolically deny him citizenship. According to the law, convicted criminals forfeit elements of their rights. Constructing the marginalized male as a natural-born criminal presents a slippery-slope scenario to rationalize the denial of rights to such males and ultimately a convenient excuse to explain the high number of police killings of young, poor males, predominantly those of Afro-Brazilian descent.

The conflict between neo-authoritarian and marginal men occurs within a symbolic space that reflects the imposition of a literal and figurative "state of exception," to borrow Giorgio Agamben's formula that denotes the paradoxical annulment of the law in the interest of "public good" (*State of Exception*). The state of exception and its attendant social and political violence guarantee the continued predominance of a neo-authoritarian masculine paradigm. In this manner, masculinity embodies an ideology that is linked to social and political structures of power (Reeser). Through the performance of masculinity in the crime films considered, structures of state and social power, justice, legality, and gender normativity are frequently reinforced and only sporadically contested, most often with little success. These crime films reflect the middle and upper classes' aesthetic tastes through their use of cutting-edge cinematic techniques and the adoption of a high-gloss, globalized aesthetic that stages the actors of social dysfunction to repress them, in turn obfuscating underlying social issues. Form thus echoes the ideological position of the middle and upper classes and promotes their sociopolitical agenda. In this sense, form and the embodiment of a "masculine aesthetic" (Bruzzi) are placed at the service of the promotion of neo-authoritarian men and masculinity.

(Neo-)Authoritarian Masculinity

Masculinity has traditionally been understood as a normative arena through which hegemonic codes of conduct are established and enforced. Both feminism and queer theory have endeavored to unearth the power structures that men have employed to assure the continued privileging of a heterosexual male sociopolitical hierarchy. Judith Butler argues that gender is "*a corporeal style*, an 'act,' as it were" (*Gender Trouble* 139). Understood through Butler's lens, gender is the result of continual social (re) enactments of gender models. The repetitive and sustained reproduction of gender creates essentialized notions of masculinity and femininity. This normalization hides the performative nature of gender and presents it "as if" it were reality. In Butler's words, "The act that one does, the act that one performs, is, in a sense, an act that has been going on before one arrived on the scene. Hence, gender is an act which has been rehearsed, much as a script . . ." ("Performative Acts" 526). It is in this sense that I employ the idea of masculinity as performance.

Butler's work focuses on the function of gender performativity and how speech acts, performative utterances, assign meaning to one's reality and thus how reality is socially constructed. The work developed within these fields to question and destabilize gendered regimes of power provides the analytical tools that are crucial to my study. The question that I am asking in this text is less that of how gender performativity, in Butler's sense, is employed to disrupt regimes of masculine domination. Instead, what concerns me is how the performance of masculinity continues to be engaged to promote male power and masculine domination. My study follows the line of questioning that David William Foster has forged with his groundbreaking 1999 research of how Brazilian film postdemocratic transition to the end of the twentieth century participated in the maintenance of masculine gender paradigms. Foster's study focuses on how the films studied reflect and participate in the construction and questioning of Brazil's national ideals of gender performativity, that is to say, stereotypes of what it means to be a man, a woman, a hero, a sexual dissident, for example. Only by revealing these gendered scripts is it possible to further intervene and dismantle structures of masculine domination in society.

The work of many masculinities theorists such as Raewyn W. Connell, Michael Kimmel, James Messerschmidt, Lynn Segal, and Stephen Whitehead has focused on deconstructing the idea of a single masculinity, refusing normative approaches to the construction of masculinity and its association with men. Understanding masculinities as a multiplicity of possible expressions can begin to break down the power structures that function through and between gender constructions. My study is theoretically grounded in Connell's classification of masculinity. Connell organizes masculinity within a hierarchy of four primary masculine identity categories—hegemonic, complicit, marginal, and subordinate—that are not exclusive but rather inconsistent markers along a changing continuum. In the Brazilian crime films that are part of this study, the binary construction and tensions between marginal and hegemonic masculinity will be my primary focus, except in the final chapter, "A Superhero of Their Own: *O Doutrinador* and Neo-Authoritarian Masculinity."

At the top of the masculine hierarchy is hegemonic masculinity, for which Connell and Messerschmidt take as their starting point Antonio Gramsci's theory of hegemony. Thus, the dominant class retains power not merely through physical force and political and economic coercion but through a combination of these vectors in conjunction with an ideological component. Ideology naturalizes the dominant classes' worldview as common sense within the other classes. Culture is a primary staging ground for struggles to attain and retain hegemony, a space that permits both normatization and contestation of various social paradigms, including gender.

Connell maintains that gender is an organizational structure that configures social practice, but she also contends that each of these patterns (hegemony, subordination, complicity, and marginalization) is mobile, in that they are not fixed points and, rather, transform and mold to changing and shifting historical conditions (76–81). For Connell,

> Hegemonic masculinity can be defined as the configuration of gender practice which embodies the currently accepted answer to the problem of the legitimacy of patriarchy, which guarantees (or is taken to guarantee) the dominant position of men and the subordination of women. . . . It is the successful claim to authority, more than direct violence, that is the mark of hegemony (though violence often underpins or supports authority). (77)

Connell points out that hegemonic masculinity necessarily subordinates both women and nonhegemonic masculinities. That being said, hegemonic masculinity does not exclusively employ forceful domination, although it can. Rather, hegemonic masculinity works through hegemony, understood through Antonio Gramsci's conceptualization of the term as "invisible power."[12] Thus, hegemonic masculinity is not necessarily the most prevalent expression, construction, or pattern of masculinity. Connell and Messerschmidt assert that hegemonic masculinity is socially dominant and its authority derives from "cultural consent, discursive centrality, institutionalization, and the marginalization of alternatives" (846).

Since neither masculinity nor ideology is a fixed concept but rather change dependent on time and place, hegemonic masculinity cannot be understood as a specific set of ahistorical traits. Historically (and regrettably often also in contemporary society), toxic traits such as violence and aggression have been constructed as markers of masculinity in many societies. While these traits may constitute part of hegemonic masculinity at a specific time and place, even if they span long periods or vast regions, they are by no means biologically innate to the construction of masculinities. Thus, one can imagine a society in which the hegemonic norm of masculinity is defined through caring qualities such as empathy. Hegemonic masculinity functions as the socially dominant paradigm of masculinity across time and space, ideologically embedded in society, and while not necessarily embodied by a majority of men, it remains the cultural ideal against which men as well as women and intersex and transgender and gender-nonconforming individuals position themselves.

Authoritarianism and Authoritarian Masculinity in Brazil

Politically, Brazil has a legacy of authoritarianism and military intervention that can be traced to the roots of the nation in the 1889 coup d'état that founded the Brazilian republic. From its initial years of political turmoil to the 1930 military junta of Getúlio Vargas to the 1964–1985 military regime, authoritarianism has intermittently irrupted into Brazil's political system, taking on distinct forms. By and large, neo-authoritarian masculinity is associated with the legacy of authoritarian state power. And the legacy of authoritarianism of the country's most recent dictatorship continues to be present in Brazil even now.

The military takeover of 1964 began the longest period of authoritarian rule in Brazilian history. That regime projected an overarching masculinist worldview. Cultural critic Idelber Avelar contends,

> The dictatorship was anchored, of course, in a masculinist and phallic interpretation of the world: breaking, entering, penetrating were constant images in the language of Golbery do Couto e Silva and other ideologues of the regime, particularly with reference to the Amazon. Military masculinity was ostensibly homophobic but also, by definition, homosocial, since it was marked by the absence of women. The voice of the regime was decidedly masculine.

> A ditadura se ancorava, por certo, numa leitura masculinista e fálica do mundo: desbravar, entrar, penetrar foram imagens constantes na linguagem de Golbery do Couto e Silva e de outros ideólogos do regime, em especial com referência à Amazônia. A masculinidade militar era ostensivamente homofóbica, mas também, por definição, homosocial, posto que marcada pela ausência da mulher. A voz do regime era decididamente masculina. ("Revisões da masculinidade" 49)

The masculinist ideals of the dictatorship were expressed most clearly during the *anos de chumbo* (leaden years) beginning in the final months of

1968 and lasting until the end of Emílio Garrastazu Médici's presidency in March 1974. In his 1970 inaugural address to the Escola Superior de Guerra (Superior War College), Médici emphasized the need to develop a more virile military and in so doing "strengthening the character [of] the Brazilian Man" (20–21, in Cowan "Sex and the Security State," 478). The masculinist stance of the regime's official ideology resulted in repression of the feminist movement (Álvarez),[13] censoring of gay subculture in the arts and alternative *boneca* publications similar to zines (Green 248–49),[14] and a general hard line, a trait associated with authoritarian power, against anything regime leaders considered subversive to its existence.

The center of Brazilian military theory and the organizational hub of the authoritarian regime was the Escola Superior de Guerra. The general working theory that circulated within the Escola Superior de Guerra was one of a feminized, weak, and vulnerable youth given over to the vices of sex and drugs (Cowan "Sex and the Security State"). In response, the school and the regime more generally called for the remasculinization of Brazil through the invigoration of its national security forces. Colonel of Artillery Germano Seidl Vidal made this point clear in a speech from 1967:

> [Basic training] will be toughening, seasoning, and structuring the young man's character. . . . Discipline weakens the impulses, advice and teachings are recorded on the spirit, and the responsibilities that touch him during guard duties . . . will transform the naive adolescent into a man.

> Vão endurecendo, temperando e estruturando o caráter do jovem . . . A disciplina amortece-lhe os ímpetos, os conselhos e os ensinamentos se gravam no espírito e as responsabilidades que lhe toca nas guardas . . . vão transformando em homem o adolescente ingênuo. (Qtd. in Cowan "Sex and the Security State," 479)[15]

During the twenty-one-year military regime, this authoritarian masculinist thread was on full display to the nation politically as well as socially. At a macro level, authoritarian father figures ruled the nation, and that model was transmitted to the micro level of individuals and family structure. Multiple generations of Brazilians were educated within this system that projected masculinist norms of gender, and sexuality and morality that privileged the authoritarian male. The masculine script the regime imposed on the nation silenced women's voices, repressed sexual nonconformity to heterosexual norms, privileged homosocial relations, and generally promoted a patriarchal structuring of society and the family.[16] The authoritarian character of masculinity defined the military men of the regime and, as seen in *Quase Dois Irmãos*, also found echoes in the ranks of the resistance movement that at times reflected some of the same masculinist tendencies. During the dictatorship and after, hegemonic masculinity inculcated countless men, women, and transgender and intersex individuals into routines of violence that became, in many ways, synonymous with the norms of masculinity.

The masculinist logic remained central to military ideology up until the 1985 transition, as evidenced by the publication in 1984 of Adolpho João de Paula Couto's *O que é subversão* by the Comissão Nacional de Moral e Civismo of the Ministério da Educação (Ministry of Education's Commission of Morality and Patriotism) (Cowan "Sex and the Security State," 476). In the treatise Couto warns against the propagation of degenerate masculinity that threatens Brazilian society, and he calls for the reassertion of a strong national manhood to save Brazil. Fast-forwarding to 2020, the message of Brazilian manhood under threat continued to pulsate in a growing number of arenas, from state security forces to the presidency, the BBB coalition to society more generally. The narrative continues to be propagated although its expression has been transformed and adapted to the contemporary sociopolitical situation. One can trace an ideological line from Vidal's speech to Couto's pamphlet to the images that fill the silver screen in Murat's *Quase Dois Irmãos*, Padilha's *Tropa de Elite*, and Gustavo Bonafé's *O Doutrinador*.

Neo-authoritarian masculinity, as I am employing it in this study, harkens back to the dictatorship and the authoritarian male who, with an iron fist, endeavored to guarantee security to those he considered part of the nation. The construction recalls Erich Fromm's 1941 category of the authoritarian character who holds a worldview that is constructed around a binary conception of power. Individuals are understood within this framework as either powerful or powerless. The authoritarian character strives to identify with the powerful; to do so, he bonds or fuses with something more substantial than himself. Fromm argues that the fusion is a sadomasochistic act because it requires the authoritarian character to be pulled in two opposing yet symbiotic directions. On the one hand, he endeavors to submit to a higher power, whether a person, institution, or idea. On the other, he struggles to dominate, control, and constrain those whom he considers powerless. Within Brazilian society, identifying with power took form in the authoritarian men aligned with the regime submitting to the power of the military institution at the same time that they considered it their duty to dominate and control those who did not conform to the regime's ideal of the nation (Cowan "Sex and the Security State" and *Securing Sex*).

My use of "neo-authoritarian masculinity" references the authoritarian masculinist character of the 1964–1985 regime. That period was characterized by a phallic understanding of the world in which feminism was repressed, the LGBTQIA+ community was censored, and male youths were seen as weak and effeminate in need of remasculinization, a discussion that I take up in my analysis of *Tropa de Elite*. The prefix "neo" signals that it is not merely the reproduction of the authoritarian male of the regime. Instead, it denotes the adaptation of the authoritarian male character within the current democratic political system. In terms of characteristics, neo-authoritarian masculinity in contemporary Brazil carries the hallmarks of Fromm's authoritarian character alongside traditional markers of masculine domination. It posits a binary view of society—the powerful and powerless, privileging of homosocial bonds, repudiation of emasculation and the feminine, rejection of the subjective, conventionalism, submission to a higher power, and valuing of aggression, power, and toughness. These examples are in no way exhaustive or exclusive.

In following the argument by Chauí and others that authoritarianism is part of the country's social fabric, neo-authoritarian masculinity thus becomes the latest cultural iteration of the resurgence of Brazil's authoritarian character. In contemporary Brazilian crime films, the neo-authoritarian male characters tap into a more powerful authority through their enactment of masculinity. That masculinity provides the ideological authority that these male characters both desire and privilege. The viewer discovers men motivated by power, aggression, violence, and fear. By tapping into the power offered by their performance of neo-authoritarian masculinity, the characters attempt to establish their own positions of power, which also guarantees middle- and upper-class hegemonic males' places in the social hierarchy. Many of these films construct the neo-authoritarian male as a necessary response to the challenging of the social hierarchy that has been evolving since Brazil's democratic transition. There are some interesting exceptions to this theme within the corpus. *O Homem do Ano* reveals how neo-authoritarian masculinity causes the neo-authoritarian male's loss of his own integrity, to use Fromm's words. That loss is expressed in anxiety, neurosis, and paranoia, thereby representing a questioning of the paradigm of neo-authoritarian masculinity itself.

In sum, the term "neo-authoritarian masculinity," as I am employing it, is a specific expression, or one might say subgenre, of hegemonic masculinity. Neo-authoritarian masculinity positions itself on a plane opposite traditional constructions of femininity, women, and homosexuality, thus imposing masculine domination. Beyond this, neo-authoritarian masculinity imparts privilege to homosocial bonds but reviles homosexual relations while demonstrating an adherence to male hierarchies. Finally, a central tenet of neo-authoritarian masculinity is the manifestation of a propensity for aggression and violence, whether literal or figurative, and more generally assigning value to qualities associated with an authoritarian male figure.

A Brief Overview

My selection criteria for the films I discuss here are multiple. First and foremost, the film's primary narrative thread must revolve around crime, criminality, and their sociopolitical consequences. Beyond this, the movies all have virile male protagonists. Additionally, I consider the cultural reputation and projection of the films, requiring that all films have relatively significant budgets and were directed by established or by up-and-coming directors who were making an entrance into more mainstream cinema at the time of their films' release. Finally, the films had to have been at least moderately successful at the box office nationally, and some even achieved a modicum of international success by virtue of being nominated for Academy Awards.

These criteria ground my discussion since crime films are never produced in a vacuum. Instead, as bell hooks (*Reel to Real*) and Nicole Rafter each has argued, crime films are shaped by and potentially shape real-world perceptions of crime. Rafter discusses how crime films participate in the formation of ideas of crime, its prevalence, and its perpetrators. Genre films tap into and dialogue with cultural beliefs, traditionally utilizing established story models that can serve to reinforce hegemonic viewpoints. In turn, the films are influenced by predominant social codes and formulate and disseminate these same beliefs in the viewing public.

Lastly, I decided to analyze individual movies rather than broaching larger groupings of films. By focusing on specific films, I develop a greater depth of analysis while linking the cinematic work to broader representational tendencies found within contemporary Brazilian cinematographic production. In sum, I develop both horizontal and vertical lines of inquiry to elucidate how Brazilian crime film participates at a symbolic level in social relations and potentially influences sociopolitical agendas.

I organize the book around six chapters. The first chapter, "Being a Man in Brazil," follows the historical development of Brazilian cinema from Cinema Novo to the end of the twentieth century, focusing on the representation of men and masculinity in films that can be broadly categorized as crime films. This brief historical overview hones in on examples of authoritarian masculinity that undergird the character construction and expression of male protagonists. This chapter is by no means exhaustive but rather an attempt to trace instances where the authoritarian character of Brazilian society that Chauí and others signal is on cinematic display.

In the second chapter, "Spectacular Men and the Violence They Perform: *Cidade de Deus*," I consider how contemporary film responds to the question of who is responsible for crime, in the recent past and implicitly also today. I demonstrate how *Cidade de Deus* is exemplary of contemporary narratives that depict urban violence, crime, and the divided city by intertwining these elements. The film accomplishes this effect by suturing the viewer into the cinematic action through the deployment of a masculine aesthetic. This engagement entices the viewer to get lost in the action (hooks *Reel to Real*). Through the obfuscation between the real and reel, the film naturalizes violence associated with the marginalized male, reinforcing constructions of social divisions. Through this sleight of hand, *Cidade de Deus* ultimately sanctions the state's deployment of violence against the marginalized male by naturalizing his criminalization.

In the third chapter, "Brotherhoods of Exception," I analyze Murat's 2004 film, *Quase Dois Irmãos*. As in *Cidade de Deus,* the director employs a teleological historical narrative to explain criminality in Brazil. The film traces a continuum between the violence of the 1964–1985 authoritarian regime and contemporary sociopolitical conditions in Brazilian society. Murat places the history of the repressive abuses of the regime in dialogue with contemporary street-crime narratives to expose the legacy of totalitarian violence and the underlying authoritarian character of Brazilian society. The sometimes violent rivalry between the film's protagonists—the senator Miguel and the drug boss Jorginho—is metonymic of the tensions between hegemonic and marginal masculinities. *Quase Dois Irmãos* reveals the authoritarian tendencies that undergird present-day social conflict, exposes the historical lineage of male violence, naturalizes the violence of the marginal male, guarantees the dominant position of hegemonic masculinity, and ensures the sustained predominance of the neo-authoritarian male.

Chapter 4, "It's a Man's World: Neo-Authoritarian Masculinity in *Tropa de Elite*," focuses on masculinity within the police force and how male rituals of violence reprise the authoritarian legacy of the military regime that governed Brazil from 1964 to 1985. The overwhelming success of *Tropa de Elite* makes it axiomatic to discussions of men, masculinity, and how the state employs violence. I examine the performance of neo-authoritarian masculinity in Padilha's film as metonymic of state power. The film differentiates the Batalhão de Operações Policiais Especiais (BOPE, Special Operations Police Battalion) from the standard military police force to effectively impose a hierarchy between men. This separation emphasizes the importance and structure of homosocial bonds between men. With this framework, the film privileges the neo-authoritarian masculinity of BOPE in juxtaposition to other male figures and masculinities such as criminals and the middle and upper classes. Thus the film imposes a power continuum that esteems neo-authoritarian masculinity embodied in BOPE. In this homosocial masculine world, the film deploys the subordination of women as a central element for the reassertion of neo-authoritarian masculinity in Brazil. These lines of inquiry converge to demonstrate how *Tropa de Elite* depicts the neo-authoritarian male as a virtual figure of salvation capable of reestablishing order and security in a society dominated by fear and insecurity.

In chapter 5, "Men on the Verge of a Nervous Breakdown," I discuss José Henrique Fonseca's *O Homem do Ano* (*The Man of the Year*, 2003). This film brings into focus questions of material and discursive violence, masculinity, socioeconomic divisions, and the problematic relation between reality and media representations of crime. Unlike the films discussed in the previous chapters that assign blame for increased criminality and violence to marginal men, *O Homem do Ano* interrogates which groups are responsible for increased societal violence, the motivating factors for this increase, and how masculinity is entwined in acts of violence. In raising these questions, *O Homem do Ano* probes into dominant public narratives about crime, revealing how they contrast with the realities that are behind violence in Brazil.

In contrast to the other films analyzed, *O Homem do Ano* reveals how the protagonist, Máiquel, uses extralegal violence to expose the instability of authoritarian masculinity and the security regime built around it.

O Homem do Ano questions narratives that posit the marginal male as the primary culprit of urban violence and uncovers the hidden power networks that promulgate those accounts. Through the unmasking of these networks of power, *O Homem do Ano* shows how violence typifies contemporary social relations. It lays bare the neurosis that infuses contemporary authoritarian masculine identities when they are constructed around violence.

The final chapter, "A Superhero of Their Own: *O Doutrinador* and Neo-Authoritarian Masculinity," delves into the world of superheroes and cinema in Brazil. In the first two decades of the century, comics and graphic novels grew in popularity and made inroads into cultural venues beyond the publishing realm. The film industry took particular notice of this trend. In this chapter I discuss Bonafé's 2018 film *O Doutrinador*, which is based on Marcelo Yuka and Luciano Cunha's 2015 homonymous graphic novel. The film is part of an ever-expanding body of superhero films that are ubiquitous internationally at the twenty-first-century cineplex. *O Doutrinador* brings the superhero to the context of 2018 Brazil, the presidential elections, and the inauguration of Bolsonaro. Employing the superhero genre and growing comic book fandom, I contend that *O Doutrinador* posits neo-authoritarian masculinity and the Doutrinador, a *justiceiro* (vigilante), as the heroic figure and society's only answer to the current social and political upheaval. In doing this, the film ultimately contributes to the country's slide to the right politically by constructing this savior figure with parallels to the rise of protofascist leaders, or as Marcia Tiburi has denominated them, "turbotechnomachonazifascistas," such as Bolsonaro both in Brazil and internationally.

My overarching aim in this book is to demonstrate how contemporary Brazilian crime film constructs the peripheral male as a natural-born criminal (*Cidade de Deus* and *Quase Dois Irmãos*). This characterization frames him as a threat to dominant society. He thus becomes the foil for the neo-authoritarian male (*Quase Dois Irmãos, Tropa de Elite*, and *O Homem do Ano*) and the pretext that society must be defended. The expression of neo-authoritarian masculinity in these films reflects on an authoritarian vein that undergirds Brazilian society (Machado da Silva, Moritz Schwarcz, Chauí, da Matta). My categorization of the male characters as neo-authoritarian highlights the links between such characters, the values they embody, and Brazil's authoritarian legacy, particularly its military dictatorship of 1964–1985. Avelar calls on the oppositional intellectual to "point out the residue left by every substitution, therefore showing the past as never simply erased by the last novelty" (*The Untimely Present* 2). I propose that masculine gender paradigms are a central form of uncovering this residue and the residual violence that accompanies it. The oppositional filmmaker can destabilize the myth of the neo-authoritarian male savior to reveal the power issues that envelop him and society.

I

Being a Man in Brazil

Masculinity in Brazilian Crime Film since Cinema Novo

Reflecting the fluidity of masculinity as a concept, representations of masculinities in Brazilian cinema have shifted since the middle of the twentieth century. Nonetheless, despite changes in the representation and expression of masculinity, a pervasive authoritarian character continues to undergird the depiction of men and masculine relations. This is particularly evident in crime film—I employ the denomination "crime-film genre" very broadly in this chapter—which I consider a privileged site to contemplate masculinities because men are overrepresented and manhood and homosocial relations are of central importance to the genre. In this chapter, I trace a chronological overview of the representation of masculinities in Brazilian crime films from Cinema Novo to the turn of the twenty-first century, with a particular final focus on the works of Beto Brant to project the discussion into the twenty-first century and to reveal this historical authoritarian undercurrent that pulsates within Brazilian cinema.

The 1960s: Cinema Novo

Cinema Novo (1960–1968/1972) is the film movement that has overwhelmingly defined Brazilian cinema nationally and internationally since its heyday in the 1960s.[1] The films of Cinema Novo foreground the struggle for social justice through the denouncement of systemic violence, social and economic inequities, and capitalist ideology. Glauber Rocha, one of the primary directors of the movement, promoted the idea of "uma camera na mão e uma ideia na cabeça" ("a camera in hand and an idea in mind"), referring to the unvarnished aesthetic of the Cinema Novo directors. Their works brought Italian neorealist cinema to the context of Brazil and Latin America, giving birth to Rocha's *estética da fome* ("aesthetic of hunger"). Rocha delineated his aesthetic vision in a 1965 speech titled "Estética da fome" he gave at the V Rassegna del Cinema Latino-Americano in Genoa, Italy (Martins Villaça 495). Rocha said the camera must transmit the violence of hunger to reflect the parched land and intensity of the dire situation that Brazil's impoverished populations faced. Cinema Novo directors translated this violence into the films' aesthetics through cinematography that is understood as a revolutionary form of visual denouncement. In the raw and at times brutal footage of these works, film critics have found a socially and politically committed cinema that contrasts with the more heavily edited and aesthetically refined cinema of Hollywood and some European traditions.[2]

Overarchingly, acute social and political criticism underpins the majority of films of Cinema Novo. Many of these same cinematic works assume a more polemic tone when read through the lens of gender and masculinities. A significant number of these films thematize the exploits of strong subversive males who confront socioeconomic disparities in their fight for a more just society. The construction of this individual draws on elements of Brazil's authoritarian character (da Matta; Chauí; Machado da Silva; Moritz Schwarcz). The cinematic productions of Cinema Novo place masculine performance on display through the protagonist's interpersonal exchanges as well as how he confronts oppressive social structures. Frequently these films present masculine power as a necessary element to respond to societal injustice, although the male protagonists' attempts are rarely successful. The films of Cinema Novo, despite championing social justice causes, thus can inadvertently reiterate and reinforce elements of the authoritarian character in Brazilian society, politics, and culture through the construction and expression of authoritarian masculinity.

Paradigmatic of this trend within Cinema Novo are the crime films *Assalto ao trem pagador* (*Assault on the Pay Train*, Roberto Farias, 1962), *Deus e o diabo na terra do sol* (*Black God, White Devil*, Glauber Rocha, 1964), *Os fuzis* (*The Guns*, Ruy Guerra, 1964), and *Terra em transe* (*Entranced Earth*, Glauber Rocha, 1967), to name a few. Themes in these crime films range from the usurpation of power by the state and its representatives (*Os fuzis* and *Terra em transe*) to urban delinquency (*Assalto ao trem pagador*) and backlands banditry (*Deus e o diabo na terra do sol*). These works were predominantly written and directed by men from an intellectual middle class (Johnson and Stam 34). Their target audience was an urban intellectual bourgeoisie. Many of these films' storylines reduce the lower-class masses to thematic elements. The poor and destitute are seldom protagonists of their own plight. Instead, the masses rely on the intervention of middle- and upper-class heroes (*Os fuzis*) or anti-heroes (*Deus e o diabo na terra do sol, Terra em transe*) to defend them. Cinema Novo thus highlights the confrontation between men of a certain class and privilege and ultimately emphasizes the strong male figure who assumes a position of power, takes control of the situation, and stands up for those he considers the weak and powerless.

An example is Gaúcho (Átila Iório), the heroic protagonist of Guerra's *Os fuzis*. Guerra's film tells two interconnected stories, both located in Milagres, Bahia, in the parched Northeast region of Brazil. The first storyline chronicles a religious leader (Maurício Loyola) who anoints an ox as a sacred animal that will lead him and his followers out of the drought by bringing much-needed rains to the afflicted region. This storyline is dominated by neorealist documentary-style shots of the impoverished local population who slowly make the pilgrimage with the revered ox through the countryside to the small town of Milagres (Miracles) in search of food and water.

Intercut with the plight of the local population is a second storyline that follows a group of military officers who arrive in Milagres to maintain law and order. They are there because the mayor owns a dry goods warehouse that is stacked with food essentials. The state security forces have been brought to town to protect the mayor's property from the famine-stricken population. The plight of the community grows more desperate, although they remain resigned to their circumstances. At the same time, the soldiers quickly tire of their assignment.

In contrast to the more documentary style of the first storyline, the second employs a narrative filmmaking style. Rather than retaining the anonymous character construction of the townspeople, the film hones in on individual character development of the soldiers, distinguishing them from the masses. Specifically, the film focuses on the intersecting lives of Mário (Nelson Xavier), a young soldier who becomes smitten with a local woman, Luísa (Maria Gladys), and Gaúcho, a truck driver and ex-soldier who eventually becomes incensed with the government officials' treatment of the resident population. Gaúcho happens to be in town because his truck broke down while passing through, and he is now waiting for replacement parts. From the outset, Gaúcho is critical of the government for sending soldiers to the area to protect food stocks rather than distribute food to the starving townspeople. As the film progresses, Gaúcho learns that Pedro (Paulo César Pereio), a soldier with whom he has tensions early on, killed a townsman as the result of a wager over his marksmanship abilities. In the end, the soldiers load the dry goods onto a truck and have them removed while the townspeople stand idly by. Concurrently, a young boy dies of starvation in his father's arms (Joel Barcellos). The greed of the state and the complacency of the population drive Gaúcho to rise up in arms against the soldiers, grab a rifle from José (Hugo Carvana), another of the soldiers, and shoot at the departing truck. His futile actions lead the soldiers to shoot him dead. The closing scenes of the film return to the holy man who slaughters the sacred cow as the mob of people descend upon the carcass in a struggle to get a piece of flesh.

Os fuzis is a film that centralizes the importance of homosocial relations and male power hierarchies from the outset. In the establishing scenes, the screen cuts between images of the peregrination of the starving townspeople, the group of soldiers bantering back and forth while eating bread and grapes in the back of a military transport truck, and Gaúcho touting his exploits with women and his ability to game the system to a fellow male traveler. These establishing scenes strip the townspeople of agency, constructing them as an undefined mass without the depth of character construction. The townspeople serve as a backdrop for the action of the film, which the opening scenes reveal as a conflict between the soldiers and Gaúcho. The dramatic tension of the film is delineated as a struggle between men, that is to say, between the government represented by the soldiers and Gaúcho, who assumes an almost heroic role in the film as the defender of the poor. Within this binary, the film delves into the realm of masculine bravado and the fight for dominance within male power hierarchies.

Following the establishing scenes, the film focuses on tensions between Gaúcho and the soldiers through the importance it gives to homosocial relations and the struggle for dominance within male power hierarchies. This is set up when Gaúcho wanders into a bar in the center of the town and finds a group of townsmen and soldiers engaged in a sort of show-and-tell about the destructive power and range of the soldiers' 7 mm bolt-action rifles. The arrogant young soldier Pedro offers townsmen a sermon on the firearm, citing an endless string of factoids. He breaks the gun down, challenging the locals to name each piece that he picks up from the disassembled weapon, and each time wagers a shot of *cachaça* to the first man to respond. Within this scene, as Pedro lectures the townsmen, his fellow soldiers José and Mário validate what he says. Their corroboration of his discourse is not vital to the information he is providing but rather consecrates his superiority within the male power hierarchy between the men in the bar.

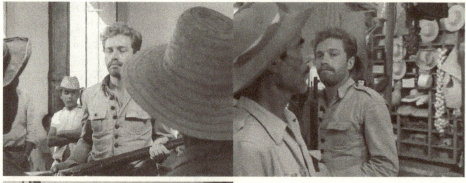

Figure 1.1. A show-and-tell of the soldiers' 7 mm bolt-action rifles in the homosocial space of the village bar. Screen grabs from *Os fuzis*.

Within this grouping, the camera privileges the bond between Pedro and Mário, cutting between the two in shot-countershot fashion, reinforcing homosocial relations and their position of power within the larger grouping of men. Yet when Mário spots Gaúcho in the back of the bar, they grin and smile at one another. Initially they are framed individually, paralleling the shot-countershot sequence of the previous scene. This time, the sequence is organized so that the camera intercuts shots of Pedro after establishing the relationship between Mário and Gaúcho. Viewers are not initially aware of their relationship. The camera visually cues them to the relationship by emphasizing the two men's parallel actions and highlighting the way they exchange glances, together jesting at Pedro, the one who is not in the know, as he holds court in the bar. In this way, the insertion of Gaúcho challenges the homosocial bond between Mário and Pedro that cemented Pedro's claim to power within the group. Incrementally, the camera maps the growing tension between Pedro and Gaúcho by cutting between the three men as they compete for Mário's affirmation. This rivalry is made tangible in Pedro's challenge to name the parts of a disassembled 7 mm rifle that Gaúcho subsequently accepts.

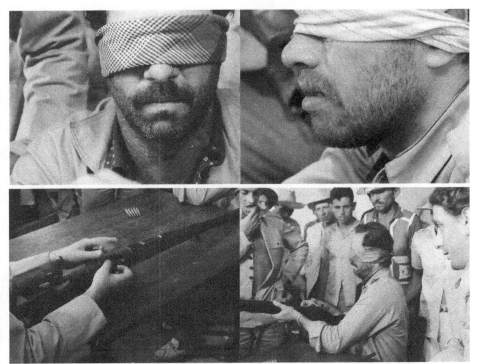

Figure 1.2. Male rivalry on display in a race to reassemble the 7 mm bolt-action rifles. Screen grabs from *Os fuzis*.

In this scene, their rivalry culminates in each man being blindfolded in a race to reassemble the 7 mm rifles that lie before them in pieces. Once again, Gaúcho beats Pedro, as before in the "name the weapon part" game. This series of scenes embodies the tensions between men within the film and the centrality of homosocial bonds and power structures. On the one hand, the men of the town stand idly around marveling at the knowledge and status of Pedro. He assumes a position of power within the group through his skills with the weapon and status as a soldier. His status sanctions his display of power and allows him to belittle the local population. When Gaúcho embarrasses Pedro publicly, he also usurps Pedro's status. Ultimately, this proves to be more egregious than initially evident because Gaúcho is an ex-soldier who had abandoned the uniform (*farda*). By leaving the military, he essentially betrayed the brotherhood that the military represents. Throughout the film, Gaúcho serves as a voice that questions what is occurring in the town and speaks truth to power. He does not directly intercede in the fight until the end of the film, once he can no longer accept the complacency of the townsmen. When he rises in arms against the soldiers, Gaúcho becomes a sacrificial hero, embodying the strong man who stands up for his convictions.

The 1970s: *Udigrudi* and *Pornochanchada*

In the later 1960s and early 1970s, the *udigrudi* film movement emerged; it also was referred to as underground or marginal cinema (*cinema marginal*). The directors of *udigrudi* were the first to embrace the concept of an *estética do lixo* (aesthetic of trash), a direct citation and rejection of Rocha's *estética da fome*. The *udigrudi* films and their more popular *pornochanchada* counterparts promoted a particularly virile form of masculinity that was overwhelmingly expressed through masculine domination of women. In these works, the strong individual male of the first wave of Cinema Novo who confronted social ills virtually vanished from the screen. This, in part, was a response to an increasingly repressive sociopolitical sphere following the 1964 coup d'état and subsequent 1968 passing of the AI-5 that ushered in the most brutal years of the dictatorship, the *anos de chumbo*.[3] Representative films such as José Mojica Marins's 1964 *À meia noite levarei sua alma* (*At Midnight I'll Take Your Soul*), his 1967 *Esta noite encarnarei no teu cadáver* (*This Night I'll Possess Your Corpse*), and Rogério Sganzerla's 1968 *O Bandido da Luz Vermelha* (*The Red-Light Bandit*) focus on the exploits of virile men. Unlike many of their *pornochanchada* counterparts, the films satirize Brazilian society with acidic brutality, calling into question everything from the political establishment to the effectiveness of the police to the social elites,[4] although they fall into some of the same trappings that, to varying degrees, they purportedly question.

    O Bandido da Luz Vermelha is a police drama that is representative of *udigrudi* cinema and the first feature-length film Sganzerla directed. The film is based on the real-life bandit João Acácio Pereira da Costa. João Acácio was a copycat criminal. His exploits were inspired by the Red-Light

Bandit, Caryl Chessman, who in 1948 terrorized Los Angeles residents in the United States. Chessman gained notoriety because he would use a red light when he robbed, assaulted, and raped his female victims. Chessman was executed in San Quentin's gas chamber in 1960. João Acácio, inspired by Chessman, terrified São Paulo's upper-class denizens in the 1960s. What stood out about his crimes, beyond imitating Chessman's use of a red flashlight in his home invasions, was the unconventional nature of his actions. Initially he would leave personal notes to his victims. As his spree progressed, he became more eccentric in his actions, such as engaging in extended conversations with his victims or forcing them to cook for him. In 1967 Acácio was found guilty of seventy-seven assaults and two homicides, and while never convicted on rape charges, he was rumored to have raped more than a hundred women (Linha Direta Justiça).[5] Acácio spent the next thirty years in jail, was released in 1997, and died later that year.

Sganzerla's film traces the exploits of Jorge (Paulo Villaça) as he sets out on a robbery spree of the exclusive neighborhoods of the city, pillaging homes and sexually exploiting the women who live in them. Jorge is an eccentric character who dines with his victims, makes daring escapes, and spends the spoils of his criminal escapades in extravagant ways. The camera follows Jorge through the city, recording not only the exaggerated nature of his exploits but also the mundane boredom that fills his days. Jorge is obsessed with sex, given to substance abuse, and represented less as a cold-blooded killer than as a depraved bon vivant. In many ways Jorge embodies the image of vulnerable youth given over to the vices of sex and drugs that circulated within the discourse of the 1964–1985 regime. These images of youthful decadence and depravity underscored the masculinist ideology of the regime and circulated through official channels such as the Escola Superior de Guerra (Cowan "Sex and the Security State"). Brazil's Superior War College was founded in 1949 and trains both military officers and select civilians. It was central to the 1964–1985 regime, providing the intellectual and technocratic backbone for the dictatorship (Cowan *Securing Sex*, 148, 274n5).

O Bandido da Luz Vermelha offers a scathing review of incompetent state security forces, jests at the vulnerability of the social elites, and creates a caricatured vision of youthful excess and degeneracy. The criticism of Brazilian society is acidic, life a nihilistic endeavor, and the bandido's death futile, when he is electrocuted by exposed wires as the police close in on him. Masculinity is dissolved and reconstructed through a consumptive nightmare in which society is projected as the bandido's oyster.

In dialogue with Sganzerla are the horror films of director José Mojica Marins, widely considered father of the genre in Brazil. The first two films of Marins's horror triptych, *À meia noite levarei sua alma* and *Esta noite encarnarei no teu cadáver*,[6] center on the diabolical figure of Zé do Caixão (José Mojica Marins), a man obsessed with the continuation of his bloodline by producing the perfect male heir. In the first film, Zé is married to Lenita (Valéria Vasquez). Much to Zé's chagrin, they are unable to conceive. Faulting Lenita, Zé ties her up, gags her, and watches as she dies from the bite of a venomous spider. With her death, he pursues Terezinha (Magda Mei), the fiancée of his friend Antônio (Nivaldo Lima). After killing Antônio, Zé rapes Terezinha. In her despair, she curses Zé and vows to return to take his soul, just before taking her own life.

Her death does not dissuade the diabolical protagonist. Zé's search for the perfect progenitor continues. He begins his pursuit of Marta (Luana), the daughter of a prominent family. Escorting her home one evening, he happens upon a gypsy (Eucaris Moraes) who offers him an ominous premonition: Satan will take his soul at midnight for his crimes. Leaving Marta at her home, Zé descends into a state of psychosis, envisioning Marta possessing his soul at his funeral procession. In an attempt to disprove the prophecy, he breaks into the mausoleum where Terezinha's and Antônio's coffins lie and opens their coffins to confirm their deaths. The film concludes with the townspeople finding Zé's half-dead body falling out of the mausoleum.

The second film, *Esta noite encarnarei no teu cadáver*, picks up with Zé returning to the small town to continue his pursuit of the perfect progeny. Very quickly he kidnaps six women from the town and locks them in his mansion. He subjects the women to a series of tests so he can determine which is the bravest and thus most fit to bear his child. Zé releases a horde of tarantulas into the women's room as they sleep. When the women awake, they are covered in arachnids. Only Marcia (Nadia Freitas) remains calm. Zé forsakes all the women except Marcia. First, he offers one woman to his hunch-backed assistant, Bruno (Nivaldo Lima), to do with her what he pleases. Bruno soon returns with the woman's limp body, explaining to Zé that she wouldn't stop screaming, so he squeezed her delicate neck, and it snapped. Zé throws the other four women into a pit and watches with Marcia as he releases a den of snakes to kill them. One of the women curses Zé as the snakes attack her. Later it is revealed that she was pregnant. At witnessing her death, Marcia refuses to have sex with Zé. She eventually kills herself after revealing to the local doctor the crimes perpetrated by

Zé. Finally, the town colonel's (Roque Rodrigues) daughter, Laura (Tina Wohlers), falls for Zé and gives herself to him. Laura and Zé's unborn child die during premature labor. Following Laura's death, Zé goes to her tomb. While there, the pregnant woman who had cursed him returns to claim his soul, and a mob of townspeople shows up to kill him after learning of his horrific acts. The film closes with Zé in a pond as the dispossessed bodies of his victims float to the surface. Zé sinks into the water as he claims to see that it is not blood but Christ that is salvation, and he implores the local priest to give him his cross.

Zé embodies Fromm's authoritarian character. In his quest to create the perfect progeny, Zé attempts to identify with something more powerful than himself, although this intention is continually frustrated. He submits himself to this quest that ultimately causes his ruination. In his quest he strives to command and control those around him through violence expressed physically with beatings, killings, and a host of sadistic acts, as well as psychologically in the fear that he intends to produce within society.[7]

Though *udigrudi* films express an underlying criticism of the nation's political elites and to varying degrees the ruling regime, they also emphasize the sexual availability of women by force and seduction, oftentimes conflating the two. In these films, men dominate women sexually, physically, and socially. What is striking in them is the degree to which male violence toward women and sexual coercion are naturalized in the protagonists. In their explicit nature, the films challenge elements of the conservative mores imposed by the dictatorship. On the other hand, they also reproduce the regime's repressive modus operandi by linking masculinity to domination and violence.

While the films of Sganzerla and Marins are more ambiguous in their message, *pornochanchadas* such as *Cangaceiras eróticas* (*The Erotic Outlaws*, Roberto Mauro, 1974), *Amadas e violentadas* (*Loved and Violated*, David Cardoso, 1976), *Seduzidas pelo demônio* (*Seduced by the Demon*, Renata Candu, 1978), *As amiguinhas* (*The Little Girlfriends*, Carlos Alberto Almeida, 1979), *O bordel, noites proibidas* (*The Brothel, Prohibited Nights*, Osvaldo Oliveira, 1980), and *A próxima vítima* (*The Next Victim*, João Batista de Andrade, 1983) shed much of *udigrudi*'s ambiguity, favoring explicit sex and scenes of violence as their central focus. *Pornochanchadas* in the 1970s and early 1980s are representative of traditional film constructions in basic terms of plot and characters without considering the quality of performance and the narrative arc minimally corresponding to the basic conventions of the narrative storytelling in their production of erotic material.[8]

These films are disconcerting on various levels, but especially disturbing is the recurrence and legitimation of violence against women. This is not a narrative exclusive to *pornochanchadas*. Elements of this storyline flicker in the reels of Cinema Novo, for example, in *Os fuzis* when Mário makes sexual overtures to Luísa or in *Terra em transe* when Paolo (Jardel Filho) delves into orgiastic decadence. These films nevertheless represent an extension and an expansion of the earlier proclivity to glorify violence and the sexual availability of women.[9]

It is worthwhile pausing for a moment to consider the degree to which violence against women in Brazil is an endemic problem that plagues the country. One of the more comprehensive studies of Brazilian society's attitudes toward violence against women is the government's 2014 Sistema de Indicadores de Percepção Social (SIPS, System of Social Perception Indicators). The study found that there has been an increase in awareness of violence against women, since 2006 with the passing of the Maria da Penha law. The overwhelming majority of Brazilians categorically rejected violence against women when directly questioned on the subject. Of respondents, 91% agreed entirely or partially with the statement "A man who hits his wife must go to jail" ("Homem que bate na esposa tem que ir para a cadeia"). When the questions were less direct, a prevailing macho attitude undergirded many of the responses. To the statement "In a fight between husband and wife, one does not get involved" ("Em briga de marido e mulher, não se mete o colher"), 81.9% totally or partially agreed. Another example is "Cases of domestic violence should only be discussed between family members" ("Casos de violência dentro de casa devem ser discutidos somente entre os membros da família"), with which 63% of respondents agreed either wholly or partially. These responses signal that while most Brazilians recognize violence against women as a problem that communities must confront, at an ideological level Brazilian society continues to be profoundly macho in its beliefs. This attitude is also represented in the number of homicides committed against women. According to the *Mapa da violência 2015: Homicídio de mulheres no Brasil* (Waiselfisz), homicides of females had risen since the 1980s from 2.3 per 100,000 to 4.8 after the first decade of the twenty-first century, placing Brazil in the top five countries in the world for the murder rate of women. In the *Anuário brasileiro de segurança pública*, the numbers accelerated with the onset of the Covid-19 pandemic. Statistics from the first semester of 2020 registered a rise of 1.9% in femicides nationally (Fórum Brasileiro de Segurança Pública 28).

In terms of political representation, women made up only 15% of either house of Congress on February 1, 2019 (77 of 513 seats in the lower house and 12 of 81 seats in the upper house), internationally ranking Brazil 132nd for the representation of women in its legislature, just behind Jordan ("Women in National Parliaments"). Throughout Brazil, women protested in significant numbers before the 2018 elections. On September 29, 2018, the #EleNão (#NotHim) political protests against Bolsonaro were the largest demonstrations by women in the history of Brazil (Rossi et al.).[10] Following the massive demonstrations, polls by IBOPE demonstrated a rise of 4% from October 26 to November 1 of intentions to vote for Bolsonaro, revealing general underlying consternation on the part of the Brazilian voting-age public toward feminism, women's rights, and citizenship ("Ibope: Bolsonaro volta").

Crime Film into the 1980s

Returning to the chronology of crime film, as the most repressive years of the dictatorship began to wane and the country transitioned back to democracy, the sexploitation genre known as *boca do lixo* was supplanted by the development of a more hard-core pornography industry.[11] Concurrently, national cinema saw a rise in police crime narratives that were focused on the urban underworld. Films such as *Lúcio Flávio: O passageiro da agonia* (*Lúcio Flávio*, Héctor Babenco, 1977), *Barra pesada* (*Heavy Hand*, Reginaldo Faria, 1977), *A república dos assassinos* (*Republic of Assassins*, Miguel Faria Jr., 1979), *O Homem da Capa Preta* (*The Man in the Black Cape*, Sérgio Rezende, 1986) reinterpreted the figure of the subversive male that had been prominent in Cinema Novo. These masculine figures, while often linked to crime, also symbolized the power of the individual to confront the institutionalized violence of the state.

Lúcio Flávio is the second feature film of the emerging film director Babenco. The film is based on the homonymous novel by José Louzeiro, who also cowrote the script. *Lúcio Flávio* takes a scathing look at crime and corruption, casting a tenuous gaze at the security apparatus in Brazil and condemning it as more corrupt and dangerous than the criminal factions of the city of Rio de Janeiro.

Beginning in the latter half of the 1970s, marginal figures such as drag queens and impoverished youths increasingly appear in films. While not assuming traditional roles of masculine power, these characters engage in violent confrontations with the corrupt authoritarian males who can be read as surrogates of the state. In Faria's film *A república dos assassinos*, Mateus Romero (Tarcísio Meira) forms a death squad of corrupt local policemen. At the opening of the film, Mateus murders Carlinhos (Tonico Pereira), the boyfriend of the drag queen Eloína (Anselmo Vasconcelos). The law ignores this act of violence, and ultimately Eloína avenges Carlinhos's murder by taking Mateus's life. The film foregrounds authoritarian masculinity as the overarching paradigm that governs masculinity and male homosocial relations while it also destabilizes the same paradigm. This destabilization has significant limitations when we consider the representation and objectification of Eloína in the film.

O Homem da Capa Preta narrates the story of Natalício Tenório Cavalcanti de Albuquerque, who was given the homonymous nickname as well as "Rei da Baixada" ("King of the Baixada") and "Deputado Pistoleiro" ("Gunslinger Congressman"). He was known to carry his machine gun Lurdinha (Little Lourdes) under a black cape when he walked the streets of the Baixada Fluminense, an inland area on the periphery of metropolitan Rio de Janeiro. In the 1950s and 1960s, he ran the Baixada and represented the state of Rio de Janeiro at the federal level. The film traces the story of Cavalcanti's rise to power, constructing him as a local hero, a man who fought against corruption, political elites, and landowners. The film presents Cavalcanti as the defender of the poor in the region. Cavalcanti is a strong man, a father figure engaged in populist politics who, rather than empowering the masses, wants to lead them. The film projects the violence of Cavalcanti as a necessary response to a rigged political system that depends on the imposition of the violence of the state. His response is embodied in three brief scenes of parallel style and framing. These scenes, similar to frames of Cinema Novo, project society's need for a strong authoritarian male figure who assumes a position of power to stand up for the weak and powerless masses. They constitute the opening sequence of the contemporary period, the final scene, and the moment Cavalcanti arrives at the statehouse following an assassination attempt as he walks the streets of the neighborhood of Duque de Caxias.

O Homem da Capa Preta opens with a series of sepia-tone film clips that succinctly plot the formative years of Cavalcanti's life and culminate in a graphic-match transition to the protagonist dressing to attend a political event. As he puts on his attire, the camera frames select articles from his apparel: bulletproof vest, white button-down shirt, gold ring, pearl tie pin, red tie, black jacket, the constitution, machine gun and clip, black cape with a red lining, and black bowler hat. In a voiceover he prays,

[May] the bed where my good Jesus slept lie over me and defend me from all danger, nothing against me, no one against me, that my enemies stay away from me, no bullet kill me, no knife take me, no evil happen to me, evil eye not weaken me, fear not make me recoil, my good Jesus.

[Que] a cama onde meu bom Jesus dormiu se deite sobre mim e me defenda de todo perigo, nada contra mim, ninguém contra mim, que meus inimigos se afastem de mim, nenhuma bala me mate, nenhuma faca me fira, não me aconteça mal algum, mal olhado não me enfraqueça, o medo não me desvaneça, meu bom Jesus.

The screen cuts to his daughters as they kiss his gold ring and he makes his way out to the expecting crowd. From the fragmented elements of these close-up frames the state senator is reconstituted, offering a crowd-level, low-angle, cowboy shot that centers him in the frame. Cavalcanti fills the screen as he begins to give his pronouncement. His speech culminates, "É para lembrar a todos que o povo de Caxias agora tem um advogado e um defensor, um advogado para impor a lei" ("I want to remind the people of Caxias that they now have an attorney and a defender, a lawyer to impose the law"). He raises his bound copy of the constitution as seen in close-up earlier. He continues, "E um defensor para fazer justiça" ("and a defender to bring justice"), pulling his machine gun, Lurdinha, from under his cape and pointing it into the air.

The second scene of interest is when Cavalcanti arrives at the statehouse following an assassination attempt on him. Taking the podium, he accuses fellow congressman Silas Gonçalves (Carlos Gregório) of employing hired guns to attempt to kill him. Silas denies the claim, and the two face off in the state building. In a shot-countershot sequence, the two argue until Silas moves out from behind his desk and microphone to stand facing Cavalcanti. The western-style "showdown at high noon" is reconfigured in the context of the halls of the statehouse. Silas pulls his jacket to the side and unstraps his holster, to which Cavalcanti responds by throwing up his cape, pointing his machine gun at the senator, and warning, "Nem mais um passo excelência, ou a Lurdinha vai funcionar" ("Not a step further, your excellency, or Lurdinha is going to go to work"). Throughout the scene,

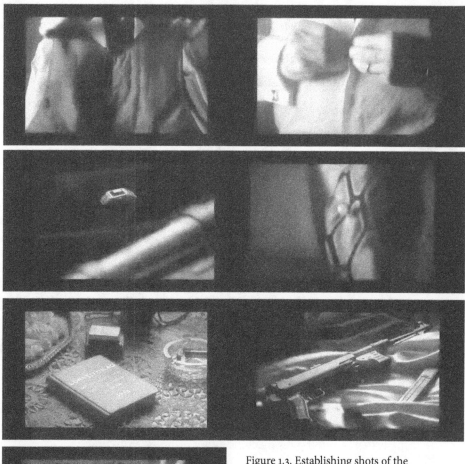

Figure 1.3. Establishing shots of the articles that define Cavalcanti: bullet-proof vest, white button-down shirt, gold ring, pearl tie pin, red tie, black jacket, the constitution, machine gun and clip, black cape with a red lining, and black bowler hat. Screen grabs from *O Homem da Capa Preta*.

the gun-slinging hero is continuously shot in a cowboy-centered framing from a low angle. Silas, alternatively, is framed from a high angle and in various instances from over the shoulder vis-à-vis Cavalcanti. The scene closes with Cavalcanti holding Lurdinha vertically to the sky, cracking a menacing smile, and leveling the gun on his opponent.

Figure 1.4. Cowboy framing of the showdown between Cavalcanti and Silas in the state building. Screen grabs from *O Homem da Capa Preta*.

The third and final scene is in the closing frames of the film, which repeat these previous two scenes in form and content. The camera frames the protagonist from a low-angle cowboy shot against the black of the night sky. He speaks to the camera:

> I don't run. Neither this revolution nor any other will make me betray my commitment to my people. If they want to get rid of me, they can. I did not get into law to be happy. I am not a communist, I am not a fascist, I am not a coward. I'm Tenório, Natalício Tenório Cavalcanti de Albuquerque, and I'm more.

> Eu não fugo. Nem essa revolução nem nenhuma outra vai me fazer trair meus compromissos com meu povo. Querem me cassar, podem cassar. Eu não fui a lei para ser feliz. Eu não sou comunista, eu não

sou fascista, eu não sou covarde. Eu sou Tenório, Natalício Tenório Cavalcanti de Albuquerque, e sou mais.

The camera tracks in to a medium close-up as Cavalcanti spins right and is seen in profile. Raising his trusted machine gun in the air, he cocks the gun's hammer and fires off a round as the muzzle flash creates a small plume of smoke. An intertitle epigraph states,

> Despite his personal courage, Tenório Cavalcanti was not larger than his time. Removed by the military in June 1964, he never ruled again politically. Today, the Man in the Black Cape lives in a suburb far from Caxias, surrounded by the humble people who always respected him.

> A pesar de sua coragem pessoal, Tenório Cavalcanti não foi maior do que seu tempo. Cassado pelos militares em junho 1964, não mais se reergueu politicamente. O Homem da Capa Preta vive hoje num subúrbio afastado de Caxias, cercado pelo povo humilde que sempre o respeitou.

All three scenes function as signposts that underscore the centrality of authoritarian masculinity in the film. They are not direct replays of the same scene; rather, they mirror one another in form and dialogue. The three scenes employ parallel framing techniques. Centered in the frame and shot from a low angle, Cavalcanti's image conveys a sense of power and strength. The cowboy-shot framing focuses on the protagonist, emphasizes the importance of the machine gun he carries, and evokes the western film genre. The prevalence of guns, male bravado, renegade justice, and a macho ethos underscores each of the scenes, recalling the heroes that this film genre has created or projected. By engaging genre film, *O Homem da Capa Preta* promotes a status quo politics in relation to the authoritarian male and masculinity. The protagonist is constructed as a salvation figure willing to confront the authority of a corrupt state, a claim that takes on particular weight in 1986 Brazil. His fight for the people, his willingness to employ violence, and the centralizing of the authoritarian male and masculinity in this struggle unite in these three scenes. They and the film ultimately project a mythical vision (Barthes) of the authoritarian male in Brazil in much the same fashion as in the films of Cinema Novo and other films I analyze in this book.

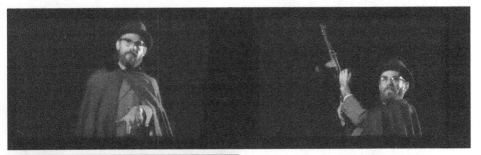

Figure 1.5. Closing frames of Cavalcanti and his trusted machine gun, Lurdinha. Screen grabs from *O Homem da Capa Preta*.

The 1990s: Into the *Retomada*

The late 1980s through the mid-1990s was a period of meager national output due to the dissolution of the state-owned Embrafilme that had produced and distributed thousands of films from its founding in 1969 to its dissolution in 1990 under Fernando Collor de Melo's administration. With the closing of Embrafilme and what seemed an unending series of national economic crises, cinematic production came to a standstill. Only six films were released in 1992.[12] Many of the crime films produced during this period focused on the construction of hypermasculinity as an ambiguous terrain (Foster *Gender and Society*). Moving into the second half of the decade with films such as *Lamarca* (Sérgio Rezende, 1994) and *Os matadores* (*Belly Up*, Beto Brant, 1997), hypermasculinity is constructed as a foundational trope of homosocial relations within Brazilian society. These films map the boundaries of hypermasculinity by signaling how masculinity, when taken to extremes, can represent a threat to Brazilian society. Many of these films fall into some of the same trappings of Cinema Novo in that they criticize institutions founded upon male violence while also relying on that same violence to confront those systems.

With the closing of Embrafilme in 1990, Brazil's national cinematic production ground to a standstill. It was only in 1993 under the administration of President Itamar Franco that the federal government introduced the new Audiovisual Law (federal law 8.685/93) to encourage investment in national cinema production through tax incentives (Nagib *New Brazilian Cinema*). The Audiovisual Law in combination with advances in digital filmmaking and the country's vibrant film culture breathed new life into Brazilian cinema, and the *cinema da retomada* period emerged. Generally, Carla Camurati's *Carlota Joaquina: Princesa do Brasil* (*Carlota Joaquina: Princess of Brazil*, 1995) marks the beginning of the *retomada*. As film production ramped up at the end of the twentieth century and beginning of the twenty-first, crime films expanded in popularity, and the neo-authoritarian male has become more prevalent moving deeper into the twenty-first century. During the initial years of the *retomada*, Brant was an emerging director who rose to prominence and whose body of work is foundational to the discussion at hand. Brant's films *Os matadores*, *Ação entre amigos* (*Friendly Fire*, 1998), and *O invasor* (*The Trespasser*, 2001) function as a particularly powerful triptych that focuses on the construction of masculinity in Brazil between the 1985 transition to democracy and the initial years of the twenty-first century. Brant's films were among a scant number of feature-length crime films released from 1979 to the turn of the century.[13]

Os matadores (1997)

Os matadores accompanies Toninho (Murilo Benício) and Alfredão (Wolney de Assis) as they pass their time in a local strip club, awaiting an unnamed man whom Carneiro (Adriano Stuart), the local crime boss, has hired them to kill. The storyline initially appears to tell two parallel stories, reconstructed through flashbacks of the two men. In these scenes, we are introduced to Toninho, a small-time Carioca thief who heists a car from the more well-to-do Zona Sul of Rio de Janeiro, where many of the city's most affluent residents live and most popular and famous beaches are. He drives to a town on the border with Paraguay to deliver the vehicle to a local used-car dealership that commissioned the theft. Upon arrival, Toninho meets Carneiro, the dealership owner, and Helena (Maria Padilha), his spouse. After dropping off the car, Toninho ventures around the central district of the town. While on the street, he happens upon Helena's fancy red sports car and discovers that she is having a torrid relationship with the boss's hired killer, Múcio (Chico Diaz). Being opportunistic, he photographs the lovers as they leave a local motel and later sells the photos to Carneiro. Subsequently, at the behest of Carneiro, Toninho signs on as a hired killer. Intertwined with this story, Alfredão recounts the tale of

Múcio and his recent demise. Alfredão reminisces about Múcio's initiation into the world of contract killing and how the two became partners. Only later do we learn that Carneiro sent Alfredão to kill Múcio after learning of his relationship with Helena. Now he has hired Toninho to kill Alfredão, doubting Alfredão's loyalty due to his bond with Múcio. As Toninho and Alfredão pass their time at the club, their intertwining stories culminate when Toninho pulls his pistol on Alfredão.

Ação entre amigos (1998)

Ação entre amigos tells the story of four friends, Miguel (Rodrigo Brassalto), Paulo (Heberson Hoerbe), Elói (Sérgio Cavalcante), and Osvaldo (Douglas Simon). As part of the resistance movement to the Brazilian dictatorship in the 1970s, they form an opposition cell that participates in the attempted armed robbery of a bank. Their plan is foiled when military officers from the secret police surround them before they can speed off in their escape vehicle. As a result, they are detained for an indeterminate time during which the state agent Correia (Leonardo Villar) tortures them. While he is in custody, Miguel's pregnant girlfriend, Lúcia (Melina Athís), who also has participated in the action, dies at the hands of Correia. He has put her in a device known as the *coroa de Cristo* ("crown of Christ") that quite literally bursts her cranium.[14]

Since their release, the group has remained in contact and reunites periodically for outings. On this specific occasion, Miguel has brought them together under the pretense of going on a fishing excursion. Once their trip gets under way, he reveals his real objective. As part of the political class, Miguel has happened across a recent photo of Correia. According to official documents, Correia had passed away some time earlier, but his body was never seen. After doing a bit of leg work, Miguel also has discovered that Correia's wife, Maria José Andrade, died three years after her husband supposedly passed away. What Miguel finds curious is that eight years earlier, her remains had been transferred to a small-town cemetery in the interior of the state by an unnamed individual. Typically, all transfers must be signed off on by a family member. Miguel has brought the group together to go to the small town, confirm that the remains are those of Correia's wife, find Correia, and ultimately exact vengeance for the deaths of Lúcia and their unborn child. Once the friends have Correia in their grasp, violence, intrigue, and betrayal consume the men as they turn on one another. Violence and Miguel's drive to exact vengeance ultimately destroy them all.

O invasor (2002)

Brant's third feature film, *O invasor*, made the rounds on the international film festival circuit in 2001 and was released in theaters in Brazil on April 5, 2002. Although *O invasor* had greater box-office success than Brant's previous two films, its ticket sales likewise lagged behind those of blockbuster hits. Nonetheless, *O invasor* incited broad discussions among film and cultural critics, particularly around questions of the moral decay of contemporary society and the overarching decadence of the urban environment. The film is set in São Paulo, frequenting the neighborhoods of Jardins, Vila Madalena, and the Zona Sul (south side) of the city.

O invasor is the story of three university friends, Ivan (Marco Ricca), Gilberto/Giba (Alexandre Borges), and Estevão (George Freire). They studied engineering together and after graduating, opened the construction firm Araújo Associados. After more than a decade working together, they have achieved positions of economic and social prominence within the community. They have also arrived at a crossroads in their business relationship over a business ethics disagreement around government contracts and dirty money. The narrative is quite close to the reality of the country then and still, with scandals such as the one that has embroiled Grupo Odebrecht, Latin America's largest construction conglomerate. Their disagreement leads Ivan and Gilberto to conspire to have Estevão killed and with him, his opposition to corrupt business ventures. The two hire Anísio to kill Estevão. What they do not foresee is Anísio's plan to impinge upon their social and material existence. From this point, Anísio begins to invade the lives of the partners, forcing them to recognize their roles as actors within this cycle of violence.

The film inserts the viewer into the fractured cityscape and what is traditionally the protected sphere of the upper middle class. The film contemplates the terrains of power that mark the present-day urban arena. In *O invasor*, the marginal male literally and figuratively invades the fortified enclave of the city's elites, revealing their complicity in the creation of their own nightmares. Violence between men is postulated as a catalyst that demands the recognition of the abject as it also endows the marginal male character with a degree of power. Anísio, the film's protagonist, penetrates the realm of the *asfalto* (asphalt) from the space of the *morro* (hill), a reference to the geographic division between rich and poor. Through his ubiquitous presence, he serves as a constant reminder of the ambiguous positioning of social and economic cleavages within contemporary society.

In the eyes of the upper classes, he poses a continual threat to the material security of the city proper by usurping its wealth and power.

Crime and Masculinity in Brant's Triptych

Taken together, Brant's triptych reveals how the lack of transitional justice in Brazil facilitated the post-transition continuation of the authoritarian masculine paradigm that prevailed during Brazil's 1964–1985 authoritarian regime. In the post-transition period, the expression of neo-authoritarian masculinity guaranteed the persistence of the violence of the military regime through the enactment of individual, institutional, and extrajudicial violence. The many accounts of police brutality, death squads, and prison violence in Brazil are representative of that violence. Brant's three films demonstrate that violence and neo-authoritarian masculinity have continued to dominate the construction and expression of masculinity in both rural and urban contexts. They suggest that neo-authoritarian masculinity continues to be a dominant paradigm of masculine identity construction in democratic Brazil. His first two films, *Os matadores* and *Ação entre amigos*, highlight the symbiotic relations between masculinity and violence in rural settings, and *O invasor* centralizes the performance of the neo-authoritarian male within the urban context.[15] Each of the three films focuses on the protagonists' attempted assimilation into a neo-authoritarian masculine order and the detrimental consequences of that masculinity. When read together, the films serve as a cautionary tale to Brazilian society of the destructive power of neo-authoritarian masculinity. Their missive is a prelude to subsequent films such as *Cidade de Deus*, *Quase Dois Irmãos*, *Tropa de Elite*, and *O Doutrinador*, a warning against neo-authoritarian masculinity as a response to the shifting sociopolitical public sphere. This theme is of importance to the project at hand because Brant's films foreground the consequences of dominant society's continuation of and assimilation into a neo-authoritarian masculine paradigm.

In the Fissures: Incomplete Transitional Justice and Neo-Authoritarian Masculinity

Brazil's transition to democratic rule in 1985 marked the end, politically, of twenty-one years of authoritarian rule. While the government returned to a democratic form of governance, it was a managed transition that began six years earlier, August 28, 1979, when President João Baptista de Oliveira Figueiredo signed law 6.683, granting amnesty to civilians but also to government figures. It states,

Amnesty is granted to all those who, during the period between September 2, 1961, and August 15, 1979, committed political or related crimes, electoral crimes, those who had their political rights suspended, and to direct and indirect employees of the Administration, of foundations linked to public power, to the employees of the Legislative and Judiciary Powers, to members of the military, and to union leaders and representatives, punished based on Institutional and Complementary Acts.

É concedida anistia a todos quantos, no período compreendido entre 02 de setembro de 1961 e 15 de agosto de 1979, cometeram crimes políticos ou conexo com estes, crimes eleitorais, aos que tiveram seus direitos políticos suspensos e aos servidores da Administração Direta e Indireta, de fundações vinculadas ao poder público, aos Servidores dos Poderes Legislativo e Judiciário, aos Militares e aos dirigentes e representantes sindicais, punidos com fundamento em Atos Institucionais e Complementares.

This law allowed for exiles to return to Brazil and gave political prisoners their freedom, but it also guaranteed immunity to military, government, and extragovernmental actors involved in the torture, killing, and disappearance of countless numbers of people, particularly from the opposition. Law 6.683 stands to this day and has been at the center of much debate. Supporters of amnesty assert that since the law was enacted prior to ratification of Brazil's 1988 Constitution, it cannot be revoked, even though it violates the terms laid out in the constitution. On the other side, opponents argue that the law amounts to a "get out of jail free card" and is protecting individuals who were responsible for grave human rights abuses between 1964 and 1985. These issues have been of particular interest since September 21, 2011, when the Câmera de Deputados (Chamber of Deputies), the lower house of Congress, approved the formation of the Comissão Nacional da Verdade (National Truth Commission). It was initially commissioned to investigate human rights violations that occurred in the country between 1946 and 1988, with most of its work focused on 1964–1985.

Brazil's Comissão Nacional da Verdade released its final *relatório* (report) on December 10, 2014. In it, the commission openly called for revoking the amnesty law because it directly conflicts with Brazilian law as spelled out in the constitution and with international treaties that Brazil has signed (Comissão Nacional da Verdade). Based on these legal claims, the Inter-American Commission on Human Rights filed case 12.879 on April 22, 2016, to challenge the continuation of the amnesty law and seek accountability for violations of human rights, specifically for the detention, torture, and death of the journalist Vladimir Herzog, among others. Herzog became a symbol of opposition to the military regime and a figure around whom to rally for human rights. The documentary *Vlado, trinta anos depois* (*Vlado, Thirty Years Later*, João Batista de Andrade) was released in 2005. The film rescues Vladimir Herzog's story and captures the fear, repression, and violence that were endemic for journalists during the dictatorship. In 2015 Felipe Mucci released his short *Vlado*, a fictionalized account of the night before Herzog's disappearance.[16]

At the local level, on December 10, 2015, the Comissão da Verdade do Rio (Truth Commission of Rio de Janeiro) released its *relatório*. This document goes a step beyond that of the national commission's report in that it not only looks back at the violations of human rights that occurred during the 1964–1985 dictatorship but also, in the concluding chapter, signals the continuation of the legacy of violence in contemporary Brazil (424–39). Thus, the Comissão da Verdade do Rio recognized the change to a democratic government that had allowed the commission to complete the *relatório*, even as the report emphasized that practices of violence the military regime employed persisted in contemporary Brazilian security forces specifically and the broader society more generally. In the representation of this legacy of violence on screen, Brazilian cinema also represents violence, understands its actors and how Brazilian society consumes this legacy of authoritarian violence, and envisions the nation's future through the projection of neo-authoritarian masculinity and men on screen.

2

Spectacular Men and the Violence They Perform

Cidade de Deus

Cidade de Deus is based on Paulo Lins's 1997 best-selling novel by the same name. Lins was born in Rio in 1958, and his family moved to the Cidade de Deus neighborhood in the 1960s. In the 1980s and 1990s he trained as an anthropologist under the direction of Alba Zaluar, renowned for her in-depth studies of marginalized groups. Through his life experiences as well as formal training, Lins gained an insider's perspective into the favela of Cidade de Deus and the lives of its inhabitants. Working from his personal and professional experiences, the Carioca novelist wrote *Cidade de Deus*, a text that incorporates elements of semifictional and testimonial narratives (Barros). In the pages of the novel, the reader very quickly notes the local vernacular of the language that heightens the feel of a firm rooting in the reality of urban Brazil during the later part of the twentieth century. Director Fernando Meirelles has explained that he originally decided to transform the novel into a film because he wanted to present this other facet of Brazilian society to the country's middle and upper classes who were ignorant of what occurred in the *morro* (hillside favela). Meirelles contends, "I would be killing two birds with one stone: I would expose a view of my country that had shocked me when I read the book, and I would give my own life a boost" (Meirelles 13). Before the film's 2002 release, Meirelles was known for directing and producing television series and publicity spots.[1] Following the national and international success of *Cidade de Deus*, the Academia Brasileira de Cinema named him Best Director in 2003, and he quickly attained world renown.[2]

Cidade de Deus, when released, was the first film from the *cinema da retomada* to break three million tickets sold nationally ("Listagem"), the highest number achieved at the box office by a Brazilian film in more than a decade. Nationally, the film grossed more than 19 million reais and internationally more than $23 million.[3] It was nominated for four Academy

Awards in 2004: best director (Meirelles and Kátia Lund), best adapted screenplay (Bráulio Mantovani), best cinematography (César Charlone), and best film editing (Daniel Rezende). *Cidade de Deus* was the first Brazilian film ever nominated in any of those categories and the first Brazilian film selected to compete for more than two Academy Awards. Meirelles clearly attained the personal boost he was seeking.

True to Meirelles's second goal as well, *Cidade de Deus* (re)ignited interest, nationally and internationally, in peripheral communities and their shocking reality of crime and the men who perpetrate it. This is not to say that the favela and favela residents, particularly men, were not previously thematized in Brazilian culture. Authors such as Nelson Rodrigues and Rubem Fonseca as well as film directors Nelson Pereira dos Santos, Roberto Farias, Carlos Diegues, and Miguel Borges created works about the favela and marginality. Internationally, a quick review of films and TV series subsequent to *Cidade de Deus* reveals a number of works that echo its depiction of peripheral communities as spaces defined by drugs and criminality, in particular, male violence. The film cast Brazil and especially Rio as a locus of drug activity on an international scale. In 2006 the protagonists of the television series *CSI: Miami*, Horatio (David Caruso) and Delko (Adam Rodriguez), travel to Rio to search out the drug dealer Antonio Riaz (Vincent Laresca).

In 2011 the *Fast and Furious* franchise released *Fast Five* (directed by Justin Lin), in which Dominic Toretto (Vin Diesel), his sister Mia Toretto (Jordana Brewster), and their friend Brian O'Conner (Paul Walker) escape legal authorities in the United States by fleeing to Rio, where they end up in a deadly confrontation with the drug lord Hernan Reyes (Joaquim de Almeida) due to a heist gone wrong. The international gangster spoof *Lillyhammer* in its third season, in 2012, jumps on the Rio drug train and sends protagonists Frank Tagliano (Steven Van Zandt), Torgeir Lien (Trond Fausa), and Roar Lien (Steinar Sagen) to the metropolis in a comedy of errors rife with drugs, violence, corrupt policing, and the exotification of Brazilian women. In the documentary world, films such as HBO's *Manda Bala* (*Send a Bullet*, Jason Kohn, 2007), Jon Blair's 2009 *Dancing with the Devil*, and Mariana Van Zeller's 2011 *City of God: Guns and Gangs*, all thematize the world of drugs and virile men in Rio's favelas.

In Brazilian cinema, the thematization of violence in peripheral communities hit an apex during the first decade of the twenty-first century. Some twenty feature films,[4] as well as a significant body of documentary films,[5] were released in that ten-year period that directly or indirectly deal with the trope of the violent male who resides in and holds sway over peripheral communities. From this corpus, *Cidade de Deus* and *Tropa de Elite* were the two best-known and most popular films produced.

Cidade de Deus ignited an impassioned debate of ethics versus aesthetics between film critics and the broader audience of moviegoers (Oliveira "An Ethic"). The tension revolved around the aestheticization and possible glorification of violence in *Cidade de Deus* versus the film as a socially conscious work in the tradition of Cinema Novo. On the one side, critics denounced the film as pure surface, lacking any critical engagement with the social and economic factors that had plagued Cidade de Deus from the community's outset. On the other side, critics argued that the film is a raw portrayal of the social and economic realities of Cidade de Deus that through a focus on narrative casts off the possibility of viewing the film through a purely aesthetic lens. By focusing on the construction of masculinity through a masculine aesthetic in the film, the aesthetic is placed at the service of the ethical to promote a neo-authoritarian stance toward crime and the marginal male on the part of hegemonic society.

Cidade de Deus employs a teleological narrative structure that naturalizes the shifting representation of the *morro* from a space of bandits with a social conscience, as proposed in movies such as Farias's 1962 *Assalto ao trem pagador*, to a terrain of savage masculinity founded on individualism and marked by lawlessness and indiscriminate violence. *Cidade de Deus* employs a masculine aesthetic that sutures viewers into the cinematic action. Blurring the lines between the reel and real (hooks) is essential to the way the film naturalizes violence associated with the marginal male subject. The consciousness created by the film does not question stereotypical constructions of social divisions but rather reinforces them. In doing so, *Cidade de Deus* condones the deployment of state-sanctioned violence against the male criminal as dominant society's response to him and his violent actions. Meirelles's film thus reproduces an us-versus-them binary logic that expunges the marginal male from dominant society and undergirds the overarching logic of the divided city (Ventura).

Cidade de Deus: A Quick Synopsis

Cidade de Deus recounts the development of the peripheral neighborhood of Cidade de Deus from its inception in the 1960s as a low-income housing project to its configuration as a space of violent confrontation between men in the 1980s. The movie is organized into three acts, sequentially portraying the peripheral community through the 1960s, 1970s, and 1980s.

In the 1960s, the film follows the story of Trio Ternura (Tenderness Trio), the three young friends Cabeleira (Jonathan Haagensen), Alicate (Jefechander Suplino), and Marreco (Renato de Souza), who commit petty crimes. The youthful gang is involved in an array of small heists as they try to avoid the authorities and gain notoriety within the community for their exploits. The film also introduces the duo Dadinho (Douglas Silva) and his childhood friend Bené (Michel de Souza Gomes) through their initial forays into the world of crime.

As the film shifts to the 1970s, Dadinho becomes Zé Pequeno (Leandro Firmino da Hora), now one of the kingpins of the narcotics trade in Cidade de Deus. He and Bené (Phellipe Haagensen) expand their business and eliminate their competitors until only Sandro Cenoura (Matheus Nachtergaele) remains. As commerce grows, Bené falls in love with Angélica (Alice Braga) and decides to leave the drug trade behind. He dreams of a country life with Angélica.

With the end of the 1970s, the unbridled savagery of the 1980s begins. Neguinho (Rubens Sabino) shoots and kills Bené. In the aftermath of Bené's murder, the battle ensues between Zé Pequeno and Sandro Cenoura, who is now allied with Mané Galinha (Seu Jorge), for control of the drug traffic that engulfs Cidade de Deus.

Marreco's brother Buscapé (Luis Otávio/Alexandre Rodrigues) is the narrator of *Cidade de Deus*. Through a combination of firsthand narration and voiceovers, Buscapé explains what it means to grow up in Cidade de Deus; he introduces characters and describes the drug trade. Through the years, Buscapé becomes a photographer, looking to art as an alternative to violence. Ironically, he is only able to establish himself as a photographer through his documentation of violence in Cidade de Deus. One could say that his narrative functions as a gallery or caption of sorts for his images and vice versa.

Keeping It Real: Authenticity

Cinema and crime narratives maintain a dialectical relation to society, oscillating between virtualization (how the mediatic image [re]produces the social) and actualization (how the image is then [re]incorporated into society) (Diken and Bagge Lausten; hooks *Reel to Real*; Rafter). MV Bill, a rapper and resident of Cidade de Deus, signaled the neighborhood's insertion into this very process when he criticized Meirelles and the film in January 2003 for humiliating the community and projecting it as a space of savage brutality (123).[6] MV Bill has remained an important figurehead and community activist in Cidade de Deus, opening the youth center Central Única das Favelas in 1999; cowriting three books; codirecting a documentary film;[7] releasing multiple rap albums; and starting the radio program *A Voz das Periferias* in 2008, to name only a few of his socially engaged projects. Beyond these efforts, he has been a voice for peripheral communities against police violence. On November 23, 2016, he vehemently denounced police raids on his apartment building. MV Bill, at the time of the release of *Cidade de Deus*, denounced the director's claims of authenticity head-on. Promotion of the film went to great lengths to claim authenticity in an effort to substantiate its purported sociopolitical agenda.

Meirelles began with Paulo Lins's 1997 novel, which is composed of an unremitting compendium of vignettes that broach the lives of some 247 characters. Mantovani, the screenwriter, transformed the seven-hundred-page novel into the intersecting narratives of Trio Ternura, of Bené and Dadinho/Zé Pequeno, and of Cenoura and Mané Galinha. Mantovani's script whittles the original narration down while purportedly remaining faithful to its spirit. The screenplay and subsequent film employ the original text as well as Lins's insider status to promote the film as a direct representation of a certain aspect of Brazilian society and correlate it with the geopolitical space of Cidade de Deus as a synecdoche for all Brazilian favelas.

To build on the claim of authenticity that Lins's novel and the setting of Cidade de Deus confer to the film, the director employed a combination of professional actors and nonprofessional actors, who had a hand in the writing of the script. In part, the dialogue of the film was constructed around sketches improvised by the nonprofessional actors during the rehearsal process. Mantovani then incorporated their improvisations into the rewritings of the script. Many critics have highlighted this process when discussing the film's supposed direct grounding in the violent realities of daily life in the peripheral spaces of the city (Nagib "Talking Bullets").[8]

The Controversy: *Cidade de Deus* and Film Genre

When considering discussions of *Cidade de Deus*, one may initially be struck by the abundance of comments of cultural critics in and outside Brazil who have reviewed the film. Non-Brazilian scholars and film critics situate the film within North American cinematic traditions that include *The Matrix* (Wachowski and Wachowski, 1999) (Rodríguez), any number of Quentin Tarantino's films (Lally), gangster films such as *Goodfellas* (Martin Scorsese, 1990) (Heard), and ghetto and hood films such as *Boyz n the Hood* (John Singleton, 1991) (Neale *Genre*; Siwi).[9]

Comments by paradigmatic directors from the hood-film genre,[10] such as Albert Hughes and Allen Hughes (*Menace II Society*, 1993), reveal striking parallels with Meirelles's assertion that he wanted to open Brazilian middle and upper classes' eyes to the deplorable social conditions prevalent in peripheral communities (13). In a 1993 interview of the Hughes brothers by Bernard Weintraub of the *New York Times* about *Menace II Society*, Albert Hughes states, "We wanted to show the realities of violence, we wanted to make a movie with a strong anti-violent theme and not like one of those Hollywood movies where hundreds of people die and everybody laughs and cheers." The directors affirmed that the hood genre, although part of the gangster- and crime-film genre, assumes a social agenda meant to confront contemporary social problems associated with violence in the urban ghetto.

While hood-film directors defend their works as social commentaries that promote social consciousness, many cultural critics argue that these films take complicated social issues (poverty, gang wars, the national war on drugs) and reduce them to spectacles for mass consumption.[11] The images of marginal spaces that circulate through these films reproduce stereotypes about the hood, African American masculinity, and spectacular violence and ultimately reduce these inner-city communities to spaces of social disorder (hooks *Teaching*, 116), as they also reduce young African American men to pathological criminals (Giroux "Racism," 56). The disjuncture between directors' claims and the critics' readings bear many similarities to the polemics that have enveloped *Cidade de Deus* and the ethics-versus-aesthetics debate.

Lúcia Nagib argues that *Cidade de Deus* avoids Americanized hood-film representations that are limited to merely "surfing the surface" or "repeating attractions" through the importance the film places on the narrative ("Talking Bullets" 246). In this line, the camera documents the socioeconomic realities of the favela and promotes social change through the revelation of a reality that is not easily accessible to those who have no direct connection or exposure to favela life. Thus, the film is a revitalization of Cinema Novo in that it recycles some of that movement's technical and thematic trademarks: the use of handheld cameras, the employment of nonprofessional actors, and the thematization and localization of the film in society's dispossessed terrains (Shaw 65–69).

Juxtaposed to these evaluations of the film is the argument that *Cidade de Deus* is premised on a "cosmetics of hunger" (Bentes). The film is a Hollywoodesque project that employs video-clip imagery to engage the spectator at an emotional level and in turn proves to be reductive of social themes of poverty, violence, and the favela.

This debate brings us back to Meirelles's professed intentions of exposing the Brazilian middle-class public to the reality of the favela and offering the audience an unfiltered experience. In that sense he reiterated the desire of Cinema Novo filmmakers to remove the barrier between the viewer and the screen through techniques such as direct diegetic sound and handheld cameras. Yet the video clip–style editing of the cinematography in *Cidade de Deus* challenges this very premise, as it serves to distance the spectator from the narrative and privilege the visual experience (Gormley 22).

Ultimately, the spectacularization of hyper-real violence (Giroux *Fugitive Cultures*; Gormley) in *Cidade de Deus* serves multiple functions. The film does more than simply surf the surface, as both director and critics have argued. Still, it falls short of demanding social visibility for peripheral communities or forwarding a claim for social justice on behalf of the residents of these spaces, as MV Bill has made painfully clear.

By honing in on the construction of masculinity within the film, one is able to observe how it employs a masculine aesthetic to anchor the hyper-real violence on screen within what is presented as concrete reality, thus conveying a political message about marginal men and masculinity in peripheral communities. This message reinforces preconceptions in hegemonic society's vision of peripheral communities in Brazil. The film constructs the marginal male as a menace to society that necessitates confrontation by the neo-authoritarian power of the state; *Quase Dois Irmãos* and *Tropa de Elite* would soon continue the resurrection of neo-authoritarian male characters.

Masculine Aesthetic: Sutured in for the Ride

Within classic cinematography, suturing is a process that stitches the spectator into the fabric of the film. Suture occurs when the viewing experience is transformed into one in which the cinematic world being represented is constructed as an encapsulated world unto itself (Heath; Silverman *The Subject*). This does not mean the spectator identifies with any specific character or necessarily assumes a participatory role in the film. Rather, suture implies that the spectator adopts the eye of the camera as the observer position. Kaja Silverman explains, "The subject's willingness to become absent to itself by permitting the fictional character to 'stand in' for, or by allowing a particular point of view to define what it sees. The operation of suture is successful at the moment that the viewing subject says, 'Yes, that's me,' or 'That's what I see'" (*The Subject* 205). In *Cidade de Deus,* the spectator adopts Buscapé's narrative point of view, accepting his account as reliable and accurate. Buscapé in this manner is complicit, enacting masculinity through his reiteration and stance as native informant that condone the film's proposed dominant masculine social norms. His complicity allows him to participate in the benefits of the hegemonic masculine paradigm (Connell 79). The presentation of the narrative voice as an authoritative insider of the peripheral community works in conjunction with the overarching discourse of authenticity that undergirds the film to construct a seamless teleological storyline. It melds the spectator's perspective with Buscapé's ambivalent stance of both fascination with and rejection of the violent males in the favela.

Buscapé's storyline is steeped in a masculine aesthetic with the unavowed yet central aim of engaging the viewer with cinematic masculinity. Following Stella Bruzzi's discussion of men's cinema, a masculine aesthetic integrates a Bordwellian neoformalist approach to cinematic style and form with models of physical, embodied spectatorship (Shaviro; Sobchack).[12] Style, mise-en-scène, framing, soundtrack, camera angle, and movement all work in conjunction with and surpass the traditional character-centered narrative. The film creates a masculine experience of "adrenaline rushes, glories and fears; conventional, character-driven forms of identification are supplanted . . . by a more abstract identification pattern rooted in an instinctive and emotional, even primal, audience response to the non-narrative textural elements" (Bruzzi 106). Spectatorship is transformed through men's cinema to surpass the scopophilic male-centered gaze suggested by Laura Mulvey. Men's cinema transcends the passive role of identification, pulling the spectator into the physicality of the experience while at the same time refusing to become purely experiential. A masculine aesthetic creates a mutable spectatorship that promotes both desiring and identifying with masculinity "conceived through, or embodied and enhanced by style and *mise en scène*" (Bruzzi 111).

Cidade de Deus progressively centralizes a masculine aesthetic to incrementally pull the spectator into this masculine cinematic experience. Cuts in the editing of the film string together the events that are narrated "as if" this were the only possible story. The silences created through editing promote cinematic cohesion, suturing the spectator into the action, especially in the 1970s and 1980s chapters. Silverman contends,

> Equally important to the cinematic organization are the operations of cutting and excluding. . . . The cut guarantees that both the preceding and the subsequent shots will function as structuring absences to the present shot. These absences make possible a signifying ensemble . . . [C]inematic coherence and plenitude emerge through multiple cuts and negations. Each image is defined through its differences . . . as well as through its denial of any discourse but its own. (*The Subject* 205)

Cidade de Deus naturalizes the favela as a mise-en-scène of male violence. This technique is deployed with the express purpose of drawing the spectator into the action.

Through suture and the centralization of a masculine aesthetic, the spectator progressively feels the threat of violence as it ravages the community on screen. The screen action engages the middle-class spectators' fears by exacerbating the threat of violence transmitted through the viewing experience. Meirelles takes the viewer on an "opium trip" (Meirelles 13), but the trip goes badly, leading the viewing public to ask what would happen if the marginal males on screen come down from the *morro*?

As violence becomes the focal point of the film, suture is more predominant as a filming technique. Suture is progressively centralized as a hallmark of a masculine aesthetic that develops concurrently through the various periods, assuming its full potential in the 1980s. The epochs are differentiated through changes in cinematic techniques of camera movement, focus, editing, color, soundtrack, and mise-en-scène. These tools are employed to naturalize the shift toward the augmentation of violence as the sole expression of marginal virility. The spectator is drawn into these changes gradually by being pulled deeper into the viewing experience and the jolt of a masculine aesthetic that dominates the screen.

In the 1960s sequence, the film begins with a warm color palette. The scenes are tinted with hues of yellow and orange that create a nostalgic feel that bathes the images. The narrative storyline remains linear during the recounting of the 1960s. The shots employ open lenses that capture the vastness of the geographic space of the recently inaugurated housing project,

Figure 2.1. Trio Ternura framed through the cattle guard of the gas truck's bumper. Screen grab from *Cidade de Deus*.

implying a future of possibilities for the residents. The framing and linear narrative work in unison with longer crane shots and smoother editing to emphasize the more idyllic environment: scenes of youths swimming in the river surrounded by the lush green of the forest and playing a pick-up game of soccer with their friends.

For this more serene setting, cinematographer César Charlone employs filming and editing techniques to create a nostalgic heroism around the youthful gang of Trio Ternura. When the camera introduces the members of Trio Ternura, a freeze frame momentarily zooms in on each member as Buscapé names them in a voiceover. The story resumes with the three walking off confidently and the narrator emphasizing their virile stance: "I was never courageous enough to follow my brother" ("Eu nunca tive coragem de seguir o meu irmão"). Across the way, a gas truck drives down a parallel street. A traveling shot first captures the boys running after it, tying bandanas around their faces, until finally, Cabeleira stands defiantly in the middle of the crossroads (and the screen), directly in front of the vehicle. The truck grinds to a halt, and from a low angle the camera frames the three boys through the square cattle guard on the truck's bumper, endowing them with grandeur. Trio Ternura, pistols outstretched, pull their bandanas down as they stand triumphantly. They overtake the driver and begin to distribute gas bottles to the community.

In this scene, Charlone explains that he and Meirelles "wanted the assault on the gas truck to be like a stagecoach holdup, with the boys and the camera running alongside the vehicle like gunmen on horseback. The boys even wore kerchiefs across their faces the way stage robbers did" (qtd. in Oppenheimer 26). By evoking the western film genre, Charlone inserts a binary logic of good versus evil into the film; his employment of conventions from that Hollywood genre creates a recognizable storyline for the viewer.

Thus, the construction of the young men presents them as bandits, conforming with character-type expectations of the western inserted into the gangster or hood film, as the two genres hold close ideological and character-type conventions (Neale *Genre*). The frontier mentality that undergirds codes of masculinity assumes mythical proportions in many western and gangster genre films. Within the timeline of *Cidade de Deus*, these mythical origins are located in the 1960s. Trio Ternura embodies the innocence of the time and place and holds the seeds of masculine violence that will devolve into the savagery of Zé Pequeno.

The gas-truck scene is also one of the first in which we can pinpoint the integration of a decisively masculine aesthetic. The scene employs traditional genre conventions such as the traveling shot that creates movement and excitement for the viewer as the camera runs alongside the boys in pursuit of the truck. The camera work surpasses the basic western conventions to suture the viewer into the scene, particularly through the use of shot-countershot. Moving from the crane shot in which Cabeleira and the others appear almost insignificant in front of the barreling truck to a low-angle tilt-up shot, these same boys now take on larger-than-life proportions. The spectator assumes the perspective of the camera to experience the adrenaline rush of the chase, the weight of the truck, and the glory of its stopping just shy of Cabeleira.

Trio Ternura's actions are the rumblings of violence that *Cidade de Deus* establishes as foundational elements of male culture in the peripheral community. Their story is one of delinquency as a prototypical male behavioral pattern, and its equation shows how the favela inculcates youths into these traditional masculine roles. In the film's early scenes, the young kids from the neighborhood are playing soccer on the community sports field. Dadinho, Bené, Buscapé, and several other boys are arguing when

Figure 2.2. Naturalizing the relation between violence and masculinity in the opening scenes of the story of Trio Ternura. Screen grabs from *Cidade de Deus*.

suddenly Cabeleira jumps into the group and grabs the ball. He begins to kick the ball in the air as the kids count the number of times he dribbles it on his foot without letting it hit the ground. Alicate and Marreco emerge, telling him to hurry up. Cabeleira punts the ball high into the air as the camera, in an opposite movement, descends to a low angle in a tilt-up shot. Cabeleira reaches into the waistline of his shorts and pulls out a handgun. The frame centers him with a heroic air in his posture, arm extended and gun drawn as he fires, foreshadowing the gas-truck holdup. A bullet cuts through the soccer ball. The image freezes, but the sound continues, when the bullet punctures the leather sphere and in white lettering "A história do Trio Ternura" ("The story of Trio Ternura") appears to the left of the ball. The freeze frame captures the deformed orb as a rush of white powder traces the path of the bullet.

The background noise goes silent and then erupts to cheers of the neighborhood kids as the punctured ball falls to the ground. The camera cuts from Cabeleira twirling the gun on his index finger in slow motion to the kids jumping up and down and shouting. In the kids' ecstatic response to Cabeleira's performance, the camera pauses briefly to frame the elation that fills young Dadinho's face. Subsequently, matching shots of Dadinho's face will repeat intermittently throughout the years as his violence and his love for it grow.

Violence embodied in the gun and the masculine prowess of Cabeleira in sports and marksmanship are centralized as something to be looked up to. The association between strength, violence, and masculinity is foregrounded as an integral part of masculine identity for the youth.

The second period, the 1970s, begins at the Motel MiAmi, where Trio Ternura, joined by Dadinho, are robbing the clientele. The evening's events quickly spiral out of control when Dadinho sets out on a killing spree, taking the lives of all the motel's patrons and personnel. The same exuberance that the camera registered in Dadinho's face at the soccer match in the 1960s is transformed into the ecstasy that fills his expression as he methodically kills everyone at Motel MiAmi. Dadinho's obsession with masculine dominance is symbolically linked to his fascination with the phallic gun and violence that culminates in the mass killing at the motel. Each of these elements, the phallic gun, the bloody massacre, and Dadinho/Zé Pequeno's incessant drive toward power and dominance, all narratively foreground prominent themes of men's cinema and technically construct a masculine aesthetic. The massacre ends the sway of influence of Trio Ternura, whose members are blamed for the killings, and it ushers in Dadinho's reign as Zé Pequeno.

With the change of regime comes the change of name. Dadinho is baptized by the local *pai de santo* as Zé Pequeno and given a necklace of red and black, the colors of the *orixá* Exu. The *pai de santo* warns Zé Pequeno, "I give you my protector. . . . You cannot have sex with the amulet on. If you have sex with the amulet on . . . you will die" ("Eu vou te dar o meu protetor. . . . Não pode furunfar com a guia. Porque se fora furunfar com a guia . . . vai morrer").[13] A novel color palette accompanies the new epoch.

The hues shift to cooler and yet more saturated tones of blue and green. This increasingly psychedelic deployment of color reflects the growing presence and influence of drugs and drug culture on the community (Oppenheimer 27). Additionally, the filming techniques and editing energize the scenes, although, as Jean Oppenheimer points out, "camera movements are freer but still respect cinematographic grammar" (27). The camera work and editing remain within the basic conventions of classic cinematic language, respecting mise-en-scène, shot, editing continuity, and so forth.

As the 1970s progress, there is a gradual change from dolly to handheld cameras. In tandem, the stability of the initial scenes is progressively shed through the incorporation of more vigorous editing in conjunction with the camera work. The scenes become shorter and more fragmented in tandem with the employment of more abrupt dialogue. These elements bring the screen alive with a masculine aesthetic that elicits an incrementally more physical response from the spectator to the action on screen. In the language of Bruzzi, there is an almost primal response as if being pulled into a world where only the strong survive. The aggression that overtakes the narrative on screen subsumes the cinematic experience as violence spills over into the non-narrative textual elements of the cinematic language. Paradigmatic of both the changes in cinematography and the prevalence of violence as defining the marginal male is a rapid series of sequential scenes of Dadinho that plot his growth into Zé Pequeno.

The transition from the 1960s to the 1970s brings a corresponding shift in tone for the new period. After the Motel MiAmi mass shooting, Buscapé recounts the beginnings of Dadinho. The screen cuts to Dadinho's confrontation with and subsequent killing of Marreco. Marreco happens upon Dadinho and Bené, who are hiding out after Dadinho's motel murder spree. Marreco is trying to get out of town since he was just caught with Paraíba's wife (Karina Falcão). As Marreco leaves, Dadinho yells to him to take his gun. When he turns to retrieve it, Dadinho shoots him while walking forward to stand over him. The camera cuts to a low angle from the ground, emulating Marreco's perspective. As Marreco is looking up the barrel of the gun, Dadinho squeezes off two more rounds. Echoing the motel scene, the camera registers the omnipotence of the gun and Dadinho's ecstasy when he uses it.

Discontinuous editing jumps the action forward in time. A matching scene parallels the previous low-angle shot. In rapid succession, discontinuous editing advances in sync with the reverberations of Dadinho's hand-

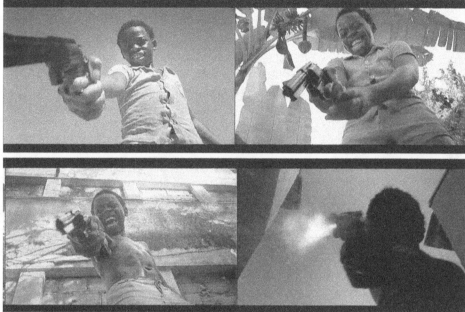

Figure 2.3. Dadinho/Zé Pequeno and the handgun, a coming-of-age story in five shots. Screen grabs from *Cidade de Deus*.

gun firing seven shots. With each cut, Dadinho grows slightly older and the setting shifts. The sequence is Dadinho's coming-of-age story, from young boy to eighteen-year-old thug. Buscapé's narrative voiceover cuts in:

> Between one shot and another, Dadinho grew up. When he turned eighteen, Dadinho was the most respected bandit in City of God. In the world of thugs, he was the most wanted in all of Rio de Janeiro.

> Entre um tiro e outro, Dadinho cresceu. Quando fez dezoito anos, Dadinho era o bandido mais respeitado na CDD. No mundo dos assaltantes, o mais procurado do Rio de Janeiro.

This sequence efficiently pulls the viewer from the 1960s into the 1970s, from Dadinho to Zé Pequeno through the use of a masculine aesthetic.

In terms of that masculine aesthetic, what one can detect in this scene is how, as the matching shots advance the sequence, they get darker to the point that Zé Pequeno's face begins to meld into the darkness of the background. This darker background also causes the muzzle flash of his pistol to become more prominent. The accompanying soundtrack builds in a crescendo that parallels these visual elements. Symbolically, the gun equates to the phallic potential of Dadinho's body as he morphs into a man. The gun, a potent symbol of masculine power, conspires with the camera to emphasize his virility and drive toward a climax as Zé's face is blacked out and the gun stands in for the man. The culmination comes in the final scene of the sequence, when Zé Pequeno is no longer alone, as the scene cuts to Bené standing beside him.

The homosocial bond between men is foregrounded; the gun, their phallus, outstretched, guides their drive toward control and domination. It is not coincidental that in the final shot, Bené's pants are unbuttoned. His genitals mark the white and red vertical striped pants. In the scene, the two young men together unload their guns into the spectator, then point their arms into the sky, firing off a couple of victory rounds. The inebriation of power and violence overtakes the screen as the dangerous marginal male has come of age.

Figure 2.4. Representing the homosocial bond between Bené and Zé Pequeno, gun, phallus, violence, power. Screen grab from *Cidade de Deus*.

In the final period of the film, the 1980s, the scenes acquire a dark mono-chromatic hue as the peripheral community is immersed in drug and gang warfare. The young men who are members of Zé Pequeno's crew shoot it out with the rival clique of Mané Galinha and Sandro Cenoura. The cin-ematic techniques of freeze frames, jump cuts, steady pans, tracking shots, and ellipsis ravage across the screen in dizzying array from the relentless, sporadic movements of the handheld camera and the shifts of the lens as it moves in and out of focus. These techniques are central to the film's de-ployment of a masculine aesthetic and can cause physical discomfort in the spectator due to the frenetic movement and constant instability of the image on screen. Meirelles explains,

> For this part of the story, we did not respect anything. . . . The camera was shaking and frequently out of focus . . . because César would be in a room with seven or eight people, panning and zooming from speaker to speaker or capturing reaction shots. The mood at this point is cold, tense and monochromatic—like an opium trip. (Qtd. in Oppenheimer 28)

The instability of the camera and the dizzying rhythm of the cinematogra-phy force the audience to feel the devastating effects of warfare by assum-ing the perspective and movements of shooter-style video games, among various techniques.

In the scenes of warfare between the factions of Zé Pequeno and Mané Galinha, the camera simulates the perspectives of both groups through cuts that frame the action from the viewpoints of the fighters. Instead of distin-guishing them, the camera melds the two factions into one bloody mass. The objective is not to have the spectator identify with either side but to feel the ravage and chaos of this savage war. Exemplary of the camera's indis-criminate insertion into the action is when Mané Galinha is shot in the leg. The camera cuts from him looking at a child soldier who had been gunned down, as the camera pans the corpse, to a shot from behind a propped-up door where a shooter discharges his weapon, to a shot framed by the slats of a burning wooden pallet as someone runs off and Mané Galinha keels over in pain. In each scene, the spectator becomes an active participant in the action, assuming the perspectives of Mané Galinha and the shooter, as well as an observer-participant watching the action, hidden behind the flames of burning refuse. The continual cuts, principally from eye-level or tilt-up shots, the shaky use of handheld cameras, and the dark color palette of the mise-en-scène create a scene of terror that evokes fear and dramatizes the devastation of this senseless war between men.

Spectacles of Men

The only space where the *asfalto* encounters the *morro* is in the photographs that Buscapé publishes in the *Jornal do Brasil*.[14] This narrative device makes the diegetic time of the film track closely with the supposed means by which news of street violence reaches the general Brazilian population. Buscapé functions as the native informant for the fictional readership of the newspaper, as he does for the spectator of the film. The voyeuristic representation in the newspaper images thus parallels the positionality of the audience. The savage men of Cidade de Deus are present as bound image-spectacles. Buscapé's photographic portrayal of Zé Pequeno and his crew is emblazoned across the front page of the *Jornal do Brasil*.

The film cuts between seven scenes of Buscapé taking the photographs, each cut culminating in a freeze-frame still. All seven images are of Zé Pequeno and his crew in cowboy framing, and each emphasizes the presence of semiautomatic guns and artillery in the foreground. In each, the weapons take on particularly phallic symbolism in their erect positioning and dominant placement within the frame. They recall the 1960s to 1970s transitional sequence of Zé Pequeno unloading his gun. However, the weapons, the symbolic phalluses, have grown, and replacing the handguns of the boys, the military-style artillery of these men implies an even greater potential for violence.

Meirelles does not leave to chance that this could be overlooked. One of the photographs appears on the front page of the *Journal do Brasil* with the headline "Traficantes da Cidade de Deus usam armas do Exército." ("Cidade de Deus Drug Traffickers Use Military-Style Weapons"). The photograph permits dominant society, the *asfalto*, the spectator, to scrutinize and study the savage marginal male, identifying him as a subject in need of control. This occurs in the newspaper and on screen through the use of freeze-frame stills. These pictures are stereotypical images of men with guns that are reproduced ad nauseam in society, evoking a masculine aesthetic reminiscent of macho culture the world over. The threat they embody is the raison d'être of the state security forces, the rationale of why Brazil needs a strong, militarized policing force that requires the return of the neo-authoritarian male.

Figure 2.5. A selection of Buscapé's images of Zé Pequeno and his crew in cowboy framing. Screen grabs from *Cidade de Deus*.

Marginal Masculinity and Violence

In 2015 the Consejo Ciudadano para la Seguridad Pública y Justicia (Citizens Council for Public Security and Criminal Justice) ranked Brazil among the most violent nations in the world. The council found that in 2015 Brazil was home to twenty-one of the fifty most violent cities in the world ("Seguridad"). A study published in 2013 found that 87% of criminal offenders in Brazil were male (Murray et al.).[15] Another study, in 2011, determined that young men ages eleven to twenty-five made up the great majority of violent-crime offenders (Ray 85). A government *Mapa da violência* (Map of violence) report from 2013 states that 92% of homicide victims in Brazil were males (Waiselfisz *Homicídios e juventude*). These numbers reveal that men are both the perpetrators and victims of the vast majority of violent crime. The prevalence of men in most indicators of violence has historically led social science literature to forward a wide variety of theories to explain the linkage between men and violence, from evolutionary rationalizations (Ray 85) to social theories that focus on learning violent behaviors from sources such as entertainment (Kruttschnitt), the breakdown of the family

(C. Brown), and economic inequality (Ray 86). In these discussions, the question of why there has historically been a strong correlation between violence and men has led researchers to debate the role of biological sex versus the role of masculinity and socialization.

Pierre Bourdieu argues that masculine domination in contemporary society is an insidious and all-encompassing socialization process:

> The biological appearances and the very real effects that have been produced in bodies and minds by a long collective labour of socialization of the biological and biologicalization of the social combine to reverse the relationship between causes and effects and to make a naturalized social construction. (*Masculine Domination* 3)

Bourdieu maintains that while the claim may be made that the male subject is innately prone to assert dominance, arguments that privilege violence as a biological trait of the male subject obviate how the socialization process serves as the catalyst for biological effects. For Bourdieu, men and masculinity are constructs of a socialization process that has profoundly influenced the evolutionary biological process to this day.

Bourdieu's ideas are helpful in understanding the construction of masculinity and the male subject in *Cidade de Deus*. The film brings to the forefront the socialization process to foreground the evolution of violence and the role of the male subject within the peripheral community at the same time that it privileges a biological argument through Zé Pequeno and his drive toward violence.

Focusing on the five central male figures (male representatives of the state, Bené, Mané Galinha, Zé Pequeno, and finally, the Caixa Baixa gang), one can plot how the film combines socialization and biological arguments regarding the marginal male subject to promote a perceived propensity toward violence. These characters reveal how the film purges any qualities beyond violence that could be associated with masculinity in the marginal male in unison with the film's devolution into a foundational discourse of fear centered on the marginal male.

The Authoritarian Man of the State

Cidade de Deus strips the storyline of virtually all sociohistoric markers that would locate the development of the Cidade de Deus neighborhood and community within the wider context of the nation. There is no mention of the military dictatorship that assumed power in 1964; the military governments of Humberto Castelo Branco (1964–1967), Artur da Costa e Silva (1967–1969), and Emílio Garrastazu Médici (1969–1974); the loosening of repression by Ernesto Geisel (1974–1978); the transition to democracy under João Baptista Figueiredo (1978–1985); the election of Tancredo Neves as president and his death before taking office (1985); or the Brasil Grande that was ushered in with the World Cup championship in 1970 and the resulting ideals of the Brazilian miracle, not to mention the economic crisis that racked the country from 1980 to 1991. The narrative elides the historical context of the nation, reproducing the spatial dislocation of Cidade de Deus from the geopolitical context of Rio de Janeiro.

Effectively easing the weight of Brazil's dictatorial past opens the possibility for the 1960s to hold the promise of a more positive futurity envisioned for the peripheral community of Cidade de Deus. It is telling that the 1960s is also the only period when state authorities are present in the peripheral community as a controlling force. *Cidade de Deus* does not present the state police in overly sympathetic terms. They are classist and racist, manipulate crime scenes to exculpate themselves of unjustified killings, and have an antagonistic relationship to the residents of Cidade de Deus. Thus, the presentation of the state forces recognizes that the institution is plagued by fundamental issues, similar to the representation of the *polícia militar* in *Tropa de Elite*. The authoritarian male of the state serves as a state-sanctioned counterbalance to the violence of the marginal male. *Cidade de Deus* focuses on the growth of violence in a marginal-male homosocial context bereft of intervention by an authoritarian state power after what the film presents as an almost golden age of 1960s innocence. Following the 1960s, state power is present in the film almost exclusively by default. Thus, as the state is sidelined, the audience accompanies the increasing violence between men; the film opens a space where viewers long for the days when the state, however problematic and limited, is portrayed as the lesser of two evils.

In conjunction with the absence of the state, father figures and the traditional family unit are practically nonexistent. Again, the only exception is in the 1960s. Buscapé and Marreco's father is present in their lives, but he is only tangentially incorporated into the storyline, similarly to the state security forces' presence. When their father (Edson Montenegro) is present, it is solely in his role as patriarch of the family. The two times that he does appear on screen are in response to Marreco getting in trouble. The first time, he finds out about Marreco's involvement with wrongdoing when

Buscapé shows up with cash. In response, their father physically disciplines Marreco and forces both sons to begin working with him selling fish in the community. The second time, Marreco was found having sex with Paraíba's wife. When the police show up at their family home looking for him, their father vows to never speak to him again. Subsequently, he does not reappear in the narrative or on screen.

The absence of male role models such as the father could be understood as an explanation for the criminal path of many of the male characters. It is telling that Buscapé is the only protagonist who does not get involved in crime and is able to get out of the *morro* through a combination of individual talent, photography, and hard work delivering the *Jornal do Brasil* and then as a photographer for the newspaper. The final scene of *Cidade de Deus* shows Buscapé leaving the favela, implying that the ultimate goal and demonstration of success is escaping the space of the *morro*. In contrast, in the novel Buscapé remains within the community and becomes a community organizer, which implies challenging and changing rather than assimilating into the status quo. It can be inferred from this that the influence of the patriarchal father who keeps his child on the straight and narrow path is the answer to the perdition of the marginal male. The father serves as a synecdoche for the state, and his heavy-handed behavior toward his sons indirectly calls for the imposition of a more neo-authoritarian stance toward the favela and the marginal male.

While the father figure disappears permanently from this point forward, the state does reappear following the shooting of Mané Galinha in the final sequences of the 1980s chapter. The narrative voice recalls, "The war was in the papers, and so the police had to take a stance" ("A guerra chegou na imprensa; a polícia teve que tomar uma atitude"). Cabeção (Maurício Marques) now heads the police force. Although he is corrupt, the return of the authoritarian male of the state brings with it a semblance of normalcy that extends to the peripheral community. The color palette of the mise-en-scène lightens, and the space regains elements of daily life. Zé Pequeno and the Caixa Baixa street kids partake in a midday cookout. While state authority is not foregrounded, the return of the state does accompany the return of daylight to the community. The presence of the state's authoritarian male, although corrupt, keeps the chaos occasioned by the violent marginal male at bay. One can understand this as a warning: while the presence of the state is problematic, in its absence, social pandemonium reigns.[16]

Bené: Feminizing the Image, Demasculinizing the Man, Sacrificing the Body

Initially Bené is Dadinho/Zé Pequeno's sidekick; the homosocial bond between them is emphasized by their always being together. Bené then begins to rupture their connection visually and ideologically when he inserts himself into consumerist-capitalist society and becomes a "playboy."[17] He gets his friend Thiago (Daniel Zettel) to buy him the latest surfer fashions that are popular with the middle- and upper-class kids of Rio's Zona Sul. In the film, his stylistic transformation occurs when the camera cuts to Bené sitting in the doorway of a housing block with the white paste of hair dye on his head. Thiago models the new clothing he purchased, to the approving smiles of Bené as Raul Seixas's song "Metamorfose ambulante" ("Walking Metamorphosis") extols the possibility of change, of becoming the opposite of oneself.

Bené's physical transformation takes on heightened significance when we consider the symbolic importance allocated to one's appearance. Society assigns sex (biological) and gender roles to individuals not by their physical attributes, genitals, but through the outward expression of how the individuals perform gender. Style, clothing, hair, and a person's way of walking all project an individual's personal expression of sex (biological) and gender. These cues are read by those with whom one interacts. The interlocution between presentation and the reading of sex and gender is culturally designated and given significance. What is considered masculine in one sphere can take on different meanings in other contexts through which one transits. In *Cidade de Deus*, the interpellation of masculinity through the outward construction of gender expression is cemented in Bené's transformation from thug to *playboy*.

Directly following Bené's makeover, the camera cuts to the beach. A large group of youths are sitting on a rock overlooking the ocean swells. Bené strolls up to them in a pair of board shorts, surfer-style choker necklace, and bleached hair. Thiago introduces Bené to Buscapé and Angélica. His new style gains him acceptance among the cool beach crowd and draws the attention of Angélica. The scene is very brief, but it demonstrates Bené's acceptance beyond gang culture and insinuates the possibility of his integration into consumerist-capitalist society by shedding his masculine guise.

When Bené returns to Cidade de Deus, he opens the door of his house and is greeted by Zé Pequeno and their crew. Their reaction to his new hairstyle and clothing—maroon and white flowered Hawaiian button-down

Figure 2.6. Bené introducing his new playboy style to Zé Pequeno and the crew. Screen grabs from *Cidade de Deus*.

shirt, jeans, and polo shoes—stands in sharp contrast to the beach scene. The gang members, all of them male, are gathered around the table counting money and dividing out dime bags of drugs. When the door swings open, a visual of Bené fills the screen.

Silence overtakes the room until Bené exclaims, "I've become a playboy" ("Virei playboy"). In a pan-left, pan-right series of answering shots, Zé Pequeno, who sits at the head of the table on the opposite end of the room, jests, "Hey, gangsters, listen to this, I have an urgent message for you. Be careful, a hen lays an egg after shaking her ass at the dance" ("Aí bandidagem, tenho um recado urgente para dar para vocês. Tomem cuidado ei, cocota bota ovo quando balança a bundinha no baile").[18] All of the others start to laugh until Bené takes a gun out of his waistline and fires it into the ceiling. Everyone takes off running except Zé Pequeno.

The message is clear: outside of the peripheral community, Bené's new style is accepted and valorized. He is the cool dude, not the hard gangster. In the context of the favela, Bené's transformation denotes his emasculation. Here the feminization of the marginal male subject is represented as dangerous and threatening. The insertion of the feminine jeopardizes the homosocial order by questioning the compulsory heteronormative structure of the gang. In these contrasting scenes, Bené's physical transformation works in conjunction with Zé Pequeno's questioning of his sexuality. When Zé Pequeno warns the others, "A hen lays an egg after shaking her ass at the dance," he publicly questions Bené's sexuality, feminizing him and placing him in a passive sexual role. The saying implies that women who go to dances are sexual objects who are available. As such, their promiscuity leads them to end up pregnant, affirming both the virile male's sexual potency and masculinity and the woman's subservient status to men. Zé Pequeno compares Bené to the woman at the dancehall because of his new feminized look and because the *playboy* is not considered as tough and manly as the thug gangster. In response, Bené reaches into his waistband and pulls out his gun, symbolically reasserting his masculinity through the menace of violence and the gun's emblematic linking to virility and the penis.[19] Despite Bené's reassertion of his masculinity, the scene foreshadows his demasculinization that will ultimately lead to his sacrifice at the hands of Neguinho.

Real Men Don't Forgive and Never Forget

Following Bené's physical transformation, he begins dating Angélica and becomes known as a cool dude. However, these changes also alter the way Bené performs masculine identity. He increasingly distances himself from the violence that is so central to the construction of marginal masculinity. This is exemplified in his role in the story of Neguinho.

Neguinho kills his girlfriend (Mary Sheila) in Cidade de Deus for supposedly cheating on him. His actions are reminiscent of the 1960s, when Paraíba killed his wife for having an affair with Marreco. The film does not dwell on the details of the events; it accepts violence against women as standard practice.[20] The camera rapidly frames the bloodied, half-naked corpse of the teenage girl in the grass just before cutting to Bené and Zé Pequeno at their residence. Zé Pequeno is kicking and punching Neguinho. He is mad only because Neguinho killed her in his territory without his permission. For that, Zé Pequeno expects Neguinho to forfeit his life. Bené saves Neguinho by grabbing him and throwing him out of the house and banishing him from Cidade de Deus. Zé Pequeno retorts, "You know what, Bené? You are very nice, girlfriend (*cumádi*). He who raises snakes, wakes up bitten, you understand" ("Sabe qual é, Bené? Tu é muito bonzinho, meu cumádi. Quem cria cobra, amanhece picado, morou"). Bené's weakness, the clemency he shows toward Neguinho, is constructed as a liability that demasculinizes him since violence is employed to guarantee male authority. When Bené spares Neguinho's life, he disassociates himself from violence and therefore also from the virile masculinity that it symbolically engenders. His leniency implies softness and forgiveness, qualities associated with the feminine and contrary to the homosocial order of the gang. Zé Pequeno makes this reading clear when he calls Bené *cumádi*, a derivation of *comadre*, instead of *cumpádi* (compadre), which normally signals a close relationship between two male friends. By using the female version, Zé Pequeno emasculates Bené.

Rupturing Homosocial Bonds

Homosocial bonding occurs within spaces that promote and are premised around the relations between men (Sedgwick). In *Cidade de Deus,* the gangs function as homosocial units or groupings exclusive to men. The social construction of gang identity in the film is formed around binary understandings of sex and gender: masculine/feminine, heterosexual/homosexual. According to this configuration, masculine identity is defined around ideals of aggression, toughness, unemotional logic, and a heterosexual matrix. In contrast, the female/feminine necessarily embodies the opposite of male/masculinity in this binary: forgiveness, weakness, emotion, and homosexuality, all qualities that are degraded to guarantee the power and privilege associated with men and masculinity. These gendered dichotomies define the gang's social structuring.

In many ways, the gang operates in a manner analogous to the traditional police or military. In *Male Fantasies*, Klaus Theweleit discusses war and the male soldier, contending that "in this world of war the repudiation of one's own body, of femininity, becomes a psychic compulsion which associates masculinity with hardness, destruction and self-denial" (xiii). In *Cidade de Deus,* the repudiation of the feminine, incrementally centralized through violence against women and between men, defines masculinity and male relations.

In the film, the feminine/female characters are progressively constructed as other to the aggressive marginal masculine ethos. Female characters are incrementally excluded from the narrative of *Cidade de Deus*. In the limited female roles of the 1960s and 1970s, women are reduced to their corporality: as the embodiment of male desire and sexual conquest (Cabeleira and Bernice [Roberta Rodrigues]), as the guarantor of a heterosexual matrix that expunges homosocial desire (Bené and Angélica), or as the site of male conflict (when Zé Pequeno rapes Mané Galinha's girlfriend [Sabrina Rosa]).

The triangulation between Angélica, Bené, and Zé Pequeno evokes the tension between men that the female character embodies. Because of her influence on Bené, Angélica represents a threat to the homosocial relations that undergird Zé Pequeno's gang. Within the homosocial structure of the gang, male bonds must repudiate anything feminine to guarantee the phallus as the "indissoluble signifier" (Theweleit xiii). The film constructs Angélica as jeopardizing the phallic bond between Zé Pequeno and Bené.

Cidade de Deus emphasizes the necessity to expunge the female and feminine from homosocial order. Zé Pequeno and Bené have grown up in Cidade de Deus from the time they were young boys. The two are thematized as a unit, a team throughout the 1960s and the first half of the 1970s. They run Cidade de Deus, with Bené functioning as a counterbalance to Zé Pequeno's unbridled aggression. But Bené's transformation and subsequently Angélica's interference, her symbolic castration of Bené (who decides to renounce his violent lifestyle), undermine the homosocial bond between the two childhood friends. This comes to a head at Bené's farewell party.

At the festivities, Bené and Angélica are sitting on the gymnasium bleachers, kissing. Zé Pequeno, who has just been turned down to dance by Mané Galinha's girlfriend, spots the two on the bleachers and approaches them, agitated from his rejection:

Zé Pequeno: What's up brother? Come here, I want to talk to you. [Zé Pequeno and Bené move away from the bleachers, out of earshot of Angélica.] There, you can't leave with that woman, no, man.

Bené: Why? I'm going to live in a cabin, smoking pot all day, you know . . . Listening to Raul Seixas.

Zé Pequeno: You're going to throw away everything we've achieved together for that bitch, my man?

Zé Pequeno: Aí meu cumpádi. Chega aí, que eu quero falar com você. Aí, tu não pode ir embora com essa mulher, não, rapaz.

Bené: Por quê? Vou morar num sítio, fumar maconha o dia inteiro, tá ligado? Escutar Raul Seixas.

Zé Pequeno: Vai jogar fora tudo que nós conquistamos por causa dessa piranha, meu irmão?

The camera underscores the construction of Angélica as a wedge between the men. Initially, when Zé Pequeno and Bené begin to argue on the gymnasium floor, the camera employs answering shots to register the emotional fervor on their faces. As the tension grows and the words "essa mulher" slide off Zé Pequeno's tongue, the screen cuts to a medium body shot that frames the two men from the waist up. Angélica, the origin of their confrontation, is visually lodged between them.

The female subject, the feminine body is posited as an obstructive force in relation to their homosocial bond. Following this argument, Bené walks away with Angélica, abandoning his band of brothers. Soon thereafter Bené will be shot dead by Neguinho at a party. In essence, Bené serves as a testament to the detrimental effects of emasculation.

Mané Galinha: Socialization and Masculine Competitions

Claudine Haroche finds that masculine virility has historically been "synonymous with strength, or at least assumes it: physical, symbolic, but also moral strength. One speaks of strength of character, considered and esteemed as an essential trait of masculinity" (403). In *Cidade de Deus,* the idea of masculine virility associated with moral and physical strength is initially embodied by Mané Galinha in the 1970s.

Figure 2.7. Angélica literally framed between men, Zé Pequeno and Bené. Screen grab from *Cidade de Deus*.

When the camera introduces this character, Buscapé has just been fired from his job as a clerk at the grocery store. In the segment titled "Falling into Crime" ("Caindo no crime"), Buscapé decides to rob a bus, and it happens that a fellow resident of Cidade de Deus, Mané Galinha, is collecting fares. When Buscapé makes this tentative step toward crime, it is Mané Galinha's example that dissuades him. Standing at the bus fare gate, Mané Galinha tells Buscapé,

> You all have to get out of there, have to study, get out of that community, man, a lot of police, many hoodlums too. . . . I studied, I went to high school, served in the military, I was the best shooter and combat fighter in my unit. At the moment I have this job because of lack of something better, but I know karate. And, if I find a gym, for sure I'll leave the favela.

> Vocês têm que sair de lá, têm que estudar, sair daquela comunidade lá, cara, muita polícia, muito bandido também. . . . Estudei, fiz colegial, servi o quartel, fui o melhor atirador-combatente da minha unidade. Agora estou com este emprego porque falta algo melhor, mas eu sei lutar caratê. E se eu escolher uma academia, com certeza eu vou sair da favela.

Mané Galinha embodies the hallmarks of masculine virility: self-control, agility, endurance, decision making, and an aptitude for the exercise of power and the power of exercise (Haroche 403). He is a heroic figure, a masculine ideal in the film whose goal is not to further his own personal power or dominate others but to improve his life prospects through hard work and within the confines of the law. Mané Galinha is situated directly in contrast to Zé Pequeno and his incessant drive toward power and male domination through the illegal exercise of violence. The repetition of the motif of abandoning the favela focuses the spectator's attention on the imperative to refute the violent paradigms of masculinity that supposedly predominate in lower-income communities such as Cidade de Deus. One can read Buscapé's initial intention of robbing the bus as a testimony to this trajectory as well as the importance of having male role models that young men can follow in order not to emulate the likes of Zé Pequeno.

However, from this point on the film follows the adage "Do as I say and not as I do." Buscapé and Mané Galinha will follow diverging paths. Buscapé will indeed look outside the community for opportunities at the newspaper, while Mané Galinha moves ever deeper into the power structure of

Cidade de Deus. His spiral into a cycle of violence that consumes his life is essentially reduced to a revenge story because of the rape of his girlfriend by Zé Pequeno and the murders of his family members. This revenge cycle is transformed into a death wish between men aimed at masculine revindication through violence.

In homosocial groups such as the military or gangs, many times male-male relationships are prioritized over male-female bonds. Men's sociosexual relations with women are constructed as means to achieve masculine status and acts that reaffirm male bonding (Flood). Women are thus configured as sites of male competition.

In *Cidade de Deus,* at Bené's going-away party, Mané Galinha's girlfriend turns down Zé Pequeno when he asks her to dance. Her rejection challenges Zé Pequeno's masculine status. In an attempt to reaffirm his standing, Zé Pequeno humiliates Mané Galinha by forcing him to strip naked on the dance floor. This initial encounter appears inconsequential since the incident ends with Mané Galinha, naked, leaving the party with his girlfriend. However, when Zé Pequeno encounters Mané Galinha's girlfriend on the street and she once again ignores him, he rapes her to reassert his masculine status in the eyes of the other gang members.

As a result of these events, in the 1980s Mané Galinha becomes one of the most ruthless killers in Cidade de Deus. Desire for revenge commands Mané Galinha's every decision. What revenge offers is the fantasy of control, which was central to his masculine identity when the camera first introduced him: studious, ex-soldier, trained in karate. All these areas imply discipline and control as well as a masculine ideal founded on a strong moral component. The disintegration of this moral component engenders violence.

The film engages a standard heroic masculine trope of Hollywood, one of moral outrage that drives a good man to extreme measures in search of justice. Initially, the spectator is meant to empathize with Mané Galinha, endowing his actions with a degree of righteousness. Thus the camera continually registers his pain through close-up framings of his face.

As Mané Galinha's battle with Zé Pequeno ravages the peripheral community, the spectator incrementally loses sympathy for the character. The original ideal of exacting vengeance, when justice is not available, is lost. In its place, the possibility of catharsis through vengeance is overwritten by the cycle of male violence premised overwhelmingly on the masculine competition between Mané Galinha and Zé Pequeno.

Zé Pequeno and the Naturalization of Violence

In *Cidade de Deus,* Zé Pequeno embodies both a socialization argument and a biological argument to explain masculine domination and its relation to violence and the marginal male. Zé Pequeno is constructed as inherently aggressive, demonstrating an intrinsic drive toward violence and power. This is initially established throughout the 1960s, when Dadinho becomes consumed with the pistol and the power that weapon represents. Subsequently, the naturalization of his incessant desire for masculine domination is affirmed when Trio Ternura along with Dadinho, before his name change, rob the Motel MiAmi.

The segment titled "History of Zé Pequeno" ("História de Zé Pequeno") begins with a cut to Dadinho in front of the Motel MiAmi. The narrative voice of Buscapé states, "Zé Pequeno always wanted to be the boss of Cidade de Deus since his childhood when he was still called Dadinho ("Zé Pequeno sempre quis ser dono de Cidade de Deus desde os tempos de moleque quando ele ainda se chamava Dadinho"). At this statement, Dadinho shoots out a small windowpane. The shattering glass is the signal for Trio Ternura that something has gone awry. The screen cuts to a flashback series of brief clips that visually recompile the story of the Trio Ternura motel robbery as told earlier in the film. The camera cuts to a door out of focus slowly swinging open inside the hotel. A man and a woman are on a large disheveled bed. The woman is sobbing as the man tries to comfort her. Dadinho crosses over the threshold of the room, his back to the camera, his body obscuring the scene. The screen cuts to a reverse shot. From the blackness of the doorway, Dadinho emerges. One hears the woman scream, the screen cuts back to an over-the-shoulder shot from behind Dadinho. The man begins to chastise the young boy, claiming that the other boys had taken all his money. As the words fall off his tongue, Dadinho lifts a pistol, and a shot-reverse-shot series registers the blasts of the gun as he kills the two patrons. The camera cuts back to a headshot of Dadinho as a broad smile engulfs his face. He begins to laugh, then turns and disappears into the darkness.

Buscapé in voiceover informs the audience, "On that night, Dadinho satisfied his desire to kill" ("Naquela noite, Dadinho matou sua vontade de matar"). The camera next encounters Dadinho walking slowly through the service area of the motel. He turns and aims his pistol at the off-camera motel workers who had been tied up during the robbery. With a smile from

Figure 2.8. Closing images that punctuate Dadinho's killing spree at the Motel MiAmi. Screen grabs from *Cidade de Deus*.

ear to ear, he fires off several rounds at the screaming employees. Dadinho walks away. There is silence.

The scene sutures the viewer into the action through the use of multiple shot-countershot sequences. The indiscriminate killing of everyone in the motel shocks the spectator, particularly since the film offers no explanation to rationalize the violence beyond Dadinho's joy in killing. The camera's multiple cuts register Dadinho's sense of ecstasy through his facial expressions. The close-up framing of his face is coupled with images of carnage at the motel, inextricably linking the two. Subsequently, over the course of the film, repetition strings together the many times the camera frames Dadinho/Zé Pequeno's delight through medium and close-up shots of his ecstatic face, intercut with scenes of violence: from the soccer field, to the motel, to the transition from the 1960s to the 1970s, to the killing of one of the Caixa Baixa street kids, to the rape of Mané Galinha's girlfriend, the list goes on. Zé Pequeno as the protagonist of the film and the representative of marginal masculinity is constructed through and by violence. In other characters, most of all Mané Galinha and Bené, we observe the detrimental effects of socialization through violence in the periphery, and the film presents Zé Pequeno as the root of that violence, the origin story from which a cycle of masculine violence infects the entirety of Cidade de Deus.

As It Ends, So It Continues

The final scenes of *Cidade de Deus* cement Mané Galinha's proverbial warning to Buscapé on the bus to get out of the favela. The state police have reestablished a semblance of order in Cidade de Deus. Mané Galinha is dead. Cenoura is in jail. Zé Pequeno has just been shot dead by a group of local street kids in the Caixa Baixa gang. Buscapé walks down the street chatting with his buddy.[21] They talk briefly about his internship as a photographer at the *Jornal do Brasil* and whether sex with the female journalist was any good. The mise-en-scène holds hope as the foreground opens into the background, where a tree at the end of the street rises above them in the sunshine. Buscapé is walking out of the shadows toward the promise of something more. He is, at least metaphorically, leaving the periphery.

The Caixa Baixa gang enters from the side of the screen. The camera slowly pivots 180 degrees as it follows the kids down the street in the opposite direction. They are discussing who they are going to kill for infractions on their turf. The physically oldest boy who first shot Zé Pequeno okays their future murders. Juxtaposed to the shot of Buscapé in the street, the alleyway leads deeper into Cidade de Deus, wedged in the shadows between the buildings.

Metaphorically, the diverging paths offer only two possibilities to the marginal male: either leave, as Buscapé demonstrates, or become the violent marginal male, the Zé Pequeno who was emblazoned on the front page of the *Jornal do Brasil*. In depicting the two paths *Cidade de Deus* reaffirms narratives that fill the pages of the daily newspapers and become the lead stories of TV news. Brazilian sociologist José Vicente Tavares dos Santos contends,

> [W]e are living on the horizon of social representations of violence to whose dissemination the mass media outlets contribute greatly, producing the dramatization of violence and propagating the spectacular, as an effect of violence exercised by the "journalistic field."

> [E]stamos vivendo em um horizonte de representações sociais da violência para cuja disseminação em muito contribuem os meios de comunicação de massa, produzindo a dramatização da violência e

difundindo sua espetacularização, enquanto um efeito da violência exercida pelo "campo jornalístico." (22)

Cidade de Deus parallels the discourse of the daily news programs that sensationalize violence for mass consumption in particular by middle- and upper-class consumers. The authority that the film claims as a means of product promotion lies in its assertion of authenticity and its insertion into an overarching social narrative about the marginal male in news headlines and more broadly in Brazilian culture. Through the employment of a masculine aesthetic and the continual repetition of violent images in the film, the real is displaced and simulacra of the marginal male are constructed. If we agree with Jean Baudrillard that communications media shape our consciousness, then it is the film, the simulacrum, that will mold the perceptions of social reality by the viewing public.

3

Brotherhoods of Exception

Power, Politics, and Masculinity in *Quase Dois Irmãos*

On May 12, 2006, fear overtook the city of São Paulo. The Primeiro Comando da Capital (Capital's First Command), a break-off faction of the Comando Vermelho (Red Command) that started in the prisons of São Paulo in the early 1990s, coordinated attacks across the city and state.[1] The criminal faction burned buses, killed state officials, and attacked private banks and public buildings. In seven days, 439 people would lose their lives in São Paulo state in this wave of violence (Adorno and Salla 7). A sense of uncertainty filled individuals in the middle- and upper-class neighborhoods of the city center, areas normally insulated from the extreme levels of violence that are routine in many low-income neighborhoods. The indiscriminate nature of the violence revealed the government's inability to protect civilians, state workers, and police alike, causing individuals to question the state's capacity to respond. The Primeiro Comando da Capital, as important power brokers within the São Paulo state prison system, were forcing dominant society to recognize their reach and authority outside of the circumscribed sphere of the prison.

Lúcia Murat's *Quase Dois Irmãos*, released two years earlier, contemplates the historic entwinement of the state and criminal gangs in Brazil. The film traces a continuum from the authoritarian state of exception during the 1964–1985 military dictatorship to contemporary neo-authoritarian expressions of masculinity in the face of shifting sociopolitical conditions in Brazil.[2] Giorgio Agamben's concept of the state of exception provides a theoretical framework for analyzing these connections and dialogues with the subject who is devoid of social, political, and civil rights, whom Agamben denominates *homo sacer*.

For Agamben, the state of exception both defines the limits of the law and elides the legal sphere. The state of exception implies the suspension of the law in order to purportedly safeguard precisely the application of law. The Italian philosopher asserts that the state of exception is "not (necessarily) a dictatorship . . . but a space devoid of law, a zone of anomie in which all legal determinations—and above all the very distinction between public and private—are deactivated" (*State of Exception* 50). In Roman law, within the state of exception, any citizen who was deemed a threat to the republic could be stripped of his rights. Nowadays, the state of exception (state of perpetual conflict, state under siege) allows for enemy combatants to be held without trial or subjected to extraordinary rendition.

There is an intimate relation between the state of exception and *homo sacer*. If the state of exception is the negation of the law for the sake of upholding it, then *homo sacer* is the individual who is at once subject to the law and excluded from it. While the law defines who *homo sacer* is, it does not afford them any legal protection. Agamben maintains that this contradiction develops from the ancient Greeks having no single word equivalent to what is currently understood as life; they employed two concepts, the biological life common to all living things (*zoë*) and political life or the life of the polis (*bios*). *Homo sacer* is stripped of their individual *bios* and thus reduced to *zoë*. Although not protected under the auspices of *bios*, the laws can be exacted from *homo sacer*. Therefore, they exist within "bare life." Agamben asserts,

> What defines the status of *homo sacer* is . . . the double exclusion into which he is taken and the violence to which he finds himself exposed. This violence—the unsanctionable killing that, in his case, anyone may commit—is classifiable neither as sacrifice nor as homicide, neither as the execution of a condemnation to death nor as sacrilege. (*Homo* 82)[3]

In *Quase Dois Irmãos*, Murat moves beyond cinematic narratives that focus exclusively either on the repression of political prisoners, such as *Zuzu Angel* (Sérgio Rezende, 2006), *Batismo de sangue* (*Baptism of Blood*, Helvécio Ratton, 2006), and *Cabra cega* (*Blind Man's Bluff*, Toni Venturi, 2004), or on the exploits of common criminals, such as *Cidade de Deus* and *O meu nome não é Johnny* (*My Name Ain't Johnny*, Mauro Lima, 2008). Murat places these narratives in dialogue with one another, signaling the legacy of totalitarian violence as part of a continuum of violence that endures to the present time.[4] Violence is embodied in the rivalry that develops between the film's two male protagonists, the state senator Miguel (Caco Ciocler/ Werner Schüemann) and the drug kingpin Jorginho (Flávio Bauraqui/

Antônio Pompêo). The men's conflict is metonymic of the tensions between the *asfalto* and the *morro* and of hegemonic and marginal masculinities, respectively. Thus, *Quase Dois Irmãos* unearths some of the roots of the present-day social conflict, exposing a lineage of male violence that ensures the sustained predominance of authoritarian masculinity, albeit in democratic disguise. The film's structure naturalizes the hegemonic masculinity represented by Miguel and its nefarious consequences for marginal masculinity and men like Jorginho.

Quase Dois Irmãos is bookended with the narrator, Miguel, explaining, "We all have two lives, the one that we dream of and the one that we live" ("Temos todos duas vidas, uma a que sonhamos e outra a que vivemos"). This line embodies the ambiguity of the film. On the one hand, the "one that we dream" points toward the idealism of utopic possibility. The 1950s embody this possibility for the narrator and, he recalls, were the foundation of the socialist ideals of the 1970s political dissidents. In the film's contemporary period, the 2000s, the phrase "one which we live" serves as an apology for his betrayal of those ideals.

Quase Dois Irmãos recounts the story of two childhood pals in Rio de Janeiro, Miguel, the son of a white middle-class family, and Jorginho, an Afro-Brazilian boy whose family lives in the Santa Marta favela. In the 1950s their fathers frequent Santa Marta's samba school, where the two adolescents meet and become buddies. The film weaves together the intersecting and diverging trajectories of their lives through the promises of social change of the 1950s, the political repression of the 1970s, and the sociopolitical disillusionment of the 2000s.

Miguel and Jorginho reencounter one another in the 1970s in prison, the Instituto Penal Cândido Mendes. The setting of the prison, as a homosocial space configured around violence and patriarchal hierarchies, proves pivotal in the men's reunion. Miguel has been imprisoned as a political dissident, while Jorginho is serving a sentence for petty street crime. The film traces their time at the prison, which coincides chronologically with the imposition of the Lei de Segurança Nacional, Decreto 898 (National Security Law, Decree 898), on September 29, 1969. This law codified punishment for crimes such as bank robbery, murder, and assault, whether the intent was political or not. In part due to the Lei de Segurança Nacional, common and political prisoners were housed together in Galeria LSN, the Lei de Segurança Nacional wing.[5] The film charts the shifting of the Galeria LSN from a cell block dominated by political prisoners in the late 1960s to one predominantly controlled by the Comando Vermelho by the 1980s.

Initially, political and common prisoners are housed together. However, as the prison population shifts and tensions grow between the two groups, the space is increasingly segregated by class and social status. This segregation occurs through the performance of different prototypes of masculinity. *Quase Dois Irmãos* examines the contact and relations between common and political prisoners and how class, race, and masculine bravado mark the interactions between the two groups.

The social tensions continue into the 2000s. Miguel is now a senator, while Jorginho is locked up in the Bangu penitentiary. From his prison cell, Jorginho controls the Morro dos Macacos favela through his nephew Deley (Renato de Souza). Miguel visits Jorginho, hoping to get his approval to build a cultural center in the favela. Juliana (Maria Flor), Miguel's daughter, is dating Deley and regularly visits him in the favela. Her relationship with Deley goes against her father's wishes. Juliana is gang-raped by Duda (Erick Oliveira) and others in a rival faction he heads, as a casualty of a turf war in the Macacos favela.

Filming Techniques and Mise-en-Scène

The storyline broaches three epochs that are marked visually through the use of distinct color palettes as well as the staging and framing of the scenes. Through a neoformalist reading of the film, color palette changes, varied constructions of the mise-en-scène, and filming techniques serve to clearly mark transitions in diachronic time.

The 1950s are constructed as staged vignettes, shot in sepia tones that bathe the images with nostalgia, paralleling the color palette choices seen in *Cidade de Deus*. The mise-en-scène of *Quase Dois Irmãos* is constrained through the sparse use of characters and props as well as shallow space composition that limits the depth of field visually, emphasizing the limitations of memory and experience. The discriminate use of props and wardrobes is a combination of predominantly whites, yellows, and browns that further heighten the effect of nostalgia evoked by the sepia tones, replicating Miguel's feelings of longing for yesteryear and his age of innocence. The use of filters and fill light diffuse the hard edges and shadows created by low-key lighting, adding to the tone of the epoch. These techniques at once centralize Miguel as the narrator and create distance from the action on screen. They serve as reminders that the story is told from Miguel's perspective while also visually implying that the promises of this era are a long-gone fantasy.

Figure 3.1. The 1950s mise-en-scène represented as staged vignettes. Screen grab from *Quase Dois Irmãos*.

The *tableau vivant* that the film composes of the 1950s suggests a momentary illusion of possible social and racial accord, at least from the perspective of the upper-middle-class narrator. The scenes suggest that Brazilian society has at least partially actualized Gilberto Freyre's idea of "racial democracy," the central tenet of his influential 1933 study *Casa-grande e senzala* (*The Masters and the Slaves*).[6] Though this ideal continues to pervade national discourse (Bastos 3–5), Murat's film exposes its many shortcomings.[7] Socioeconomic and racial tensions operate in the background of the 1950s narrative, foreshadowing the conflicts of the 1970s and beyond.

The 1970s are constructed around a muted or gray color palette in which cool blue and green hues predominate and transmit the oppressive atmosphere within the prison walls and in Brazil more generally. The country is in the throes of the military dictatorship. The scenes are dominated by medium and close-up shots framed by bars, internal windows, and walls, constant reminders of the prison space the protagonists inhabit. Many of the shots emphasize a shallow depth of field to transmit the protagonists' spatial and sociopolitical confinement. The depth of field then shifts as the integration of the common and political prisoners becomes more pronounced. The camera increasingly moves out from the individual cells and lingers in the common corridor of Galeria LSN, a long passageway lined with solid metal cell doors on either side. The doors become smaller as the narrative progresses and the depth of field increases, visually parallel-ing the rising tensions and expanding gulf between common and political prisoners.

In general, the scenes employ high-key lighting, with only a few excep-tions, emphasizing the vacuous yet constricting space of the prison that contains very few props, as one would expect of the prisoners' quarters. These details not only highlight the conditions in which the prisoners are housed but also register the heightened importance of the inmates' bodies and their interpersonal relations within the constricted, barren space.

Lastly, in the 2000s, the use of more intense and saturated colors in conjunction with high-key lighting and the increased prevalence of hand-held cameras add movement to the screen and heighten the visual engage-ment of the spectator. The progressively chaotic and unstable nature of the filming techniques visually echoes the escalating tensions that confront the protagonists as they once again cross paths. A more visually tumultuous mise-en-scène draws the spectator into the developing action. At a meta-phorical level, these decisions create the feeling of daily life being gradually more agitated within the cityscape. If one understands the 1950s as an age of innocence and the 1970s as the gray or dark leaden years of the dictatorship, the vibrancy of the contemporary period simultaneously holds the promise of the future, the weight of history, and the vitality and frustrations of the actual moment.

Figure 3.2. The mise-en-scène of the common corridor of Galeria LSN at the Instituto Penal Cândido Mendes. Screen grab from *Quase Dois Irmãos*.

The 1950s: Masculine Dreams and Racial Tensions

The 1950s sequence opens with the boy Miguel (Brunno Abrahão) in his bedroom getting ready to sleep as his mother (Cristina Aché) reads the story of Cinderella. This scene is crosscut with the young boy imagining Cinderella and the Prince, two Afro-Brazilian samba dancers, elegantly dressed in white, twirling across a dirt-floor stage, a red and white *escola de samba* (samba school) flag tussling in the wind.[8] Miguel inquires, "But Mom, what samba are they dancing?" ("Mas mãe, qual é o samba que dançavam?"). The storyline cuts to the 2000s, graphically pairing the red and white flag of the sambistas with a twirling blue and gold samba-school flag during Rio de Janeiro's *carnaval* celebrations, visually linking the 1950s to the present. The storyline also juxtaposes Miguel's childhood idealism with his current reality when he is informed of his daughter's rape during the *carnaval* festivities, although this connection is made only at the close of the film when the opening scenes are revisited.

Miguel's dreamlike sequence portrays an idealistic vision of socioeconomic and racial harmony between men. The image projects the samba school as a space of unity or coming together of the *asfalto* and the *morro*, rich and poor, Blacks and whites. Men are united over their passion for samba. Miguel's and Jorginho's fathers spend late evenings and weekends together playing music at the samba school, sharing *feijoadas* on Sundays, and generally making revelry. In the 1950s, the homosocial bonds between the two men are focalized, while class and racial tensions are pushed from the fore by emphasizing their camaraderie. The establishing scene of the 1950s sets the tone. The two men are at the samba school sitting around drinking. In the carousing, Jorginho's dad opens the scene with the initial verse of Cartola's samba "Quem me vê sorrindo" ("Who Sees Me Smiling").[9] With the second verse, Miguel's father joins in. The camera frames the two men in the center of this *tableau vivant*.

The mise-en-scène highlights their homosocial bonds. The narrative voice corroborates what one visually sees: "My childhood dreams" ("Os meus sonhos de infância"). But as Miguel narrates, "I could see another life other than the one we were living, pointing to all that would happen" ("Eu já podia ver outra vida a que vivemos, apontando para tudo o que viria acontecer"). The rupture to which Miguel refers in his voiceover is embodied in the female characters' reaction to their husbands' homosocial bonds.

Through crosscutting, the film highlights the fathers' analogous circumstances. After their late night at the samba school, the two men with their

Figure 3.3. Miguel's and Jorginho's fathers at the samba school in the favela Santa Marta. Screen grab from *Quase Dois Irmãos*.

sleepy young boys confront their wives, who are less than pleased with the men's evening of carousing. The wives chastise the men not only for having the children out late but also on the detrimental effects of hanging out with each other. In this manner, women assume a dual function in the 1950s as guarantors of social norms and a force of resistance to homosocial relations between men of different socioeconomic status. The opening scene of the 1950s at the samba school establishes a parallel between the fathers' friendship and their sons' bonds and cements the importance of the homosocial bonds between the young boys. Yet these initial scenes also prefigure the tensions between men that will come to the fore later in the film.

In their discussion of homosociality, Nils Hammarén and Thomas Johansson distinguish between horizontal and vertical, hierarchical homosociality. Horizontal homosociality is founded on principles of friendship, emotional support, and intimacy, while vertical, hierarchical homosociality is focused on the maintenance of power structures and the continuation of a hegemonic masculine order. This conceptual framework is useful to understand how the homosocial bonds between the two boys shift between the 1950s and the initial period of the 1970s. In the opening scenes, the young boys' homosocial bonds are built around horizontal homosociality. The camera develops these intimate bonds that unite them. When the two boys are dancing samba together, the camera frames them in a full body shot, foregrounding their figures in the midst of other samba school patrons.

Both boys embody the promise of a more egalitarian future in Brazil. Miguel sees himself as having attempted to continue his father's legacy of trying to confront socioeconomic and racial divisions. However, what he reproduces is a patriarchal system that actually maintains the status quo. This is apparent through a more critical reading of the relations between the fathers and not the boys' idealism. What undergirds the fathers' relationship is the vertical homosocial bond between the two men. In the cross-cut sequence of the women chastising the men, Jorginho's and Miguel's mothers expose the hierarchies of power that govern the relations between them. It is the historical legacy of white elite samba composers profiting from sambas written by their poorer Afro-Brazilian counterparts. Richard Parker argues,

> This invasion of the schools by the middle and upper classes has been interpreted in different ways. It has been seen as a sign of the incorporation of the marginal *sambista* into the structure of the global society, as evidence of the hegemonic appropriation of a popular form of black expression by the white elite, and as a product of the inclusion and *communitas* of the *carnaval* itself. (176–77)

Thus, Miguel's father's (and subsequently his own) sociopolitical positioning on the surface may appear to confront social biases but continues a historical legacy of appropriation, assimilation, and scapegoating. In the 1970s, when Miguel and Jorginho reencounter one another, it appears that horizontal homosocial bonds unite them, but very quickly a vertical, hierarchical homosocial configuration becomes apparent.

The 1970s: Masculine Tensions and Racial Dreams

The 1970s are the historical period that is given the most screen time in *Quase Dois Irmãos*. And in many ways this period is central to understanding the film. The setting, the Instituto Penal Cândido Mendes, was a men's prison throughout much of the twentieth century.

During the 1964–1985 military dictatorship, the prison complex held common and political prisoners, although the state did not recognize the political status of political prisoners locked up at Ilha Grande. This was not an issue specific to the prisoners of Ilha Grande but rather the government's modus operandi generally in relation to political detainees in the late 1960s and early 1970s.[10] The Brazilian government employed the prison system to negate political rights to individuals, effectively transforming the prisons and by extension, the nation into terrains governed by a state of exception (Agamben).

Under the authoritarian regime, the government progressively imposed an ever-deepening state of exception on the country. In 1964, following the ousting of President João Goulart from power, initial laws were passed that targeted the administration of the deposed president. Ato Institucional no. 1, passed on April 9, 1964, little more than a week after Goulart was deposed, transferred power from the president of the republic to the military commanders, repealed legislative term mandates, negated juridical process, and suspended the political rights of individuals.

Once former government employees of the Goulart administration were removed, the newly imposed military government passed a series of decrees that imposed an ever more repressive regime on the Brazilian citizenry. Each decree built upon the previous one to form concentric circles that enveloped Brazilian society.[11] In 1967, the Lei de Segurança Nacional, Decree 314, instituted a broader definition of its scope:

National security encompasses, essentially, measures directed toward the preservation of external and internal security, including the prevention and repression of adverse psychological war and revolutionary or subversive war.

A segurança nacional compreende, essencialmente, medidas destinadas à preservação da segurança externa e interna, inclusive a prevenção e repressão da guerra psicológica adversa e da guerra revolucionária ou subversiva.

With that, national security became the country's supreme law, trumping the rights of the citizenry.

The Lei de Segurança Nacional opened the door for a series of more repressive institutional acts that began with Ato Institucional no. 5, AI-5, of December 13, 1968,[12] and ended with the final installment of the series, no. 17, of October 14, 1969.[13] These institutional acts superseded both judicial review and the nation's constitution. Over the course of two and a half years in 1967–1969, these institutional acts were imposed to legalize the use of repressive measures by the state against its own citizens (Dassin).

At the height of the military dictatorship, in the late 1960s and early 1970s, political prisoners were detained, tortured, and disappeared under these decrees. According to the recently released report by the National Truth Commission, 434 individuals were either murdered or disappeared. Human rights abuses were validated by the state's legal framework. AI-5, issued by President Artur da Costa e Silva under the pretext of national security, suspended the writ of habeas corpus and exempted executive decrees from judicial review. AI-5 permitted the government to detain and imprison anyone, and prisoners had no legal recourse to question or challenge their incarceration. The rule of law effectively transformed these individuals into *homines sacri*.[14] They were stripped of *bios*, reduced to *zoë*, and under the auspices of AI-5 no longer protected under the law yet subjected to it. To date, no official data have been compiled on the exact number of political prisoners held during the dictatorship. Unofficial data compiled by Danyelle Nilin Gonçalves in 2006 indicate that 25,000 political prisoners were held over the twenty-one-year period.[15]

State of Exception and Political Prisoners in *Quase Dois Irmãos*

Quase Dois Irmãos focuses on the erasure of political life (*bios*) within the dictatorial context and shows how this framework is subsequently superimposed from political to common prisoners during the democratic transition. Unlike films such as *Cabra cega, Batismo de sangue,* and *O que é isso, companheiro?* (*Four Days in September*, Bruno Barreto, 1997), the filmic gaze in *Quase Dois Irmãos* does not privilege solely the *zoë* of the supposed subversives. Instead, it establishes a correlation between political prisoners and common detainees, casting them all as *homines sacri*. Erased from the legal purview and yet subject to it, political and common prisoners form an abject brotherhood of *homines sacri*. At first, homosocial bonds unite the two groups of men in their antagonism toward state power, but as the state's repression wanes and power structures shift, their homosocial bonds are transformed into a terrain of contention.

The government's denial of the inmates' status as political prisoners is evident in the opening scenes from the 1970s storyline, before the integration of common prisoners into the narrative. Miguel and his cell mate, Peninha (Fernando Alves Pinto), have just come back from the prison yard, where they retrieved several contraband newspaper articles. When the two return to their cell, Miguel pulls the clippings from his waistband. The headline asserts, "There are no political prisoners in the country" ("Não há presos políticos no país"). The frame cuts to a headshot of Peninha as he ironically professes, "You don't exist, I don't exist" ("Você não existe, eu não existo"). As Miguel begins to read silently, the camera lingers and the initial playfulness of the scene is shed. Miguel's face, as it emerges above the newspapers, registers a sense of pain and preoccupation. He informs Peninha, "They killed Marilena" ("Mataram a Marilena"). Peninha stares blankly and reaches for the article. The camera zooms in on the headlines: "Dantesque Night of Terror" ("Noite dantesca depois do terror"). Headshots of "The First Suspects" ("Os primeiros suspeitos") fill the front page. The exposé shows a mug shot of Marilena, Peninha's former partner. Although the image affirms their political existence, *bios*, through the prisoners' acknowledgment of her activism, the headlines deny her political existence (and by extension the prisoners' existence) vis-à-vis the state's construction of the event as one of terror, officially negating a political agenda as motivation for her actions.

The newspaper headline scene initially draws the spectator into the intimate space of the prisoners' daily lives. It opens with them playing a game of soccer in the prison courtyard, then shows the collective effort of the inmates to smuggle news contraband into the prison, and finally pulls the viewer into the personal terrain of Miguel and Peninha's cell. This contextualization leads the viewer to engage with the daily functioning of the prison, where the state attempts to reduce life to *zoë* while inmates struggle to maintain a sense of *bios* in no small measure through the privileging of the homosocial bonds that unite them.

It is the homosocial bonds between Miguel and Peninha that are central to their resistance to the repressive tactics of the state. This is highlighted not only in their being constructed as an almost inseparable pair throughout the 1970s but also in their actions, which show a heightened degree of intimacy. Miguel playfully swats Peninha when he first arrives back at their cell from the prison yard with the newspaper clippings. The two men find comfort and strength in one another and their friendship. It is through their bond that they jointly face the repressive tactics of the regime.

Biopolitics and Repression

Biopolitics can both construct and invalidate the subject's *bios*.[16] Therefore, the individual body becomes a primary staging ground of the law, as both a site of enforcement of the law and of resistance to the law. *Quase Dois Irmãos* reveals how the inmates' everyday corporality such as dietary and hygiene questions is transformed into vectors in the axis of a struggle for power between the military and prison authorities and the prisoners.

Through their bodies, the state attempts to control the prisoner's subjectivity and weaken them as sociopolitical beings. Practices of vigilance, confinement, and punitive subjugation such as beatings and torture, common in authoritarian regimes and penal systems, are meant to replace *bios* with pure *zoë*.

The regime's intent is to limit life to the body, a surface that can bear the full brunt of the law. Representatives of the state assert their position of power by attempting to construct the prisoners' masculinity as inferior through the employment of mechanisms that connote a loss of control. The inmates are stripped, tortured, and placed in solitary confinement. This demonstration of power imposes on the prisoners the hypermasculine ideals favored by the military regime.

As an example, the events surrounding Miguel's and Peninha's solitary confinement illustrate how the principle works. Upon learning of the death of their comrade Marilena, Miguel and the inmates of the Galeria LSN decide to protest their physical and social isolation (they are not given access to media outlets nor other informational materials) as well as their lack of recognition as political prisoners. In protest, the inmates sign a petition to the director of the Ilha Grande penitentiary demanding official recognition as political prisoners and access to daily newspapers. To place pressure on the government to recognize their demands, Miguel and Peninha stage a distraction during visiting hours so that Ana (Jerusa Franco), Miguel's girlfriend, can smuggle a copy of their letter of protest out of the prison. As punishment for the disturbance, Miguel and Peninha are stripped, and each is placed in solitary confinement.

The film represents the inmates' time in solitary confinement visually by stripping the detainees of their physical garments and the suppression of *bios* in an attempt to reduce them to a state of *homo sacer*. In the scene following the commotion in the visitation area of the prison, the camera cuts to the guards dragging Miguel and Peninha down a dark windowless corridor and throwing them into solitary holding cells. The guards slam the solid metal doors, and through diegetic sound one hears the jingle of keys lock the men in the dank rooms. The camera lingers in the minimally lit corridor, registering the black of the two doors that are barely discernable against the subtle variations of the black and dark-gray hues of the walls. Nondiegetic noise, a high-pitched sustained squeal, creates a sound bridge between the outside shot of the doors and the cut to the inside of the cells. Low-key lighting, focused solely on the bodies of the detainees, draws attention to the contours of their flesh.

The camera mimics the vigilance of the state apparatus by isolating the individual within the frame and centralizing the body as the site of state control. The prolonged high-pitched sound in combination with Miguel's and Peninha's pacing bodies creates an almost dizzying effect that communicates the claustrophobic nature of their surroundings and the passage of time. The frame cuts to a shot of Miguel's dirty hands and blackened fingernails as they slowly emerge from beneath a blanket that minimally covers his body slouched on the floor, leaning against the wall.

The scene draws the attention of the spectator to the mechanism of control that the regime applies to the physical bodies of the inmates. In juxtaposition to these apparatuses, the homosocial bonds between Miguel and Peninha serve as a source of strength and resistance. The two men are visually paired here and throughout many of the Ilha Grande scenes. The prisoners employ their bodies as locations of resistance, such as through a hunger strike. The hunger strike of the political prisoners in the film references actual hunger strikes that occurred during the dictatorship.

On October 13, 1978, the Brazilian Congress passed constitutional Amendment 11, revoked AI-5, and restored habeas corpus after ten years. The amendment took effect on January 1, 1979. With AI-5 recently defeated, discussions around passing a possible amnesty law began to circulate. However, the amnesty law the government was proposing, in its original iteration, did not extend amnesty to all political prisoners. In light of this, on July 22, 1979, prisoners at the Presídio Frei Caneca in Rio began a hunger strike that would spread to other prisons throughout the country. The hunger strike resulted in the National Congress passing the Lei de Anistia on August 11, 1979. Under this law, while the government officials responsible for torture and killings were given amnesty, prisoners convicted of "crimes of blood" ("crimes de sangue") such as kidnappings, terrorism, and armed robbery remained imprisoned. This was the largest hunger strike ever to take place in Brazil. While it began in mid-1979, its rumblings were already a matter concern for the dictatorship in 1977, when female political prisoners at the Bangu women's prison began a hunger strike, demanding a transfer to the Presidio Político Frei Caneca. In solidarity with their hunger strike, prisoners from the men's prisons Frei Caneca in Rio de Janeiro and Lemos de Brito in Salvador also participated. This grabbed the attention of authorities who were concerned it could spread throughout the country. On November 8, 1977, Senator Amaral Peixoto made a *pronunciamento* (pronouncement) requesting that the president of the republic find a solution to the hunger strike.[17]

Hunger strikes are political acts that transform the body into a site of resistance in an attempt to reaffirm the excluded or negated political voice (*bios*) of the prisoner. The hunger strike transforms the act of self-starvation into a public act—the release of a list of demands to the general public—that reinserts the prisoner into the wider polis and imposes a temporal element that negates the possibility of continuous deferral of action. The state must respond to the action because the strike is literally transformed into a question of life and death that has a definitive temporal endpoint.

The act of resistance can be recircumscribed from the individual to a collective or wider social context. An example is found in the following statement from members of the Provisional Irish Republican Army who participated in the 1981 hunger strikes by political prisoners in Northern Ireland:

> From the moment we entered the H-blocks we had used our bodies as a protest weapon. It came from an understanding that the Brits were using our bodies to break us. It wasn't just a prison movement. We began to identify with the oppressed all over the world. That's how full the circle had become. (Qtd. in Feldman 232)

In Murat's film, one can understand the strike not solely as an act of individual prisoners but also as the attempted reassertion of the political voice, the *bios*, of the leftist resistance into the political framework of the country. In this way the body becomes a site of contention and contestation between the individual and the state. However, the film swiftly moves from focalizing these tensions to examining the divisions that develop within the prison population, principally between common and political prisoners. This thematic shift is reflected in a change from an approximation focused on the biopolitics of corporality and the physical control of bodies to a biopolitics of gender.

Prison: A Petri Dish of Masculinity

One can better understand the transition from a biopolitics of the body to a biopolitics of gender by drawing a parallel with the distinction between sex and gender. Sex normally refers to the biological designation of the sexed body. This is traditionally constructed as a binary, male/female, although recently there has been a push to recognize the sexed body as existing within a continuum rather than a simple binary.[18]

Gender, on the other hand, references the sociocultural sense and expression of the sexed body. Jemima Repo in *The Biopolitics of Gender* argues for the need to reconsider gender through the lens of biopower and how it has been deployed as a mechanism of power since the 1950s, particularly in the final quarter of the twentieth century. Repo positions her work as a progression of Michel Foucault's now canonical analyses of modern discourses of power, the body, and sexuality.

Foucault attempts to decenter the regimes of power that are employed within society to control the sexed body. He contends that sexuality is rooted in biopolitical power regimes with the intent of controlling the sexualized body, ultimately regulating whole populations. Expanding on Foucault's work, Repo proposes that the deployment of gender has created a new arena within the "life-administering" (as understood by Foucault) function of power. This began at the same moment that a series of crises, specifically the post–World War II crisis of masculinity, had struck the western world.[19] Repo notes, "The invention of gender linked this new technology of social control [gender] with the sexual apparatus" (19).

Concentrating on the shift from the biopolitics of the body to a biopolitics of gender in *Quase Dois Irmãos* reveals how gender functions as a central mechanism of control in Brazilian society over the past half-century. The prison and the military state apparatus are two important institutions when considering gender relations between men as biopolitical mechanisms of control.

Within the Brazilian penitentiary system, just as with most penal systems worldwide, men constitute the overwhelming majority of the inmate population.[20] Thus, the space of the prison takes on heightened significance in discussing questions of men and masculinities. Don Sabo and colleagues, in their work on the US prison population, contend that prison is an ultramasculine world where nobody talks about masculinity.[21] They find that the prison complex and the individuals it employs and incarcerates essentially ignore the centrality of masculinity and men's relations in reference to how men are detained, the functioning and organization of the homosocial community inside the detention centers, and prisoners' ability to reintegrate into society upon release (Sabo et al. 3). Prison has traditionally been a sex-segregated space, overwhelmingly populated and administered by men, although the number of women within the prison complex is rising quickly, as prisoners and as guards and administrators. The prison is a space configured around sex segregation, homosocial ordering, patriarchal hierarchies, and violence, thus locating it as a traditionally representative patriarchal institution (Sabo et al. 7–8). Accordingly, these homosocial spaces of the prison but also military institutions are pivotal in the formulation of masculinities because the space exacerbates the construction and expression of masculinities that one can locate beyond the prison walls. Within this structuring, hegemonic masculinity is expressed overwhelmingly through intermale violence and dominance hierarchies constituted around divisions of class, race, and sexuality (Sabo et al. 5–6).

Ilha Grande: Masculinities in Conflict

In Murat's film, the prison works as a microcosm of masculine relations in Brazil during the 1970s. *Quase Dois Irmãos* illuminates how relations between men were predominantly configured and how they changed with the decline of the dictatorship. The film shows that some of the building blocks of tensions between men of different classes were set during the military regime and the subsequent democratic transition. With the transition, parts of the repressive governmental structure assimilated into the democratic regime, but also the authoritarian male was subsumed into new expressions of hegemonic masculinity, which consolidated the privileged position of the white middle- and upper-class male in society. The devolving relationship between Jorginho and Miguel in prison is representative of these changes.

In the 1970s, when the audience reencounters Jorginho, he has been detained and is awaiting transfer from the mainland to Ilha Grande prison. Jorginho is thrown into a detention cell with a group of political prisoners awaiting transfer to the Lei de Segurança wing. When Jorginho is put in the holding pen with the other men, a voiceover of Miguel offers an evaluation of the situation: "Perhaps Jorginho's life was a foretold tragedy that we helped write" ("A vida de Jorginho talvez tinha sido uma tragédia anunciada que nós ajudamos a escrever"). The narrative voice purports to recognize the participation of the middle and upper classes in contemporary social, economic, and racial divisions in Brazil. Nonetheless, the "talvez" ("perhaps") in this statement opens a space for Miguel and the middle- and upper-class viewing public to expunge their participation through the film's naturalizing of violence, which is connected to the marginal male subject. In this way, the political dissidents' role in Jorginho's tragedy is contained, limited to the Comando Vermelho's appropriation of the organizing principles that the political dissidents employed.

Figure 3.4. Jorginho in the holding cell with the political prisoner: "Who's the sheriff of this fucking place?" Screen grab from *Quase Dois Irmãos*.

When Jorginho is thrown into the cell, he backs into a corner, holding his shoes in his hands, and inquires, "Who's the sheriff of this fucking place?" ("Quem é o sherife dessa porra?"). The response from political prisoner Marcos (Charles Fricks) is that there is no sheriff. "Everyone is equal" ("Somos todos iguais"). While in theory the prisoners preach equality, it is made clear to Jorginho that this theoretical equality has tangible limits. Specifically, another political prisoner, Aluísio (Bruce Gomlevsky), establishes that at the prison there is a collective of 150 political prisoners and three rules: you can't rob, engage in pederasty, or smoke marijuana. Jorginho scoffs at the idea that in jail they prohibit smoking pot. Marcos tells Jorginho that the prison is for political prisoners, so he can disagree but better consider what he is going to do against the others.

At a linguistic level, the inmates' discourse formally advocates equality within the prison population. However, the differentiated status between the political prisoners in juxtaposition to Jorginho, a common prisoner, is emphasized by the mise-en-scène and filming techniques. These visual indicators contradict the political prisoners' formal discourses of equality.

Throughout the scene, the cell remains spatially divided between the two groups. When Jorginho first enters the cell, Marcos stares intently at him. Subsequently, the camera tracks Marcos as he stands up and moves toward Jorginho and the camera. The focus is on Marcos's face as the camera tracks in, visually endowing him with power. As he announces that there is not a sheriff, a crane shot reiterates division through the spatial composition of the cell. Successively, there is a cut to a downward-tilt shot that traces Jorginho's standing body pressed against the wall, first tossing his shoes down and then sliding to a sitting position. In a quick shot-countershot sequence, the camera pulls the political prisoners inward at the same time that it emphasizes Jorginho backed against the wall. As Marcos explains the rules to Jorginho, the camera backs out to an over-the-shoulder shot framing, reproducing Marcos's perspective, visually inviting the viewer to identify with the political prisoners' viewpoint. In this fashion the camera boxes Jorginho in, visually controlling him. The scene creates a back-and-forth pull between linguistically insinuating the possibility of the incorporation while visually reaffirming Jorginho as "other" to the white middle-class political prisoners, between tenuous inclusion and intimidation.

The scene embodies an observation by Sabo: "The masculinity that surfaces in the prison is more an attitude, a hazy cluster of concerns and expectations that get translated into emotion and physical movement in ways that never quite come clear" (63). The scene foregrounds Jorginho as the political prisoners' other. He is the only Afro-Brazilian detained for an unspecified common crime, and his understanding of how prison and masculine relations function deviates from the perception of the predominantly white upper- and middle-class men with whom he is housed. When the camera cuts from the scene, Jorginho squats in a corner of the cell while the group of political prisoners occupies the other side. In the final shot-countershot, Marcos and the political inmates stare intently at Jorginho while he diverts his gaze downward from them. What we witness are the initial pressures for Jorginho to assimilate to the political prisoners' hegemonic masculine paradigm while registering him as an outsider to their group.

Ilha Grande: Masculinity, Race, and Biopolitics

Jorginho is part of an initial small cohort of common prisoners who were placed in the Galeria LSN wing of the prison under the Lei de Segurança Nacional decree. Upon his arrival at Ilha Grande, the political prisoners had begun a hunger strike and are circulating pragmatic information on how to care for oneself physically. The political detainees encourage the common prisoners to join their resistance efforts and cross the terrain of contravention into that of subversion.

The film denotes how the newly arrived common prisoners jest at the collective's efforts, reiterating their differentiation, thematized in the main-land holding-cell scene. When Jorginho receives instructions for the hun-ger strike, he and his cell mate sit on their lower bunk reading the norms that should be applied: exert the least amount of energy feasible, sleep as much as possible, and drink saltwater several times daily. They respond with explicatives "Fuck! Damn!" ("Porra! Caralho!"), smiling and laugh-ing at the idea. Jorginho goes on to ask, "So this means that I'll have to go hungry, drink water like a camel, and sleep like an old goat" ("Quer dizer que eu vou ter que passar fome, beber água que nem um camelo e dormir feito um bode velho"). Jorginho bleats like a goat as the two men keel over in laughter. The film cuts to Miguel and Peninha preparing a mixture of saltwater when we hear the guards pulling Jorginho from his cell.

The guards (Hugo Leonardo and Rafael Nannheimer) find Jorginho in possession of a document that outlines the norms of the hunger strike and attempt to ensure that he not ally himself with the political detainees. They employ a biopolitical "matrix of domination" (Hill Collins) in which race and class are employed in unison with brute force and physical depriva-tion to refute Jorginho's insertion into *bios* through his identification with the *coletivo*: "Black motherfucker. You mean you also like going on hunger strikes. You'll see what happens" ("Negro filho da puta. Quer dizer que também gosta de fazer greve de fome. Vai ver o que acontecer"). The guards drag Jorginho into a separate room and beat him until blood runs down his chest and face. As he lands multiple blows to Jorginho's face and body, the main guard exclaims, "Shameless black man. Black subversives do not exist!" ("Negro sem vergonha. Negro subversivo não existe!"). The back-ground is blacked out, and the visual focus is centralized on the tortured body of the prisoner through the use of hard-focalized lighting. Jorginho is stripped down to his underpants, his body limp and bleeding. This con-trasts visually with the guards who stand erect as they beat and jab him with their billy club, an obvious phallic reference.

What one witnesses is the violation of Jorginho's body by the guards. He is emasculated and thus projected as embodying an inferior masculinity, subjected to the brutalization of the guards. This is the only torture scene of the film. The scene highlights the tearing down of Jorginho's mascu-line identity at the end when they drag him out of the room unconscious and bleeding. He has become a passive body. There are parallels between Jorginho's torture and Marilena's death. Both denote the infliction of the law by bypassing it. Their torture and her death are at once legitimated, as a mechanism employed by the state to defend against enemies of the state and of society, and denied, as in the state's denial of detaining political prisoners. Although the existence of common inmates is not contradicted, they are in effect legally invisible due to their racial and socioeconomic status and their emasculation, projected as inferior to the political prisoners.

Jorginho's torture stands in juxtaposition to the solitary confinement of Miguel and Peninha, whose homosocial bonds are a source of strength and resistance. While the former is passively dragged away by the guards, the political prisoners walk out of their solitary confinement. They maintain a measure of masculine agency.

It is at this moment that Jorginho is pulled into the collective. His torture opens the possibility of identification with the political prisoners. The members of the collective begin to beat on their doors and denounce that the guards "took one of the guys from the collective" ("levaram um do coletivo"). Miguel confronts the guards directly, attempting to assert a sense of *bios* for the group. He protests that guards took someone from one of the cells up front and beat him. He says, "There are no common prisoners in this cell block, he is part of the collective. If he disappears it is the administration's responsibility" ("Não tem preso comum não, ele faz parte do coletivo. Se ele desaparecer é responsabilidade da administração"). When the political detainees are able to stop Jorginho's torture, he accepts the rules of their collective. He, in effect, submits to their masculine rituals.

It is during this time frame that Jorginho integrates into the hegemonic masculine paradigm of the middle- and upper-class political detainees. The film emphasizes this shift first by eliminating almost all references to common prisoners. Besides Jorginho, common prisoners are absent on screen, and the narrative ceases to differentiate between common and political prisoners. Common prisoners only reappear on screen when the power dynamic of the cell block begins to shift with the arrival of a new cohort of common prisoners.

Second, Jorginho becomes part of the homosocial grouping of Miguel and Peninha after the scene of Jorginho being beaten. This is almost immediately brought to the fore with the shift to Miguel, Peninha, and Jorginho playing a samba in their cell. Their musical foray points toward a rekindling of the previous bonds that Miguel and Jorginho shared in their childhood at the Santa Marta samba school.

Nonetheless, these horizontal homosocial bonds constructed around emotional support and intimacy that focus on the men sharing music and fellowship in their cells very quickly shift to the imposition of vertical homosocial bonds meant to guarantee male hierarchies and established power structures within the prison. This transition is accomplished by pairing what begins as the group of men casually singing samba to kill time and segues into Miguel, Peninha, and Jorginho "disappearing" the inmate João's (Paulo Hamilton) cat, Trotsky.

Set to the playful rhythm of Peninha's guitar, the three men bag the cat in a pillowcase as they hiss and torment it. The film cuts to João when he stumbles upon Miguel, Peninha, and Jorginho in the showers and asks them the whereabouts of his cat. In jest, they make cat sounds, hissing, purring, and the like. Gradually their bullying takes a serious turn. Miguel confronts João, scolding him for feeding the cat from his allotted milk ration because *companheiros* are starving in Vietnam. Their cruel treatment of the cat mirrors the violence of the state and centralizes violence as a ritual of male bonding. Beyond this, it serves to guarantee the hierarchical power structure between the inmates. The three men have attained dominant status in the cell block, therefore establishing the social and masculine norms that are then imposed upon the other inmates (Connell; Connell and Messerschmidt).

A second incident cements the development of these vertical homosocial bonds around a hegemonic masculine paradigm vis-à-vis women. After Miguel learns that his girlfriend, Ana, has left him for another man, Jorginho tries to cheer him up. This time, rather than functioning as a band of brothers who confront nonconforming men and impose a hegemonic masculine paradigm over them, as was the case with João, they unite through the denigration of women.

Jorginho pulls Ana's picture from the wall and sits next to Miguel in his bunk. Jorginho begins cursing the photograph, exclaiming, "Motherfucker" ("Filha da puta").[22] He invites Miguel to join in. Their exclamations assume a growing crescendo as they cuss at the photo. Jorginho begins tapping out a samba rhythm on the tambourine to "motherfucker." Very quickly this rhythm segues into the film's opening musical score "Quem me vê sorrindo" ("Who Sees Me Smiling"). The juxtaposition prioritizes male homosocial bonds in counterposition to male-female relations. It also recalls their childhood memories of the Santa Marta samba school, the bonds that united their fathers, and a legacy of male-female tension.

This moment of male bonding repeats the previous ideals of camaraderie that the viewer witnessed in the disappeared cat scene at the same time that it focalizes the rekindling of the childhood bond that Miguel and Jorginho shared. We could argue that these scenes construct Jorginho as complicit, participating in the benefits garnered through his incorporation into the hegemonic masculine paradigm of the Galeria LSN prisoners (Connell 79). For example, the political prisoners have negotiated concrete privileges not given to the other prisoners such as visitation rights. Miguel will later reference these benefits to chastise the common prisoners in an attempt to convince them to join the political detainees as tension grows within the cell block.

Through elliptical editing, a sound bridge of samba is employed to mark the passing of time. Miguel and Jorginho are sitting on Miguel's bed; their singing of Cartola's "Quem me vê sorrindo" continues. The camera pans right across the length of the bed to Peninha, who enters the cell strumming his guitar. The sound bridge accompanies the camera as it pans back left. Miguel and Jorginho have shifted physical positions, and their attire has changed. It is the day of Peninha's release. The breaking apart of Miguel and Peninha's homosocial prison bond is the beginning of the end of the political prisoners' hegemonic masculine order as the composition of the prison population shifts. With the changing prison population, the dominant masculine paradigm that privileged the upper- and middle-class white male also is transformed, and a struggle for power ensues.

Between Men in Prison: Negating the *Bios* of Common Prisoners, Transferring the State of Exception

Demetrakis Demetriou argues that hegemonic masculinity is not simply an oppositional force that pits itself against all nonhegemonic masculinities; he maintains that hegemonic masculinity is constantly reinventing and renegotiating itself to retain its position of power. Demetriou contends that masculinity adopts what is outside of or counterhegemonic to it, progressively incorporating elements of the outside into a hegemonic bloc with the aim of retaining and reproducing the status quo's masculine power structure.

When a new group of common prisoners and their leader, Pingão (Badu Santana), join the Galeria LSN cell block, the intent of the *coletivo* is for the new prisoners to assimilate to the established group's power structure, as Jorginho had. However, when it becomes obvious that the new group is not willing to conform, the *coletivo* centralizes masculinity as a ground of contention that molds their response to the newcomers. The political prisoners struggle to retain power by increasingly embracing violence and incorporating external power markers to preserve their hegemonic status. The spectator can see this playing out in the early encounters between the two groups. Paradigmatic is the scene following Jorginho's warm reception of Pingão and the other common prisoners. The film cuts to Pingão explaining to the other common inmates how to play dice. They are about ready to place their bets when Miguel and other members of the *coletivo* arrive to explain the rules of the Galeria LSN to the new arrivals. The film focuses on the *coletivo*'s welcome party and cuts to Miguel as he explains, "Hi comrade, those of us here are part of the representatives of our collective. We hope that you will integrate quickly so that we have more strength to fight against repression" ("Aí companheiro, nós aqui fazemos parte da representação do coletivo. Nós desejamos que vocês se integrem rápido para a gente ter mais força para lutar contra a repressão").

In a shot-countershot close-up sequence, the camera tracks the conversation. Pingão responds, "So you are the ones who run this shithole" ("Então são vocês que mandam nesta porra"). Pingão's understanding of the situation is framed within traditional configurations of prison power structures in which a sheriff runs the prison wing, makes all decisions, and apportions goods and services. In response, Aluísio, whom Jorginho initially encountered in the transfer-holding cell, notes that decisions are not made by a sheriff: "Here, we only have one representative elected by the collective. Do you understand? This whole boss, sheriff thing does not work here. Here, decisions are voted on by the collective" ("Aqui tem só uma representação eleita pelo coletivo. Me está entendendo? Essa coisa de mandar, de xerife não tem aqui não. Aqui as decisões são votadas pelo coletivo"). Tensions escalate when Pingão responds, "My brother, it works like this. I am a smart man, you understand. This fucking voting thing is for those who have a voter's card. I'm a bum, a killer!" ("Meu irmão, o caso é o seguinte. Eu sou sabido, morou. Essa porra de votação é para quem tem título de votação. Eu sou vagabundo, matador!").

The reference to voter registration distances the common prisoners from the political platform of those who are already there. Pingão's response challenges the hegemonic masculine paradigm of the upper- and middle-class political prisoners. He inflames tensions through his emphasis on hypermasculine norms constructed around violence and male bravado. In light of the changing demographics, the narrative implies that the newly arrived common prisoners are a threat to the democratic principles that are at least discursively central to the political prisoners' platform.

The subsequent argument between Miguel and Pingão reflects a repositioning of the political prisoners to Pingão's incitement of violence as a central element of masculine expression in the Galeria LSN. Miguel cautions,

"This prison has rules. . . . Everyone here has kidnapped, everyone here has stolen, has killed" ("Esta cadeia tem normas. . . . Todo mundo aqui já sequestrou, todo mundo aqui já roubou, já matou"), to which Pingão jests, "They have stolen what, my brother, . . . candy from a baby? Killed a cockroach in the corner?" ("Roubou que, meu irmão, . . . doce de criança? Matou barata no canto?"). A fistfight between Miguel and Pingão breaks out until Jorginho steps in and imposes order. The latent violence that undergirded Miguel, Peninha, and Jorginho's disappearance of João's cat Trotsky is brought to the surface. Violence is transformed into the language between men.

After this encounter, the *coletivo* incorporates more violent methods into their masculine self-definition, reflecting an increasingly authoritarian masculinity toward the common prisoners. When the *coletivo* is threatened with relinquishing their power, they reproduce a logic that echoes that of the dictatorship to guarantee their privileged position. Interestingly, João, the only racial minority within the political prisoner collective, is the sole voice that recognizes the similarities between the *coletivo*'s response to the common prisoners and the regime's to political dissidents.

Thus, while the *coletivo* at first preaches an ideology of inclusion, the body language and underlying tension that pulsate in the scene refute the men's discourse. In their hypocrisy one can find parallels with the gap between public discourse and socioeconomic and spatial divisions beyond the walls of the prison. This scene initiates what results in the complete segregation of the two groups. Jorginho subsequently derides Miguel:

> I thought we are all equal. We have to unite. My child will attend the same school as yours. Our destinies are the same. We will live the same way as you. Fuck, my brother, you all don't even want to live with us inside here. They are bastards, that is true. When you need something, everyone is equal. Now you send a letter to the prison director to separate, . . . rich there, poor here; white there, black here. Don't fuck with me.

> Pensei que nós somos todos iguais. A gente tem que se unir. Meu filho vai estudar na mesma escola que o teu. O nosso destino é o mesmo. Nós vamos viver da mesma forma que vocês. Porra, meu irmão, vocês nem aqui dentro querem morar com a gente. São safados, isso sim. Quando precisar de alguma coisa, todo mundo é igual. Agora mandam carta para o diretor para separar . . . rico para lá, pobre para cá; branco para lá, preto para cá. Não fode, porra.

In his monologue, Jorginho signals the gap between ideological discourse and reality when the middle and upper classes are confronted with forgoing their position of privilege. After a wall is erected in the common hall area to segregate the common and political prisoners, Jorginho adorns the central cement column of the common prisoners' space with bright red letters: "Proletarian political prisoners" ("Políticos proletários"). The new Comando Vermelho wing assumes the discourse of the *coletivo,* applying their organizational techniques to the constitution of the common prisoner bloc. At the same time, the political prisoners have now assumed a neo-authoritarian role that has parallels with the dictatorial regime.

Under the 1964–1985 regime, left-leaning middle- and upper-class youths such as Miguel and Peninha were identified as threats by the regime and thus persecuted, imprisoned, and disappeared. In the film, as it transitions into the 1980s and the end of the regime, the upper- and middle-class prisoners have assumed this same stance by identifying the lower classes as an inherent threat to the social and political structure.

Returning to the ideas of Sabo and colleagues, the prison is a homosocial space that is paramount in the formulation of masculinities, gender, and power relations both inside and beyond the prison walls. What the viewer witnesses in *Quase Dois Irmãos* is the transference of the authoritarian mores from the regime into the future middle-class political elites. It is the continuation of neo-authoritarian masculinity incorporated within a contemporary sociopolitical hierarchy that privileges divisions of class, race, and masculinity (Sabo et al. 5–6).

Sociologist Loïc Wacquant argues that the penalization of poverty in Brazilian society is the continuation of a status quo politics inherited from the most recent dictatorship ("Toward a Dictatorship" 199; "Militarization" 60). In the spatial segregation of the prison that *Quase Dois Irmãos* depicts, we find a parallel to the widening social divisions that become more pronounced throughout the 1980s and 1990s and into the 2000s. This has led to the configuration of the urban space as a *cidade partida*, a divided city, a reality that now scars the sociospatial composition of Brazilian metropolitan centers.[23] The spatial segregation of the city has been rationalized by the social and political elites in part through the demonization of the marginal male and the naturalization of his propensity toward violence.

Into the Twenty-First Century: From the Prison to the Streets

By the time of the film's final segment, set in the 2000s, Miguel has internalized a neo-authoritarian masculine mindset that originally drove the political prisoners to segregate the LSN prison block in the 1970s. While his position as a senator in a democratically elected government and his calm demeanor on screen appear to contradict an authoritarian mindset, the reproduction of the codes that he incorporated during his time in prison continue to guide his worldview. This is apparent in his conversation with Jorginho at the Bangu prison.

Miguel wants to discuss the possibility of constructing a cultural center in the favela: "We have received international financing to build cultural centers in poor communities. If you support me, I can get one for the Macacos favela" ("Nós conseguimos financiamento internacional para centros culturais em comunidades carentes. Se você me apoiar, eu posso conseguir um para o morro de Macacos"). At first glance, the initiative gives the impression of being grounded in Miguel's continuation of his fight for the social good that undergirded his resistance to the dictatorship. However, his discourse is couched in a paternalistic system of social assistance that, by the end of his presentation of the project, reveals the continuation of the same hegemonic neo-authoritarian episteme that drove him to call for segregation at Ilha Grande. As he continues, the viewer becomes privy to his true conviction about the youth of the favela: "It could be an alternative for that group of unemployed little punk asses" ("Pode ser uma alternativa para esse bando de moleques desempregados").

Antonio Gramsci has argued that cultural hegemony comprises the norms and mores that guide our everyday lives, the "common sense" framework that organizes how we navigate the world. However, the Italian philosopher asserts, these everyday mores are anything but common sense; they are the invisible political foundations that facilitate the imposition of systems of control within populations (*Prison Notebooks*). Within this episteme, hegemonic masculinity is not achieved simply through the imposition of violence, nor is it necessarily the most virile expression of masculinity. Rather, hegemonic masculinity is the controlling paradigm of masculinity, a dominant cultural pattern that subordinates other masculinities (and femininities) to it (Connell; Connell and Messerschmidt). The film shows how this dominant cultural pattern has shifted by the early 2000s to maintain the subordination of the marginal male. Miguel has naturalized this framework, a position that permits him to retain his social and political dominance. The filming techniques work in conjunction with the construction of the characters to transmit this ideal.

Mise-en-Scène Framing Prison

To understand how the marginal male is cast in a subordinate position in the contemporary period, we need to comprehend how the film organizes the scene sequences to guide the spectator's reading of the narrative. While the 1970s receive the most screen time, it is the 2000s that serve as the anchor point that structures the film. More specifically, the film employs the conversation between Miguel and Jorginho at the Presídio de Segurança Máxima Bangu (maximum-security prison at Bangu) in 2004 to evoke flashbacks to the 1950s and 1970s in conjunction with the narration of contemporaneous events, all of which develop the thematic points that arise out of Miguel and Jorginho's conversation. Their exchange is cut into nine scene segments that proceed chronologically.[24]

The mise-en-scène of the Bangu prison scenes establishes the tone of this organizing narrative. When the scene opens, it is with a tracking shot of a formal pair of black, shiny, leather shoes moving across the screen. White vertical bars divide the foreground of the camera from the background, where a person whom the viewer later identifies as Miguel is passing. The camera cuts to a headshot framing of Miguel's face as he stares intently at the camera. The prison bars cast hesitant shadows on the wall behind him. The screen cuts to a matching shot of Jorginho, only he stands behind the white bars of the prison cell that frame him, eyes cast downward. The parallel framing visually implies their spatial proximity but also their intersecting lives. They are "almost brothers," whose meaning the viewer will only come to understand as the film progresses.

Initially, the camera remains outside the cell and employs the bars in the foreground to block-frame the shots, a constant reminder of the enclosed space. When the camera ventures into the cell, Jorginho remains framed by the metal bars. Miguel, on the other hand, is framed against the flat background of the wall, freeing him from the confines of the prison and visually distancing him, even if only momentarily, from the prison space.

The men's wardrobes work in tandem with the framing. Miguel dons a formal black suit, white shirt, black tie, and black leather shoes. His outfit contrasts with the surrounding beige walls and white bars of the prison. He is a representative of the state, a *deputado*, which Jorginho underscores by referring to him by his title and refusing the more personal use of his name.

Figure 3.5. Parallel framing of Jorginho and Miguel at Bangu prison. Screen grabs from *Quase Dois Irmãos*.

Jorginho, in contrast, is wearing a beige polo with dark navy-blue and white vertical stripes. While not a traditional prison jumpsuit, his attire visually reproduces his surroundings, the beige of the shirt blending into the beige wall of the background and the broad vertical white and blue stripes echoing the prison bars. The visual parallels between the space and Jorginho's wardrobe cast him as a natural presence within the prison. He is on display, to be observed and considered a cautionary case study of what the middle and upper classes can expect of the marginal male.

Masculine Panic: Protecting Middle-Class Women from the Marginal Male

A well-worn trope within colonial literature is that of the threatened white woman from the dominant socioeconomic group who must be protected from the ravishment of the savage native man. *Quase Dois Irmãos* taps into this narrative to augment a sense of risk to hegemonic middle- and upper-class masculinity. In the film this is achieved through various lines of development. First, the middle and upper classes are progressively associated with female characters. Juliana and her girlfriends are the face of the middle- and upper-class youth. The film does not introduce any middle- or upper-class young men. The film emasculates the entire socioeconomic stratum. At the same time, Miguel, the sole middle-class male of the contemporary narrative, is in metaphorical terms castrated since he is unable to control or contain his daughter and thus incapable of protecting her from the menace of the marginal male.

In juxtaposition to these women, the youth of the favela are projected as ever more synonymous with the hypermasculine peripheral male: Deley, Duda, and the young men in their gangs.[25] Their interactions are marked by violence, the objectification of women, and a general disregard for the rule of state law, of which Miguel is a representative; the young men impose a hierarchical masculine order through gang culture. At the same time, young women from the favela replicate this patriarchal hypermasculine order. Specifically, there is a group of young women (Adriele de Oliveira, Jaina Christina, Jéssica Santos, and Joana Serafim), led by Mina de Fé (Pâmela Bispo), whose primary role within the film is to defend their men, in this scene Deley, from outside women, here Juliana. Mina de Fé and Juliana are Deley's lovers, and the two women have a growing rivalry over him. In their encounters, the storyline moves from tension at the opening *baile funk* to physical confrontation when Mina de Fé throws Juliana to the ground during an altercation. Juliana is dominated by representatives of the favela: Deley, Mina de Fé, and ultimately Duda.

While we encounter Juliana and her friends only a couple of times, the middle-class schoolgirls are clearly visually differentiated from Mina de Fé and the other young women from the favela. This is most obvious when, following an argument between Juliana and Deley, Juliana and her friends are leaving the favela and run into Mina de Fé and her gang. As the middle-class women walk down the steep stairs, they are all wearing jeans or jean skirts and T-shirts. They are carrying backpacks, and a couple of them have notebooks in their hands. The visual clues provided by the wardrobe and props emphasize a degree of discretion in terms of attire and the objectification of their bodies. They are identified with education—they are carrying school items—and endowed with an air of immature youthfulness. In contrast, Mina and her girlfriends are all wearing halter tops and high-cut shorts. Their props are their bodies. While these indicators are somewhat

Figure 3.6. Visually differentiating the middle-class Juliana and her friends from Mina de Fé and the other young women from the favela through casting, wardrobe, and other elements of the mise-en-scène. Screen grab from *Quase Dois Irmãos*.

subtle, they unmistakably differentiate the two groups of women, creating a sense of vulnerability that is linked to the *asfalto*.

The confrontation between the women is a result of Juliana's sexually charged relationship with Deley, which the film constructs as putting her at risk. Thus, Miguel, and by extension the viewer of the film, are asked to protect her. In the only intimate sex scene of the film, Deley and Juliana are at his place having sex when his scout (Bernardo Santos) interrupts them because Duda killed a street vendor to send a warning and challenge to Deley's authority. Deley throws Juliana out, making clear that she is not his priority.

> Deley: Something happened. Get your stuff and go.
> Juliana: No, my big black man, let's get back to it.
> Deley: I told you to go. Fuck! Get your stuff and go. Please, don't complicate things.
> Juliana: I come all the way up here, climb all those stairs, and you tell me to go?
> Deley: Fuck you! I've already told you and I'll say it once more: get your stuff and get out!
> Juliana: Don't talk to me like that.
> Deley: I will if I want to. For the last time: get your stuff and get out!
> Juliana: Watch how you talk to me. I'm not one of your little girls from the favela.
> Deley: Who do you think you are, a fucking princess? You're just another girl. Listen to me. I'm going down and if I see you here again, I'll beat you! I'll throw you out of that fucking window!

> Deley: Puta, tenho uma imprevista. Pega as tuas coisas e vai embora.
> Juliana: Ah não negão, vamos voltar.
> Deley: Já falei para tu ir embora, caralho. Pega as tuas coisas e vai embora. Por favor, para não complicar.
> Juliana: Porra, Deley, vem até aqui, subir essa escadaria para tu me mandar embora, cara?
> Deley: Foda-se, eu já falei para você e é a última vez que te repito: Pega as tuas coisas e vai embora, caralho!
> Juliana: Foda-se, não fala assim comigo, não.
> Deley: É dai, falo do jeito que eu quiser. Pega as tuas coisas e vai embora. Não vou ficar repetindo, não.
> Juliana: Como é que fala comigo. Eu não só ninguém do morro não.

Deley: Quem você pensa que é, meu irmão? Uma princesa de merda? Você é só mais uma. E olha só aí, eu vou descer e se eu te ver aqui de novo eu vou te rebentar. Eu vou te jogar pela essa janela, caralho!

Deley's verbal and physical violence toward Juliana highlights the disposability of the female, the feminine within the hypermasculine frame of the favela. Once Juliana leaves the favela, female characters are eliminated from the scenes, and the violence between the opposing gangs escalates as the hypermasculine marginal males battle for control of Macacos. Juliana will only reappear in the favela and on screen in the final sequences of the film, when she is raped by Duda and his gang and is admitted to the hospital unconscious and violated.

A Cautionary Tale

In the final buildup to Juliana's rape, there is an interesting crescendo effect in the film. This buildup naturalizes the violence within the marginal classes and serves as a warning to its ominous consequences for Brazil's elites. The finale begins with a cut to the end of the 1970s. Jorginho and his group have killed Pingão and all his men to assert their dominance and power over the newly installed Comando Vermelho wing. Pingão and his crew's bodies lie on the floor on display in front of the gated doorway that divides the common and political prisoners. The camera dollies backward from the steel gate on the political prisoners' side. The common prisoners stand over the dead bodies. As the political prisoners approach the massacre, the camera continues to pull back. The screen cuts to a pan of the dead bodies and then tilts up. The screen cuts again to answering shots of Miguel and Jorginho standing on opposite sides of the dividing metal bars. They are both framed from eye level in close-up.

What is most telling are the expressions on their faces. When Miguel raises his eyes from the scene of carnage, his face shows surprise, sadness, and regret; he is frozen by the cold and calculated violence that Jorginho exacted upon his rivals. In contrast, the screen cuts to Jorginho, in a match framing. He does not look down but rather stares unflinchingly at Miguel, the camera's point of view shot. In the shot-countershot sequence, Miguel makes eye contact, and Jorginho's face lights up in a smile. This is the final scene of the 1970s.

The scene cites the match scene from Bangu prison when Miguel and Jorginho first meet in 2004. From this point, the film cuts back to Deley moving through the *morro* with his gang, weapons drawn, in search of Duda. By cutting directly to the war between Deley's and Duda's factions in the contemporary period, the film evokes the historical narrative of the story, foreshadows the violence to come, and posits the marginal male as naturally expressing a hypermasculine ethos that is constructed around violence.

The film ends by intercutting unnamed assailants murdering Jorginho in his cell, Duda and his crew gang-raping Juliana, and Miguel's frustrated attempt to transit through Rio during *carnaval* to get to the hospital. The scenes culminate with an ominous air, shot at night and having shed the previously vibrant color palette of the earlier contemporary scenes. Additionally, the extreme use of handheld cameras disorients the viewer through continual movement on screen. As Duda and his gang rape Juliana, the viewer initially hears them calling her "little slut" ("putinha"). Very quickly, the diegetic sound is cut and an instrumental version of the theme music "Somos quase irmãos" ("We Are Almost Brothers") plays. The camera witnesses Juliana screaming, the marginal male grabbing and violating her. The music score brings us back to the beginning of the film to witness the brutal reality of the life that has erased Miguel's idealism.

The focus on reality illuminates the epigraph of the film. As the sun rises, Miguel enters the hospital room where Juliana lies unconscious in bed. He approaches her and caresses her hand as his mother assures him, "Everything will be alright" ("Tudo vai ficar bem"). The scene fades again to an all-white screen in counterposition to the darkness of the previous scenes in the favela. The film ends with a pan of a Rio skyline populated by the white façades of middle- and upper-class apartment buildings in a medium long shot with the green hills of the city in the background. As the camera pans right and climbs the *morro*, the chaotic nature of the self-constructed housing of favelas occupies the foreground as the Cristo Redentor statue rises above the skyline. In a voiceover we return to the opening lines: "We all have two lives, the one that we dream of and the one that we live." This final scene summarizes the argument of the film. Juliana represents symbolically the emasculation of the middle and upper classes, a synecdoche of their vulnerability. In the violence that befalls her lies a cautionary tale, one that promotes the continuation and the strengthening of a neo-authoritarian male mindset in contemporary Brazilian society.

The 2006 bombings and mayhem in São Paulo that were provoked by the Primeiro Comando da Capital renewed debates around human rights and their application to common prisoners that have sprung up in Brazil since the transition to democratic rule in 1985. After the transition, the campaigns for human rights that had focused almost exclusively on political prisoners shifted their gaze to common prisoners and the application of those rights to this largely disenfranchised group. The common adage that equates human rights to "privileges for bandits" (Caldeira 340–46; Holston *Insurgent Citizenship*, 300–309) is emblematic of the debates that have dominated the country since the 1980s. A case in point is that of Franco Montoro, who was the first democratically elected governor of São Paulo post-transition and part of the transition back to democratic rule in Brazil. His platform as governor, from 1983 to 1987, was constructed around the promise of a return to the rule of law, the confronting of police abuses, and the betterment of prison conditions in the state. Montoro appointed Carlos Dias, a lawyer versed in the defense of political prisoners and human rights issues, as his secretary of justice. Dias pledged to "humanize the prisons" (Caldeira 342).

While Montoro and Dias struggled for human rights to gain a stronger foothold within governmental institutions and society more generally, crime was on the rise. The middle and upper classes took notice of this phenomenon. The sense of a breakdown in personal and public security garnered a backlash from the privileged classes and resonated within the mass media outlets. Rising fear and increased crime rates served (and still serve) as counterdiscourses to the initiatives of the former governor and were seen as a legitimating force for the negation of citizenship to marginal individuals and the continuation of a punitive approach to crime. The statistics reveal Brazilian society's approach to criminality. From 1980 to 2010, the prison population more than doubled every ten years, from 37,000 in 1980 to 90,000 in 1990 and to 232,000 in 2000, rising to almost 500,000 in 2010 and 750,000 in 2018. In 2015, approximately 37.5% of all incarcerated individuals were pretrial detainees ("Brazil" *World Prison Brief*). The numbers demonstrate that the binary structuring of Brazilian justice continues into the twenty-first century, and films such as *Quase Dois Irmãos* promote the status quo through the advancement of neo-authoritarian understanding of masculinity in Brazil.

4

It's a Man's World

Neo-Authoritarian Masculinity in *Tropa de Elite*

June 13, 2013, São Paulo, Brazil. Avenida Paulista was beginning to fill. The protesters had forced the closure of this central thoroughfare in São Paulo. Metro stops from Clínicas onward were shut down by police to limit access to the looming demonstrations for "fear of violence." The crossroads of Avenida Paulista, Avenida Dr. Arnaldo, Avenida Rebouças, and Avenida Consolação were a sea of state security forces. The forces expanded northwest down Avenida Dr. Arnaldo. Spanning out in the opposite direction down Avenida Paulista, the growing numbers of protesters reached as far as the eye could see. The tension in the air was palpable.

As I made my way back to the flat where I was staying a couple of blocks from the commotion, the security forces began pushing their way down Paulista. Arriving back at the flat, I clicked on the evening newscasts to follow what was happening on Avenida Paulista. The images that filled the screen showed the streets that I had just walked by. However, the protests that I had witnessed firsthand, while massive and agitated, did not coincide with the video clips of aggression and destruction that streamed over the networks. In subsequent days, daily newscasts streamed an unending loop of images of vandalism: shattered windows, large rocks and bricks lying among shards of glass, and masked youth destroying and pillaging private property. It is not that this did not occur, but there was a gap between the media's representations of the manifestations and what I had witnessed firsthand on the streets.

Discussions of the violence that "accompanied" the protests marked many conversations as individuals, particularly from the upper and middle classes, were in a panic about "the situation." The broadcast images confirmed fears that the upheaval was not about the increase in bus and metro fares but an excuse appropriated by criminal factions and lawless individuals who wanted to rob, steal, and otherwise plunder the middle- and upper-class bastions of the city.

The police crackdown on the protesters was thus presented not as the suppression of free speech but as the government protecting and securing the middle and upper classes against these anonymous yet socially, racially, and gender-marked bandits. The violent tactics used by the police to repress lower-class demonstrators obeyed a familiar modus operandi of the exaggerated response and deployment of an arsenal of increasingly military-style weaponry, from riot gear, batons, and riot shields to tear gas, rubber bullets, water canons, and stun grenades as well as violent assaults on groups and individual protesters.

Tropa de Elite is axiomatic to discussions of masculinity and violence in Brazilian film at the beginning of the twenty-first century and dialogues directly with the images broadcast on the night of June 13, 2013, and beyond. If ticket sales are any indication of the general public's endorsement of a film, then *Tropa de Elite* caused quite the sensation. It was the highest-grossing box-office success in Brazilian cinema the year of its release, and this after a pirate copy was leaked nationwide three months prior to the film's official release. The film even had an impact on the general public's acceptance of the Batalhão de Operações Policiais Especiais (BOPE, Special Operations Police Battalion), according to Rio de Janeiro police forces. In a television interview on the popular variety program *Fantástico* on September 23, 2007, Ubiratan Angelo, general commander of the military police in Rio de Janeiro at the time, praised the film for changing the public image of the police. He said youths playing cops and robbers had begun vying to be BOPE agents rather than drug dealers in their daily role-playing ("Fantástico").

Kingstone and Power's *Democratic Brazil Revisited* establishes that between 2000 and 2007, just prior to *Tropa de Elite*'s release, democratic rule and ideals were consolidated in Brazil. This strengthening also marked an erosion of authoritarian power through the further dismantling of several dictatorial structures in Brazilian society. These changes implied a contesting of the traditionally privileged position of dominant patriarchal culture and authoritarian power. Tellingly, police reform was not part of the restructuring. José Padilha's *Tropa de Elite* constructs masculinity as a metonymy for state power in society. In this framework, the protagonist's assertion of neo-authoritarian masculinity symbolizes a repositioning of Brazil's authoritarian legacy to address the social, political, and cultural changes taking place at the beginning of the twenty-first century. The film ultimately promotes the vindication of the authoritarian male as a response to the sociopolitical anxieties of the middle and upper classes in the face of a changing society that challenges their traditional position of privilege. *Tropa de Elite* explores a continuum of violence whose foundations can be traced to the legacy of authoritarian rule in Brazil, with its latest incarnation being the 1964–1985 dictatorship. Padilha's film reiterates this legacy through the configuration of masculinity and relations between men.

The film's protagonist, Capitão Nascimento (Wagner Moura), undergoes a crisis of masculinity that reflects shifting social relations in Brazil. His character embodies authoritarian power as it is represented through the state. His loss of power, or the implied threat thereof, causes a profound personal crisis that extends into social institutions. The resolution is clear: the reassertion of authoritarian power and its correlating performance of masculinity. The narrative posits neo-authoritarian masculinity as the response to both contemporary issues of crime and insecurity in Brazil and to profound social changes that have affected the privileged position of men, such as the growing assertion of women in social, economic, and political realms.

Tropa de Elite takes as its background story BOPE's preparations for the visit of Pope John Paul II to Rio de Janeiro in 1997. The narrative focuses on Capitão Roberto Nascimento, the unit's commander. His wife, Rosane (Maria Ribeiro), is pregnant and about to give birth to their first child. In the first-person narration of Capitão Nascimento, the pressures of work in combination with current life changes are causing him to experience a high degree of anxiety.

In light of this pressure, Nascimento is searching for a qualified replacement for his position. He finds two new BOPE recruits, Neto (Caio Junqueira) and Matias (André Matias), whom he identifies as possible replacements. The film follows the training and rites of passage of Neto and Matias as they move from the ranks of basic *polícia militar* (PM, military police) officers to members of the elite BOPE force. The two are juxtaposed to their peer Fábio (Milhem Cortaz), who is unable to fulfill the requirements of BOPE recruits and drops out during training. Through this process, we accompany Matias's and Neto's initial frustrations with their appointed positions in the military police; the romantic involvement of Matias with Maria (Fernanda Machado), a woman from the Carioca upper middle class; the brutal training protocol of BOPE; the death of Neto at the hands of Baiano (Fábio Lago), the drug kingpin of the Morro dos Macacos favela; the vengeance of Neto's death and Matias's rise to captain. While at first Capitão Nascimento is tormented by panic attacks, once he assumes his role as patriarch of his family and indisputable commander of the battalion, he is able to overcome what he calls his "sickness" and reestablish order and security. His personal healing through reasserting his authority also promises to contain the solution to the ills afflicting the social body.

The film is narrated from the perspective of Capitão Nascimento. The use of a first-person voiceover establishes Nascimento's authority to both communicate and interpret the events in which he participates and we witness. Nascimento narrates the events in retrospect, theoretically giving him critical distance. As a result, the narrative voice creates a pact with the audience that Nascimento is performing a candid and authentic retelling of events. Idelber Avelar argues that *Tropa de Elite*'s narrative technique amounts to an honest recounting of Nascimento's story to the degree that the film does not try to hide behind a "neutral documentary style" ("*Tropa*"). I would argue that no documentary film is ever neutral in its style and construction,[1] although many would like the spectator to believe this. Padilha does not attempt to gloss over the non-neutrality but constructs Nascimento through total exposure: he is narrator, subject of the camera, and protagonist of the storyline.

Authenticity is central to the power and authority of *Tropa de Elite*.[2] Though the film does not claim documentary status, that the images and sounds are footage from real life, it nevertheless employs various narrative and cinematic tools to establish authenticity and to link the story to actual events. In this sense, *Tropa de Elite* blurs the line between fiction and nonfiction filmmaking. By obfuscating this distinction, the film engages contemporary Brazilian society's preoccupation with the rising rates of violence—whether real or perceived—that the media represent daily in television and newspaper headlines (Beato). Authenticity and authority are fundamental to the argument that the film sells to spectators: mainly, the need to empower a more neo-authoritarian masculinity as a response to social issues.

Even before the film introduces the narrator-protagonist, authenticity is centralized and established. At the outset, *Tropa de Elite* offers a disclaimer:

This film is based on accounts by twelve officers and a psychiatrist in Rio de Janeiro's police force. According to them, the accounts are real.

The footage with the officers' and the psychiatrist's statements was destroyed. (*Elite Squad* DVD)

Bráulio Mantovani adapted the screenplay from *Elite da tropa* by the anthropologist and former National Secretary of Public Security Luiz Eduardo Soares and ex-BOPE members André Batista and Rodrigo Pimentel. Their 2006 book is a fictionalized recounting of the two men's time in the Rio de Janeiro BOPE police battalion. Thus, the film claims to present a semifictionalized testimonial by BOPE officers. The fictionalized realism that the cinematic work employs as a claim of authenticity establishes the veracity of the narrative as a sort of metastory of sociopolitical issues that are ever present in twenty-first-century Brazil.

In the film, what the viewer witnesses are BOPE's preparations for the visit of Pope John Paul II to Rio de Janeiro on October 2–6, 1997, for the Second World Meeting with Families. Following the initial attention-grabbing, adrenaline-pumped *baile funk* establishing scene, the storyline rewinds to an earlier moment to establish the beginning of the narrative through the integration of real-life found footage of the pope's visit. The incorporation of this found footage confers a heightened degree of truth and reliability to our narrator.

Filming Techniques

Tropa de Elite follows the cinematic style of many Brazilian crime films that emerged in the first decade of the twenty-first century, such as *Cidade de Deus* and *O Homem do Ano*. These productions are all marked by the use of high-contrast lighting, saturated colors, energetic camera work, and aggressive editing complemented by strong musical soundtracks to create intense film-viewing experiences. To varying degrees, these cinematic works suture the viewer into the film with the intention of inviting him to lose himself in the spectacle on screen.[3]

Tropa de Elite is no exception. The establishing scene sets the tone. The film opens with the agitated movement of a handheld camera in the midst of a *baile funk*. The pulsating funk beats of MC Júnior and MC Leonardo's funk "Rap das armas" ("Weapons' Rap") overlay the saturated colors of the *baile* in a montage sequence whose rhythmic editing cuts sync with the opening credits of the primary cast members. This opening scene is overrun by a title screen wipe: a blood-red, bullet-riddled *Tropa de Elite* emblazoned against a black background, accompanied by the high-energy rock rhythms of Tihuana's title track "Tropa de Elite." The title screen and soundtrack initiate BOPE's invasion of the Babilônia favela. These establishing scenes immerse the viewer in a high-octane cinematic experience from the first frame of the film with the promise of an action-packed crime thriller.

Tropa de Elite does not disappoint. What is immediately obvious in Lula Carvalho's camera work is the predominance of medium and close-up framing of the characters in cowboy shots and choker close-ups. The use of these more intimate camera shots inserts the viewer into the personal spaces of the characters. This in part reflects the first-person narration of the storyline, reminding us that this is a biased accounting of events from the perspective of BOPE members. At the same time, it creates a vibrant, action-packed film because the camera does not simply register the events from afar but participates in them and invites the viewer to lose himself in the action; it breaks down critical distance and sutures the spectator into the position of the neo-authoritarian male.

In doing so, *Tropa de Elite* legitimizes neo-authoritarian masculinity by presenting the members of BOPE and their version of hegemonic masculinity as the "currently most honored way of being a man." The hegemonic positioning of neo-authoritarian masculinity requires "all other men to position themselves in relation to it" (Connell and Messerschmidt 832). This positioning is not left to chance. *Tropa de Elite* deploys film form to locate all other men—the military police, drug dealers, lower classes, and upper and middle classes—in relation to BOPE, always valuing the perspective of the latter. This relation continuously reiterates that authoritarian male order is preferable to democratic social chaos and violence.

BOPE: Power Differentiation

In *Tropa de Elite* and on the streets of present-day Rio de Janeiro, BOPE is a special-forces unit within the military police. The military police is a national reserve unit that can be mobilized and integrated into the armed forces in times of war, and thus it retains federal status. However, in their daily activities, military police form the backbone of general policing in states and cities. Military police in each state have developed individual special-forces tactical units. BOPE is one such unit, in Rio de Janeiro state. Since these special-forces units are configured according to the needs of each state, the organization and specific duties of each elite response team vary in terms of duties performed as well as their names: BOPE in Rio de

Janeiro and Belo Horizonte; Rondas Ostensivas Tobias de Aguiar (ROTA, Tobias de Aguiar Ostensive Rounds), Comandos e Operações Especiais (COE, Commandos and Special Operations), and Grupo de Ações Táticas Especiais (GATE, Special Tactical Action Group) in São Paulo, for example.

Historically in Brazil, one of the first federal special-forces units was the Departamento de Ordem Política e Social (DOPS, Department of Political and Social Order), formed in the 1920s as part of the civil police force. DOPS assumed a central role as the civilian police force's political and social repression arm first in the Estado Novo under the Getúlio Vargas regime (1937–1945) and subsequently during the 1964–1985 authoritarian regime. That later regime created the Destacamento de Operações de Informações–Centro de Operações de Defesa Interna (DOI-CODI, Department of Information and Operations–Center of Internal Defense Operations) in 1969, during the *anos de chumbo* (leaden years) in Brazil. The DOI-CODI was founded out of the power structure of the armed forces. The DOI-CODI and DOPS were the two primary units of the 1964–1985 authoritarian government's repression apparatus, overwhelmingly responsible for the torture and disappearances of supposed subversives in Brazil.

With the 1985 transition to democracy, Brazil's armed forces did not undergo a complete restructuring, an anomaly in the region. Within the context of Brazil, one of the most contentious recommendations of the Comissão Nacional da Verdade (National Truth Commission) as well as multiple human rights organizations is the demand that the police demilitarize. Although the DOI-CODI and the majority of the state DOPS were closed, the federal and state security structures and leadership remained in place. As such, these organizations represent the military and policing heritage of the authoritarian regime today. A continuum exists between the methods employed and the overarching approach to urban policing of current police tactical units specialized in urban warfare, such as BOPE, and the repressive policing units of the most recent authoritarian regime, such as DOPS and DOI-CODI.[4] The "maximum force" mentality of contemporary state-level special-forces units is part of the legacy of the 1964–1985 authoritarian regime and is reflected in *Tropa de Elite*.

Tropa de Elite, set in 1997, establishes a hierarchy of authoritarian order within the state security forces in Rio de Janeiro as a guiding principal of accepting BOPE's authority. Much of Brazilian society then held and still holds a fundamental distrust of state security forces. In 2014, according to the Índice de Confiança na Justiça Brasileira (Index of Confidence in

Brazilian Justice), approximately 66% of respondents to a national poll said they lacked confidence in the work of the Brazilian police (Cunha et al.).[5] Thus, Padilha's film needs to differentiate the members of BOPE from the general police forces to establish their authority and affirm the viewers' confidence in the film's narrator.

Michel Foucault, in *Discipline and Punish*, argues that power relations are pivotal to processes of social stratification. In culture and society, differentiation serves to create groups, and it is through the establishment of these clusters that power is allocated based on collective distinctions. These power differentials can be observed inside police and military institutions. Within state security forces, power hierarchies exist both at the individual level and through institutionalized categorization.

Frank Barrett has studied power hierarchies based upon the deployment of constructions of masculinity within the US Navy. He argues that hegemonic masculinity in the armed forces is constructed around several central strands whose configurations vary according to the individual. Barrett maintains that the central themes of these identity strands within the military are "risk taking; discipline; excitement associated with operation of powerful technology; tolerance of degradation; stoic endurance of hardship; tenacity and perseverance in the face of difficult physical trials; rational calculation; absence of emotion; and technological mastery" (95). The author observes that each "organizational community" within the US Navy employs varying configurations of these identity strands to construct and impose masculine power strategies. These organizational communities vie to incrementally secure more powerful positions internally within their group and in relation to other groups.

Tropa de Elite relies on institutionalized power differentiation between the standard military police units and BOPE to condone the latter's policing tactics that are rooted in a legacy of authoritarianism. The film establishes clear lines that distinguish the organizational community of BOPE from that of the standard military police, placing BOPE in a more powerful position. This distinction begins with BOPE's status as a special-forces unit within the military police. In real life and in the film, BOPE's differentiation from the standard *polícia militar* is emphasized symbolically and most visibly in their use of all-black uniforms, vehicles, and weapons and their emblem: a skull impaled by a knife through the top of the cranium with two pistols crossed behind it against a black background encircled by a red border. According to the official website of Rio de Janeiro's BOPE, the all-black uniform as well as the black background of the unit's emblem represent the permanence of battle. Visually, the emblem and blacked-out motif infuse their look with a more ominous air. The red that encircles the black sphere in the background is the red of bloodshed. The skull stands for both knowledge and death. It is interesting to note that the *caveira* (skull) was the symbol adopted by the São Paulo death squads led by Sérgio Paranhos Fleury.[6] The knife embedded in the cranium symbolizes human resilience, victory over death. Finally, the two golden handguns are representational of the military police.[7] As Capitão Nascimento informs us and the historical evocation of Fleury's death squads confirms, these elements carry symbolic weight meant to invoke fear in the *marginais* the special units posit as their antagonists.

The *caveira* symbol figures prominently in the film. The logo is emblazoned on the chest of BOPE uniforms, berets, vehicles, and bodies; Neto tattoos the *caveira* on his forearm. The term "caveira" features prominently as a linguistic device in the film. When members respond to one another with a simple "caveira," they are signifying an affirmative response. Assenting through the *caveira* condones the dominant status of BOPE and validates their expression of neo-authoritarian masculinity as a legitimate means to (re)empower dominant society or, better said, a society dominated by neo-authoritarian men.

Corruption

Tropa de Elite also differentiates BOPE based on their incorruptibility and employs this to condone their use of violence. The film roots incorruptibility in individual honor and discipline that is placed at the service of BOPE's professionalism and competence. The film links these qualities and the success of an anticorruption platform to the leadership of a strong authoritarian male figure.

The first half of the film focuses on Neto's and Matias's rebellion against the corrupt status quo within their military police unit. They recently assumed new positions as officers in charge of the mechanics garage and the Department of Radio and Statistics, respectively. They incur the ire of their commanders because they are competent at organizing and overseeing their offices, they are honest, and they take on the system by organizing a plan to redirect their commanders' payoff money to underfunded divisions of the police force, specifically the repair of police vehicles. Neto's and

Matias's incorruptibility and the punishment they receive because of it lead them to enlist in the BOPE training camp.

When the BOPE officers receive the list of incoming trainees, their conversation reinforces the idea that the force is beyond corruption. The scene projects BOPE as the saviors or heroes who can clean up corrupt state security forces and by extension, Brazilian society. In the scene, Nascimento and his fellow officers sit around a conference table reviewing one by one the names of the incoming cadets. The various commanders detail the problems of each potential trainee: one is corrupt; another is a "marginal"; another is pimping women in Copacabana. Nascimento, who is in charge of the training camp, replies respectively about each: "He'll become a statistic," "He'll become *caveira* bubblegum," "Leave him to me" ("Vai virar estatística," "Vai virar chiclete de caveira," "Deixa ele comigo"). This process continues until the names Neto and Matias are read; they hold promise as future BOPE members. BOPE officer Renan says the two initiates are "awesome" ("ótimos") and "began well" ("começaram bem") when BOPE declared war in the Babilônia favela. Renan, Capitão Nascimento, and the other officers are positioned as gatekeepers of good, the righteous force of BOPE, symbols of neo-authoritarian masculinity to which the selected rookies must aspire.

The strict moral code that Capitão Nascimento and BOPE impose within their ranks is the foundation that supposedly guides their moral compass in the battle against criminal factions and the decadence of Brazilian society. The film asks the viewing public to trust BOPE and Capitão Nascimento to guarantee the law, and it condones their transgression of it. BOPE demands that the spectator confide in the authoritarian male figure in a time that purportedly requires extraordinary measures.[8]

The imposition of strong moral codes and the objective of rooting out corruption by a strong authoritarian male figure also provides a historical link to the 1964–1985 military dictatorship. Heloísa Maria Murgel Starling contends,

The 1964 coup justified a significant part of its functionality by producing a kind of intervention *ex machina* capable of ending corruption and guaranteeing that the military believed themselves to be the good punitive order.

O golpe de 1964 justificou parte importante de sua funcionalidade ao produzir uma espécie de intervenção *ex machina* capaz de acabar com os corruptos e garantir aquilo que os militares acreditavam ser a boa ordem punitiva. (251–52)

Part of the rationale of the 1964 coup was that the strong hand of the regime was needed to regenerate society and change a decadent ruling order. High Commander of the Armed Forces General José Canavarro Pereira declared, "We will not let up in our fight against subversion and corruption in the country" ("Não esmoreceremos na nossa luta contra a subversão e a corrupção no país") (qtd. in Gaspari 162).[9] The regime viewed corruption as an indicator of moral decadence.[10]

Tropa de Elite forwards a parallel line of reasoning. Capitão Nascimento is presented in the film "as if" he were a paragon of virtue. He has attained, just as the torturer, untouchable status. He is given license to torture people at will, although torture is forbidden by the Brazilian constitution; his violation of that prohibition is evidenced in the various times he is seen "bagging" subjects during interrogations, that is, suffocating them by placing plastic bags over their heads. For Neto and Matias, their path to success is also clear; they must emulate their captain through their expression of neo-authoritarian masculinity embodied in their unrestrained violence toward criminals.

Neto, who assumes command of the operation to secure the favela of Babilônia for the pope's visit, is portrayed as a killing machine. This is made clear when Nascimento boasts that Neto "killed more than thirty crooks in the first week" ("Matou mais de trinta vagabundos na primeira semana"). Matias shows greater restraint in his actions at first. However, as he is initiated into this brotherhood of men, his incremental acceptance and enactment of violence, which culminates in his killing of Baiano, guarantees his ascension to the rank of captain by the end of the film.

Training Masculine Hierarchies

For standard military police to rise in the ranks and become members of BOPE, they first had to complete the BOPE training camp. In the film, the initiation process of the training camp closely parallels the central tenets that Barrett identifies as fundamental to the construction of masculine identity within the armed forces (95). Over the course of the BOPE training camp, the cadets move from the most basic of these tenets, tolerance of degradation and stoic endurance of hardship, through mastery of technology, finally arriving at rational calculation and absence of emotion. In each of the trials the BOPE cadets face, the trainers push them to drop out of the program. Only the real man can overcome the hurdles of the trial and become a BOPE officer.

A cadet's ability to endure the trials of the camp assumes a twofold meaning. It reaffirms the storyline's argument that BOPE is made up exclusively of trustworthy men who have demonstrated both physical and psychological endurance. They can be entrusted to guarantee the law although this requires BOPE to surpass the limits of the law. The tests also are meant to create bonds between the men and institute a hierarchy of masculine power within their ranks.

Tropa de Elite establishes such a hierarchy among cadets in the opening scene of the training camp. As the initiates stand against the black background of the dead of night with hard lighting illuminating their faces, rifles, and uniforms, Nascimento informs the viewer in a voiceover,

> Neto decided to join BOPE because he liked war. Matias went along because he believed in the law. The corrupt guy came with them. If Fábio stayed in the battalion, the colonel would kill him. Poor thing. The guy did not know that next to me, the colonel was a girl.

> O Neto decidiu entrar para o BOPE porque ele gostava de guerra. Matias ia junto porque ele acreditava na lei. O corrupto veio com eles. Se o Fábio ficasse no batalhão, o coronel matava ele. Coitado. O cara não sabia que perto de mim, o coronel era uma moça.

In this statement the delineation of a hierarchy of masculine power is established that is then developed throughout the scene. Neto and Matias possess what are presented as necessary kernels of neo-authoritarian masculinity that will allow them to join BOPE. Neto's masculine identity is constructed around violence. For Matias, it is the ideal of discipline. Between them, our narrator prioritizes violence over discipline. However, we will discover that violence can be learned. Fábio, along with Coronel Otávio (Marcello Escorel), is transformed into a synecdoche for the *polícia militar*. Both men are emasculated through Nascimento's use of "moça" ("girl") and serve as foils for the construction of the ideals of hegemonic neo-authoritarian masculinity promoted by BOPE.

The hierarchy is reiterated in the filming techniques. The men stand in formation holding their rifles across their chests. Neto is the first candidate in line. The camera visually privileges the violence he represents. The camera dollies backward. Matias stands in formation alongside Neto, emphasizing discipline. As the camera passes by them, it pans slightly to frame their faces. They are violence instrumentalized at the service of neo-authoritarian masculinity, holding the promise of a secure society. The camera continues to pull back before reaching Fábio. When the camera reaches Fábio, it interrogates his profile in an extreme close-up. The heightened visual examination of Fábio mimics the scrutinizing eye of Capitão Nascimento. Fábio, just as all the cadets, is under the lens. As spectators, we are meant to understand through and confide in the discerning gaze of Nascimento—and by extension BOPE leadership—to know that they weed out all initiates who do not measure up to the masculine standards demanded of BOPE.

Charlotte Hooper finds that in order for hegemonic masculinity to affirm its dominance, it relies on femininity and other subordinate masculinities as others within a binary that legitimizes its authority. This binary privileges values associated with dominant masculinity. Hooper maintains, "As masculinity is the valued term, it can be argued that femininity is merely a residual category, a foil or Other for masculinity to define itself against" (43). If we follow Hooper's line of argumentation, the masculine/feminine dichotomy holds within it a host of other pairings—strong/weak, tough/tender, aggressor/victim, order/anarchy, war/peace (43), and these likewise are naturalized, privileging a phallocentric ordering of terms.[11]

Figure 4.1. Matias, Neto, and Fábio standing in formation in the opening scene of the BOPE training-camp sequence. Screen grab from *Tropa de Elite*.

Figure 4.2. The ever-expanding BOPE mock cemetery for fallen recruits who symboli-cally bury their hats in graves marked by tombstones. Screen grabs from *Tropa de Elite*.

Within the space of *Tropa de Elite*, hegemonic neo-authoritarian mascu-linity kills off the emasculated other. This occurs in relation to the elimina-tion of the female characters to guarantee an unalloyed male homosocial order as well as the purging of male characters who are deemed as not measuring up to the paradigms of neo-authoritarian masculinity and can therefore not partake in the hegemonic masculine order.

Over the course of the boot camp, BOPE officials erect a mock cemetery for all the fallen initiates, those who surrender in the face of the mental and physical tests they face. Those recruits must bury their hats in holes marked by mock tombstones. Those who do not complete the training are projected as lesser men.[12] When Fábio drops out of the camp, Nascimento exclaims, "Fuck the weak and the corrupt" ("Que se fodam os fracos e os corruptos"). Fábio is killed off symbolically, purging weakness and emasculation from the ordering of neo-authoritarian masculinity. This ritual also promotes the association of neo-authoritarian masculinity with action and returns us to the privileging of Neto for his propensity for violence. Nascimento points out that once Neto assumed command of the squad, he "liked action" ("gos-tava de ação").

Neo-Authoritarian Masculinity and Phallic Connotations of the Weapons of War

Stéphane Audoin-Rouzeau argues that historically there is a parallel between the expanding crisis of military masculinity in the first half of the twentieth century, an increasing sexualization of military masculinity, and an intensified concentration on the phallic connotations of the weapons of war within the Western Hemisphere. The symbolic appropriation of the weapons of war reaffirms the male subject's virility and homosocial bonding.[13] The cinematic canon of war films has cemented the bond between military masculinity, weapons, and sexuality. One only need recall Stanley Kubrick's 1987 Vietnam War film *Full Metal Jacket*. I refer to the scene in which the cadets, all wearing white undershirts and boxers, march in the barracks quarters in two mirrored circles. Each cadet stands with one hand holding a rifle on his shoulder while the other hand clutches his genitalia. The trainees chant: "This is my rifle. This is my gun. This is for fighting. This is for fun." Every time the cadets iterate "fun," they double-pump their genitalia. The scene visually embodies Audoin-Rouzeau's argument of the shifting positioning of modern weaponry to assume phallic status associated with a soldier's affirmation of his virility. It is the virility and strength of the neo-authoritarian male in association with his weapon that *Tropa de Elite* emphasizes.

In *Tropa de Elite,* during incursions of BOPE members into the favela, the soldiers always have their rifles poised on their shoulders, in a combat-

Figure 4.3. Scenes from the BOPE firearms training. Screen grabs from *Tropa de Elite.*

Figure 4.4. Over-the-shoulder shots that suture the spectator into the firearms action, recalling first-person perspective in shooter video games. Screen grabs from *Tropa de Elite*.

ready stance. Their relation to favela residents is mediated through their weapons rather than through dialogue. In the film, the weapon visually endorses neo-authoritarian masculinity by emphasizing the ideal of phallic male power as innate to BOPE forces. The sequence of gun-training scenes establishes this power dynamic.

The arms-training sequence lasts around six and a half minutes and moves between nine scenes, seven of which centralize BOPE's weapons of war. The scenes occur in quick succession, beginning with Neto, shirtless, in his room, pivoting 180 degrees from right to left to right, discharging his unloaded handgun with each gyration. The camera, next to him, shifts from a close-up of his head to a cowboy framing of him in the full-length wall mirror, pistol drawn. He unloads seven imaginary rounds in quick succession.

The film cuts to target practice using a sound bridge between the click of the empty handgun magazine and the acute sound of live rifle-ammunition rounds firing, centralizing the weapon and with it Neto's and Matias's inculcation into the violent ethos of BOPE. Now Neto is wearing the camouflage uniform of the cadets and holds a semiautomatic rifle in his hand. According to our narrator, there are only three cadets left, and he needs to choose between Neto and Matias. The sound of the bullets discharging in rapid fire dominates the scene and establishes an agile rhythm while augmenting the screen tension.

The camera dollies around Nascimento, Neto, and Matias, cutting quickly between multiple camera perspectives along the 180-degree axis of action. The two trainees fire off two rounds every few meters, closing in on their target. At the end, after they holster their weapons, Nascimento congratulates Neto on a job well done, pointing out that it was easier because Neto is using Nascimento's rifle. The successive scenes lead us through the trainees climbing Pão de Açúcar (Sugarloaf peak), to night tactical training through a maze of shipping containers, to their initial incursion into a favela that resembles a war-torn landscape, and finally to Neto assuming control of the team, killing "marginais" and securing the Babilônia favela.

What we witness in these scenes is the disciplining of the cadets' bodies and control of their weapons. Before their training, they were inexperienced, untrained, and naïve, in other words, naked and vulnerable like Neto's body. As they advance, the visual representation of their bodies changes from naked to camouflage to the black of BOPE. Their weapons also progress from unloaded handguns to live-round long rifles to the semiautomatic weapons of BOPE. The soldier and the weapon become integrated, the black of the gun bleeding into the black of the BOPE uniform, one an extension of the other and both cementing the brotherhood of men.

Homosocial Bonding and BOPE

The BOPE training camp is a space that prioritizes the formation of relationships between cadets to promote cohesion within the troops. The film centralizes homosocial bonding in the transformation of the cadets from boys of the *polícia militar* into men of BOPE. *Tropa de Elite* emphasizes this transition through the structuring of the camp, where the recruits are assigned numbers (01, 02, 03, and so forth) to replace their individual names. Their anonymity breaks down individuality and underscores their membership in and identification with this group of men. Other examples that emphasize their bonding as a band of brothers are the call-and-response songs the cadets sing while marching and a host of situations and exercises in which they are bound together by making the group responsible for the actions of each individual and the individual for the actions of the group.

Psychotherapist Christina Wieland argues in *The Fascist State of Mind* that breaking down individuality while emphasizing cohesion and masculinity through rituals and symbols creates a "manic phantasy of supermasculinity—a masculinity bigger than life and truly omnipotent. This manufacturing of masculinity is a real 'masquerade of masculinity'" (42).

Figure 4.5. BOPE cadets in a semicircle around the pot of beans and rice the commanders have dumped on the ground in front of them. Screen grabs from *Tropa de Elite*.

Creating cohesion through a masquerade of masculinity is the focus of the chow scene, when the cadets in full gear wait for the captains to serve food.

Capitão Nascimento asks 06, Neto, as sheriff of the unit, how long the group will need to eat. Neto requests ten minutes, but the commander only gives them ten seconds to eat. He wants "to see this ground clean" ("ver esse chão limpo"). The traditional beans and rice are served by dumping the whole pot of food onto the ground. All cadets are held accountable for finishing the food, an impossible task. When they are unsuccessful, the commander chastises them. Nascimento points out that 02, Fábio, did not eat. In response, 02 says he could not "reach the food." In front of the other cadets he is told to clean the ground of food or the squad will spend the night in the bog. The commanders reprimand Fábio for his lack of allegiance to the group. His example inculcates the importance of group cohesion and performance in the interest of the unit rather than the individual. When Fábio vomits as he kneels down to eat the food, the commanders obligate the group to eat the vomit-strewn chow. From this point, the scene cuts to the cadets marching in the bog.

In the food scene, filming techniques underscore the importance of group cohesion by cutting between crane shots of the scene where the individual soldiers are only identifiable as part of the group and over-the-shoulder medium framing shots when Nascimento castigates Fábio. From the crane shot, Fábio appears to form part of the unit, but the scrutiny of the medium shots highlights his slouched body position in juxtaposition to the others, who stand at attention. The camera accentuates his lack of integration into the group.

Contemporary military theory maintains that cohesion through rituals of masculine bonding and camaraderie is fundamental to military perfor-

mance and effectiveness (Kronsell 59–63). Building trust and camaraderie through these rituals between men supposedly motivates them to fight
and helps in battle readiness. Traditionally, this has also meant that women
have been segregated from these homosocial military networks.

A later scene depicts those dynamics, after Baiano and his gang kill Neto,
by then a BOPE officer, for venturing into their territory. The mise-en-
scène of Neto's funeral centralizes the force of homosocial bonds and the
exclusion of women. The scene opens with Nascimento in a funeral march
to drape a flag with the BOPE skull logo over the Brazilian flag that cloaks
Neto's coffin.[14] The camera pans his movements from eye level and then assumes a bird's-eye position above the foot of the coffin. The men of BOPE
occupy the left side of the frame; the general military police officers and
other men fill the right side of the frame. Women stand at the head of the
coffin, visually distanced by the camera. As the wake ends, the men continue to flank the coffin, as women drop flowers on the coffin and leave.

This scene is fraught with symbolism. Women are conspicuously segregated from the homosocial groupings of men. The stoic nature and the
absence of any outward demonstration of emotion by the men—in juxtaposition to the women, who cry, sob, and drop flowers—fulfills the tenets
of the emotional hierarchies between military men, according to Barrett's
study. Nascimento's voiceover makes clear that it is these bonds that fuel
Matias's drive to avenge Neto's murder. It is telling that from the funeral
scene we cut to Matias and Nascimento torturing Rose, Baiano's girlfriend,
to locate the drug kingpin. The female characters Rosane and Maria are
expunged from the narrative following the funeral. With the middle-class
women eliminated, females from the favela are incorporated as part of the
threat that emanates from it and against which BOPE is fighting. This is
one of the first scenes in which Matias directly assumes the role of torturer.
The funeral can be read as symbolically marking his inculcation into and
acceptance of neo-authoritarian masculinity and the extreme methods of
BOPE.

Masculine Power and the Criminals

The vision of the favela established in the film dialogues directly with mass
media representations and stereotypes of the *morro* as a violent space. This
image stands in contrast to the middle- and upper-class enclaves of the
asfalto. The designation of the urban space in Brazil as a divided arena

between the *asfalto/morro*, rich/poor, city/favela has been the theme of a significant body of academic literature in Brazil (Ventura; Caldeira; Koonings and Kruijt) and has proven recurrent in cultural production.[15] Within this binary configuration, the favela is traditionally constructed as the negative term, particularly when viewed through the lens of the middle and upper classes. In the opening scene of *Tropa de Elite*, the viewer experiences the favela as a locus of criminal activity, where guns and drugs are commonplace. Padilha's film also suggests that residents endure a totalitarian organizational structure imposed by drug-dealing criminal factions.

The establishing scene of *Tropa de Elite* demarcates the power landscape in Rio de Janeiro as an arena of military conflict and by extension, Brazil as a war zone rife with civil conflict between criminals and state security forces. The film opens with a chaotic visual montage of a *baile funk* in the favela, intercut with the opening credits. A handheld camera whirls around, registering incomplete snapshots of the *baile*. Between fragmented bodies and swirling lights, the conspicuous firepower of those in attendance stands out. The soundtrack blasts "Rap das armas." The song's chorus extols conflict: "To come up here on the hill even BOPE trembles / We don't have a soft spot for the military, civil police, or PM" ("Pra subir aqui no morro até a BOPE treme / Não tem mole pro exército, civil nem pra PM"). The soundtrack presents the favela as a no-go zone where state security forces are not welcome. The voiceover of Capitão Nascimento cuts into the scene:

> In my city we have more than seven hundred favelas, almost all dominated by drug dealers armed to the teeth. FMK, Uzi, AR-15, and so on. Elsewhere in the world such weapons are used in war; here, they are the weapons of crime.

> Em minha cidade tem mais de setecentas favelas, quase todas dominadas por traficantes armados até os dentes. FMK, Uzi, AR-15, e por aí vai. No resto do mundo esse tipo de armamento é usado na guerra, aqui são as armas do crime.

The diegetic sound of MC Júnior and MC Leonardo's funk verses in "Rap das armas" reinforce what the film depicts:

> Here comes someone with an AR-15 and someone else with 12 in hand / Here come two more with pistols and another with 28 specials / One guy walks with a URU in front of him, escorting the paddy wagon / There are two more in the rear, but they have a Glock in their hands.

Vem um de AR-15 e outro de 12 na mão / Vem mais dois de pistola e outro com 2-oitão / Um vai de URU na frente, escoltando o camburão / Tem mais dois na retaguarda, mas tão de Glock na mão.

The song, in conjunction with the parade of firearms that we witness on display at the *baile funk,* legitimate Nascimento's claims about the pervasiveness of guns and violence in the favela.

The film establishes from the outset the criminals' reign over the favelas and the inability of traditional police to control criminality due to substandard training and corruption. The criminal factions of the favela can be understood through Raewyn Connell and James Messerschmidt's rubric of marginal masculinity. Throughout the film, they deploy elements that also underscore neo-authoritarian masculinity. Thus the criminals in *Tropa de Elite* also demonstrate a hierarchical structuring of men, a propensity for violence, a heightened degree of male bravado, and so forth. These characteristics attributed to the criminal parallel those ascribed to BOPE but represented as a degraded expression because it is not placed at the service of the middle and upper classes. This representation is necessary because it serves to explain the need for BOPE's growing aggressiveness toward the marginal figures, emphasizing the importance of an ever more authoritarian masculine stance toward criminality and to highlight the incorruptibility of BOPE.

According to Connell's rubric of masculinity, the representation of criminal elements in the film falls within the designation of marginalized masculinity due to the characters' subordinate class and racial status. We can consider the construction of the criminals' masculinity in terms of a degradation or perversion of neo-authoritarian masculinity, with BOPE being the paradigm of its expression. For the neo-authoritarian logic of the film to work, the criminals must assume a form of neo-authoritarian masculinity and cannot be emasculated as the middle class is. The criminals must command a strong masculine presence to evoke the necessarily heightened neo-authoritarian stance of BOPE to fight fire with fire. The criminals are a dangerous and formidable rival whose violence seemingly necessitates BOPE's use of more extreme aggressive tactics. Yet while the criminal factions represent a formidable threat, they are also depicted as less competent, lacking the training, mastery, discipline, tenacity, and perseverance (Barrett) of BOPE. There is an interesting feedback loop in the film in which the incremental escalation of violence on the part of the criminals is paralleled by the severity of force that BOPE employs, particularly in the character development of Matias.

Demetrakis Demetriou expands Connell's concept of hegemonic masculinity, problematizing the normalization of these categories. Demetriou points out that Connell fails to consider how these categories change over time according to the interactions between masculinities in society. Within these shifting masculine paradigms, the hegemonic order struggles to retain power.[16] What Demetriou postulates is the idea of a "dialectical pragmatism" of intramasculinity, an internal hegemony within masculine relations. Thus, hegemonic masculinity appropriates elements of other masculinities over time to usurp any nodes of power they develop and retain its position of dominance. We can understand the escalation of violence in Padilha's film through Demetriou's dialectical pragmatism and how it plays out in the figure of Matias.

During the opening scenes of the film, when BOPE overtakes the favela, Nascimento questions a *fogueteiro* (scout) (Brian Amorim).[17] Ultimately, he decides to release the boy. In the days following their incursion into the favela, the *fogueteiro*'s mother (Rosana Barros) comes to BOPE headquarters to plead with Nascimento to get her son's body back. We do not witness the murder of the boy. The mother's request to bury the body of her son engages the audience at an emotional level, demonstrating the cruelty of the drug kingpin of the favela through his lack of common decency or respect for any type of rules of engagement. Normally in armed conflict, particularly between states, it is considered a right under international and domestic law that the corpse of a deceased family member be returned.[18]

The disappearance of her son carries particular historical weight in Brazil, where during the 1964–1985 dictatorship people were disappeared by the government. One could read this scene as a way of distinguishing or distancing BOPE from the unacceptable practices of the 1964–1985 dictatorship, associating these methods with criminal factions. Nascimento thus affirms his righteousness when he returns to the favela to attempt to recover the boy's corpse. By indirectly engaging Brazil's historical memory, the film begins to parse out diverging aspects of authoritarianism, differentiating between BOPE's supposed results-driven use of interrogation, for example, in juxtaposition to the criminals' brutal deployment of authoritarian methods to the detriment of dominant society and common decency.

This same idea is repeated when Baiano takes retribution on Roberta (Fernanda de Freitas) and Rodrigues (André Mauro), volunteers at a local nongovernmental organization (NGO) in the Macacos favela, in retaliation for Matias's presence in the favela. Baiano faults them for allowing the military police to enter his territory without his permission. In Baiano's logic, this error leads to the killing of Neto and BOPE's ensuing search for Baiano. The scene opens with Roberta and Rodrigues crying. Within seconds we see the blood spray from Roberta's head as Baiano shoots her between the eyes while she kneels on the ground. Successively, Rodrigues, ensnared in tires, is doused with gasoline and set ablaze. Baiano's soldiers call out for Rodrigues to burn, as his body is engulfed in flames and his screams pierce the scene. This sequence of shots hits a particularly visceral nerve, since this is a method of execution by drug lords in Brazil that has taken on almost mythical status in the general public's imagination.[19] Similar to the first example, this scene underscores the lack of any type of objective purpose behind the violence beyond retaliation. Both scenes are constructed to represent cruel, senseless violence. The former, however, alludes to the historical legacy of disappearances in Brazil, while the latter engages the audience on a more visceral level by showing the criminals' cruelty unfiltered.

One should also consider that the first scene can more easily be written off by dominant society because it can be categorized as violence between criminals. Elite and middle-class society in Brazil is generally more accepting of violence when violence is contained within the space of the favela or affects the lower socioeconomic classes. However, in the second example, Baiano's ire is released upon two middle-class youths. This touches a particular vein because the target audience—those who can afford to go to the multiplex, purchase a ticket, and watch the film on the big screen—can identify with these characters. As the violence from the criminal factions escalates, so too does the violence of the future captain of BOPE, Matias.

Augmenting Violence

Violence is a core value and trait of neo-authoritarian masculinity in *Tropa de Elite* and is centralized from the outset of the film.[20] Violence is construed as an integral part of masculinity but also as a necessary response to criminality in Rio de Janeiro and Brazil more generally. The BOPE members within the favela, a *zone of exception*, are given full license to kill, torture, or otherwise violate the rights of the favela residents.[21] Favela residents are reduced to *homines sacri* (Agamben *Homo Sacer*), individuals not recognized as part of the polis and therefore not afforded the rights of citizenship, as I signal in my analysis of *Quase Dois Irmãos*. Because they are subjects of the law but not protected by it, they can be tortured as well as killed. Torture forms the backbone of BOPE's policing strategy.

The final scene of the film is the culmination in its depiction of torture and killing as well as in how it establishes violence as a fundamental element of neo-authoritarian masculinity in BOPE. Though BOPE represents the law, the scene also suggests that law is an impediment to justice. In this scene, Nascimento and Matias are searching for Baiano. BOPE officer Renan tells Nascimento, "It's going to turn into shit. . . . The residents are watching everything that we are doing. . . . I don't agree with torture" ("Vai dar merda. . . . Os moradores estão vendo tudo aí o que a gente está fazendo. . . . Eu não concordo com a tortura"). Renan's resistance to finding Neto's killer by any means necessary is dismissed by the protagonists as both a betrayal of the homosocial bonds between men and a final push to emphasize the necessary severity that society requires of the neo-authoritarian male to impose the rule of law. Nascimento's response to Renan is, "The guy killed Neto. I came up to get the guy and I'm going to break the guy today" ("O cara matou Neto. Eu subi para buscar o cara e vou quebrar o cara hoje"). The entire film places a high degree of emphasis on the homosocial bonds between members of BOPE. Within military circles, homosocial bonding is considered to correlate directly to troop readiness and willingness to fight in war. As such, Matias's disposition to avenge Neto can also be read as his readiness to fight against the criminal factions by employing any means necessary.

Nascimento and Matias, in their search for Baiano, encounter a young man who is part of Baiano's network. They take him to the edge of a cliff for interrogation. The interrogation begins with Nascimento slapping the kid and asking, "Where is Baiano?" ("Cadê o Baiano?"). Then he orders the boy bagged. In a shot-countershot sequence, the camera cuts from Nascimento to the boy's head in a clear plastic bag, then back. In the time-space of the cut, Matias replaces the captain on screen and assumes the role of interrogator, choking and slapping the kid, repeating, "Where is Baiano?" Blood-soaked plastic bags litter the ground. When these interrogation methods don't work, the men threaten sexual violence. The same scenario progression repeats itself: Nascimento begins, grabbing a broomstick and ordering a pair of BOPE officers to pull the boy's pants down. Matias takes the broomstick and gets behind the boy, preparing to anally penetrate him. The threat of being sodomized breaks him.

The scene emphasizes Matias mimicking the active, aggressive role of Nascimento. In contrast to the beginning of the film, when Matias professed

Figure 4.6. Baiano's POV up the barrel of the shotgun of Matias. The framing cuts from chest up to shoulders up to choker close-up. Screen grabs from *Tropa de Elite*.

a profound belief in the rule of law, he has now adopted a neo-authoritarian stance toward policing in Rio de Janeiro and understands the purported need for a strong disciplinary male figure who will get the job done. The two officers find Baiano, and the scene closes with Matias staring down the barrel of a 12-gauge shotgun at Baiano's face. The camera assumes the point of view of Baiano, the framing cuts from chest up to shoulders up to a choker close-up view of Matias. The shotgun fills the screen prominently. Matias cocks the hammer, the screen cuts to white, and we hear the shotgun fire. It is the final shot. Justice has been served, Neto avenged, the drug kingpin eliminated, and dominant order reestablished.

These final scenes of open torture and violence can be considered the most troublesome of the film because they condone violence as a valid tactic against individuals the state considers *homines sacri* and in effect strip them of any legal protections. This view is underscored in the final scene, which shows how favela residents witness the abuses and yet have no recourse and, according to the film, no right to stop it. They are beholden to the law but not protected by it. Human Rights Watch released a report in 2014 denouncing the continued problem of torture in Brazil against marginalized individuals ("Brasil: Reformas"). In light of such reports, representations take on even greater meaning, and films such as *Tropa de Elite* become even more problematic in their portrayals of violence and torture in the state's war against crime.

Masculine Power and the Middle Class

In *Tropa de Elite,* middle-class males are the only group of men (juxtaposed to BOPE, PMs, and drug dealers) who are not represented through the lens of homosocial affiliation. Instead, they are emasculated through their association with women and their inability to enact the violence that the film associates with masculine ideals of domination. The construction of the middle class in the film echoes how the 1964–1985 authoritarian regime viewed middle-class university students. During the dictatorship, the military regime emasculated university students as vulnerable youth drawn to the vices of drugs, subject to physical degeneration, and given to questionable influences (Cowan "Sex and the Security State," 467–68). This narrative suggested that the students required the strong hand of the regime to guide them toward the correct path, to strengthen their bodies and their will to resist those conditions.

In *Tropa de Elite,* university students exhibit many of the same defects that the military regime attributed to middle-class youths. In one of the first scenes, at the university law school, Matias is in a working group with Edu (Paulo Vilela), Maria, and Roberta. They are going to present on Foucault's *Discipline and Punish* in class. To prepare for the presentation, the four meet up at the NGO Núcleo de Democratização da Cultura (Center for the Democratization of Culture) in the Macacos favela where Edu, Maria, and Roberta volunteer. The scene is interesting because the only active participant is Matias, who gives an overly simplistic summary of the work to his classmates. Edu lights up a joint and passes it around. As Edu, Roberta, and Maria get high and giggle about the excellent quality of the weed, Matias remains focused on the lesson. In the end, Maria chastises Edu for not having done his part to prepare for the talk. The scene establishes middle-class youths as spoiled rich kids who are more concerned with popularity and fun than taking their studies or the work of the NGO seriously.

The authority and positive influence of the neo-authoritarian male, Matias, is reiterated when the group leaves the study session. Maria stops to chastise Romerito (Allan Guilherme), a local boy in Macacos favela, because he isn't studying. She claims he doesn't like to study. Matias notices Romerito has difficulty shooting the marbles straight in a game of ringer they are playing. Matias gives Romerito a quick eye exam and discovers that he has vision problems. As previously, the film anchors itself in a binary division that underscores the benevolence and positive influence of the neo-authoritarian male.

In contrast to Matias, Edu is an allegory of the decadent middle-class Brazilian males in the film. He is constructed in stereotypical terms as the middle-class student who smokes marijuana, sells pot at the university to his friends, but is insulated from the repercussions of his actions by class privilege. Volunteering at the Núcleo de Democratização da Cultura, Edu has access to the favela. The NGO exists with the blessing of Baiano, *o dono do morro* (king of the hill). The NGO's presence in the favela facilitates Edu's access to marijuana that he distributes through Márcio (Erick Oliveira), who runs the photocopy shop on campus. The film constructs Edu as the popular cool kid in the university. This is exemplified in the first scene following the evening study session at the NGO. The camera cuts to Edu as he strolls across campus. Most of the students say "hi" to him, patting him on the back or bumping hands with him. The scene is set to the music of Sangue da Cidade's "Brilhar a minha estrela" ("My Shining Star"). The song's reggae beat adds a smooth vibe to the scene, conjuring reggae's stereotypical association with marijuana.

As the students feed their vices, though, they also choose to remain oblivious to the effects of their actions, focusing on "what is beautiful" ("no que é bonito"), as Sangue da Cidade's song suggests. The film assumes a well-worn argument in Brazilian society, exemplified in Nascimento's narrative voice asking, "How many children will we have to lose to the drug trade so that a playboy can roll a joint?" ("Quantas crianças a gente vai ter que perder para o tráfico só para um playboy rolar um baseado?"). Nascimento's focus is solely on the criminalization of illicit drugs. It does not recognize any other social, political, or economic dimensions to the drug trade or levels of violence.[22] He argues that penalization and the heavy hand of BOPE are the only ways to break the cycle of drug violence.

While in the first study session scene Matias ignores the students smoking weed, after the death of Neto and his entrance into BOPE, Matias becomes the enforcer of the law. During a peace march by students, Matias goes to the university, beats up Edu, confiscates the marijuana from Márcio, and takes Márcio away at gunpoint. The scene underscores the distance between the middle-class students, who are dressed in white, and Matias, who wears the all-black outfit of BOPE. The black and white color juxtaposition of their wardrobes symbolically points to the film's underlying binary construction of violence in contemporary Brazil and references the permanence of battle symbolized in BOPE's black outfit. This battle, the film indicates, has multiple fronts, one of which is the middle and upper classes' hypocritical stance echoed in their call for peace. *Tropa de Elite* maintains that their hypocrisy masks the reality of what the country needs, the reaffirmation of a strong neo-authoritarian male figure to reestablish order.

In terms of masculinity, the scene suggests the emasculation of the middle-class male. In the final moments, Edu lies face down on the ground, groveling in pain. It is Maria who attempts to stand up to Matias, but she is pushed away, incapacitated in her resistance to the neo-authoritarian male. Matias represents the neo-authoritarian violence that, the film suggests, Edu and Maria need to guarantee their security and yet denounce as treading on their constitutional rights.

Women and Men

Tropa de Elite focuses on the reassertion of hegemonic neo-authoritarian masculinity. The film initially locates hegemonic masculinity, linked to male power and dominance, in a state of crisis in relation to the female characters. Women are at once an impetus for the male protagonist's crisis of masculinity and the catalyst the film employs to substantiate the reassertion of neo-authoritarian masculinity.

Masculinity in modern society has been constructed around a gender binary that assumes as its opposite femininity. Within traditional binary conceptualizations of masculinity and femininity, the two are inextricably linked, one being dependent upon the other to give meaning to each term. This binary framework reduces these two identity markers to essentialist definitions and attempts to naturalize the link between masculinity and the male body on the one hand and femininity and the female body on the other. Thus, normative social constructions of sex and gender force the individual into paradigms of masculine and feminine that are subsequently employed as restrictive mechanisms to control understandings of the sexed body, individual expressions of gender identity, and the overall social and political roles assigned to men and women. *Tropa de Elite* incorporates a limited cast of female protagonists and allots even less screen time to the development of their characters. This being said, these women represent a constant threat to masculine authority and the film progressively marginalizes women as the male protagonists assume an ever more neo-authoritarian stance.

Maria, Matias's girlfriend, is one of only two female characters of significance in the storyline of the film. Maria and Matias, after meeting in their law school class, begin a romantic relationship. However, Matias never informs Maria that he is a member of the military police or BOPE. Matias's charade is only revealed when Baiano discovers a picture of the young officer under the headline "Slaughter in Babilônia" ("Chacina no Babilônia") in the daily paper *Agora no Rio* and takes retribution on Roberta and Rodrigues. It is interesting to note that while Matias is in a relationship with Maria, he retains faith in the law, and his inculcation into the use of violence and torture remains at bay. The rupture in their romantic relationship also marks the moment of his induction into the enactment of the violence of BOPE and his complete dedication to the homosocial bonds that link this band of brothers. At this moment his desire to avenge the killing of his childhood friend Neto converges with his complete inculcation into the homosocial order of BOPE. The purging of female characters at this point also expunges any semblance of control over the violence that the male protagonists enact.

A parallel situation plays out with Rosane, Capitão Nascimento's wife, the second female character who figures into the storyline. When Rosane is given screen time, an underlying tension juxtaposes her relationship with Nascimento to his homosocial relations as a member of BOPE. The tension between men and women is constructed early on and escalates throughout the film.

Our first encounter of Rosane, beyond her voice on the other end of a telephone, follows the opening credits, when Nascimento returns home late at night. The narrative voice explains, "My life was getting more difficult by the minute" ("A minha vida estava ficando cada vez mais difícil"). The voiceover accompanies the image of Nascimento as he walks into their bedroom and touches the pregnant belly of Rosane as she sleeps. The next morning, the camera, in a reestablishing shot, accompanies Rosane and Nascimento into the kitchen as he gets ready to leave for work. The camera frames the two in choker close-up, pivoting along the axis of action as they banter back and forth about his long work hours. Looking at Rosane, Nascimento asks, "What do you want me to do, stop working?" ("Você quer que faça o que, pare de trabalhar?"). Rosane responds, "If I would have known that you were not going to get out, I never would have gotten pregnant" ("Se soubesse que você não ia sair, não tinha engravidado"). Nascimento's gaze is now directed downward. After a long silence on his part, he simply responds with "Tchau." The frame cuts to the *polícia militar* headquarters. Nascimento in a voiceover states, "War always charges a price, and when the price is too high, it is time to get out" ("A guerra sempre cobra o seu preço, e quando o preço é alto demais, é hora de pular fora").

The idea of war here takes on a double meaning in the context of the film. There is the war in the streets that is the conflict between BOPE and the criminal gangs that operate in Rio de Janeiro. At the same time, there is a second war in the private sphere of the home. It is a struggle for power between men and women. Nascimento's understanding of these wars reflects the traditional gendered binary work/home. These categories are premised around and reinforce stereotypical constructions of masculinity and femininity. For this binary to function it requires a naturalized division between men and women in which men give priority to work while women focus on the family. The film locates the price that this more personal war exacts in the initial exchange between Rosane and Nascimento. The scene juxtaposes the opening scenes—men are associated with authority, work, action—to the space of the home, where women stifle these pursuits. In this battle of forces, the film constructs Rosane as symbolically castrating Capitão Nascimento. She forces him to decide between continuing working or having a child. This binary construction flips the traditional question of work/life balance normally imposed upon women. Following the logic of the film, Rosane forces Nascimento into a submissive position with regard to the family. This choice is reflected in his silence and downward gaze rather than looking at her at the closing of the scene. Nascimento transforms silence, traditionally a trope associated with the stoic male, into a tool of empowerment by refusing to engage with Rosane. The scene closes as he walks out to join his battalion. Rosane's continual emasculation of the protagonist as portrayed in the scene emblematizes the role of women as a countervailing force in the struggles of neo-authoritarian masculinity.

The crisis of neo-authoritarian masculinity is highlighted in Capitão Nascimento's first panic attack, suffered on screen while he is rock climbing (top roping) with Rosane. She belays him from below. The camera takes a full body shot of Nascimento clutching the rock as a woman nimbly scales the rock face to his left, moving smoothly past him. The camera cuts to Rosane asking from below if he is alright and then cuts back to him, his face buried in the rock façade as the female climber stops, inquires if he is okay, and then continues her ascent when he replies nervously, yes. Nascimento does not look at her or at Rosane but peers to the right off screen, visibly shaken.

This is the only scene where women constitute the majority on screen. This scene is a metaphor for women's changing roles in Brazilian society. Men have traditionally occupied most positions of power in the country. Nonetheless, at the turn of the twenty-first century, society and the labor markets began undergoing drastic changes as women gained a stronger foothold economically as well as socially and politically.

In Brazilian society, women have made strides toward gaining formal parity and social justice along gender lines. With the 1985 transition to democracy, women began to advocate for greater social equity in Brazil. As a result, the 1988 Constitution included provisions such as granting equal rights to men and women, establishing antidiscrimination laws, and recognizing the rights of domestic workers (Lovell). In 1996 the Brazilian Congress passed electoral laws that require electoral lists have 30% female candidates. These are important gains but are marked by ambiguity. These laws have not translated into the tangible results they were designed to achieve. The legislative, judiciary, and executive branches of government have retained their patriarchal structure, which has curbed the impact of gender equity in government (Alcântara and Sardenberg). The proportion of women holding seats in the upper and lower houses of Congress in 2014 was only 9% in the lower house and 16% in the upper house (Viñas 43), far below the required percentage of female candidates. Their underrepresentation reflects how women have been predominantly kept from positions of power (Alcântara and Sardenberg), experience a lack of equality in access to jobs (Lovell), and experience high degrees of gender-based violence in the form of sexual, physical, and psychological abuse (Schraiber et al.),[23] demonstrating that Brazil has continued to be a fundamentally patriarchal society.

Dilma Rousseff was elected Brazil's first female president in 2010 and reelected in 2014 to the highest position of government. Her impeachment and events during the subsequent administrations too numerous to delineate here reveal the tenuousness of her achievements and the continuation of patriarchal ordering. The gains women have made are not as sweeping and rapid as many believe they should be. Even so, as women make advances toward achieving gender equity and social justice, the traditional patriarchal structure finds itself under heightened threat in terms of the privileges allotted to men solely on the basis of their biological sex designation. It is this threat that the female rock climber symbolizes in *Tropa de Elite*. The film offers a singular response to the destabilization of traditional male privilege represented by the slow yet notable ascent of women: the reaffirmation of neo-authoritarian masculinity.

Exemplary of how the film privileges neo-authoritarian masculinity and represents women as symbolically castrating men are another two sequential interactions between Rosane and Nascimento toward the end of the film. In the first, after a disappointing day of training with Neto, Nascimento returns home. At home, he has a panic attack and takes anti-anxiety medication. Rosane, having woken up from his rustling in the bathroom, opens the lavatory door. Nascimento, standing in front of the medicine-cabinet mirror, takes his anti-anxiety medication, stares down at the sink, unable to face his own reflection, repeating, "This thing here is not a problem. Everyone takes this thing here . . . It is not a problem" ("Este aqui não tem problema nenhum. Todo mundo toma ese aqui. . . . Não tem problema nenhum"). Her response is to tell him, "You're not going to need this anymore. You're going to get out and everything will pass. . . . You're going to get out of BOPE" ("Você não vai mais precisar tomar. Você vai sair e tudo vai passar. . . . Você vai sair do BOPE"). For her, BOPE is the cause of his anxiety. She begins to pressure him to leave BOPE. However, for Nascimento, there is not a future outside of BOPE. He says, "I'm going to get out to go where?" ("Vou sair para onde?"). As she follows him to the living room, asking him if he is going to quit and chastising him because he now has a family, they get into an argument. In the action of the scene, Nascimento yields to her advice. It is her decision that he will leave BOPE. At the close of the scene, Nascimento hunches over, sobbing on Rosane's shoulder as she holds him and repeats, "Everything is going to be alright" ("Vai dar tudo certo"). The narrative voiceover cuts in to the final frames:

> There was only one thing that pissed me off more than a mistake during one of my tactical operations: it was Rosane telling me what I had to do. . . . Even worse is that sometimes, even though I knew she was wrong, I obeyed.

> Só tinha uma coisa que me deixava mais puto que erro na minha operação, era Rosane dizendo para mim o que eu tinha que fazer. . . . Pior que às vezes, mesmo sabendo que ela estava errada, eu obedecia.

This scene repeats elements of the previous kitchen segment. Once again, Nascimento and Rosane get into an argument about his continuation in BOPE in light of his newborn son. But the tension has escalated. Previously, Nascimento retained a degree of power by firstly falling silent and secondly, ending the conversation by leaving for work. This time, however, Rosane assumes a more dominant stance, beginning with her insistence that leaving BOPE will cure him. As the argument intensifies, Rosane takes on an ever more assertive position, to the point that she tells Nascimento that Neto deserves a second chance. More telling than even the dialogue is the

Figure 4.7. Nascimento berates Rosane when he returns home after learning of Neto's death. Screen grab from *Tropa de Elite*.

body language. It is Nascimento who attempts to walk away from Rosane, and she pursues him until he breaks down crying in her arms. Visually, the film implies that she takes the power of decision from him in terms of leaving BOPE as well as confirming Neto as his replacement. In hindsight, the narrative voice attempts to reimpose a masculine order by claiming that he knew she was wrong but followed her indications anyway. The narrative voice employs the scene almost as a cautionary tale, asserting that a stronger, more authoritarian stance would have been the proper response from the protagonist at that moment.

While these two scenes impose the will of Rosane, the couple's final altercation reaffirms a neo-authoritarian stance for Nascimento. He once again returns home in the late hours of the night. In contrast to the previous familial scenes, Rosane is awake and reading on the couch. Before she is able to say anything beyond "How are you?" ("Tudo bem?"), Nascimento confronts her:

> Do not open your mouth to speak about my job in this house. . . . You will not speak anymore about my work in this house. Do you understand? It is me who runs this shit here, and you will not open your mouth to talk about my battalion in this house. Do you understand? You got it? I'm the one who runs this shit here!

> Não abra a boca para falar do meu trabalho nesta casa. . . . Você não fala mais do meu trabalho nesta casa. Você está entendendo? Quem

manda nesta porra aqui sou eu e você não vai abrir a boca para falar sobre o meu batalhão nesta casa. Você está entendendo? Você entendeu? Quem manda nesta porra aqui sou eu!

He assumes a neo-authoritarian position that mirrors his exchanges with the *marginais* in the favela. While he does not slap his wife as he does to favela residents, his body language and hand gestures mimic his brutal dealings with them; he stands above her and points his finger in her face, moving closer to her with each shake of his hand. His head, in a similar movement as during interrogations, snaps up and down as he barks commands at her. Visually, the scene is differentiated; during interrogations, the camera usually holds a medium to close-up shot; now, the camera has retreated to just past a cowboy shot, framing the scene from a slight distance, placing the viewer in a more distant position from the action. This viewing position allows the spectator to spatially locate Nascimento as he stands over Rosane in the mise-en-scène. The physicality of the exchange is reduced as compared to the scenes of torture, while the hierarchy between the two genders is emphasized. It is significant that the scene ends with Nascimento going into the bathroom and dumping his anti-anxiety medication down the drain. This is the first time he is able to overcome his panic attacks.

Tellingly, his hand does not tremble but is firm and steady. The implication is that the crisis that was afflicting Nascimento was not panic attacks due to a high-stress job; it can be read instead as stress caused by the repression of his masculinity. The film contends that men flourish in the face of high-stress, action-filled, violent situations, and it is not those but rather the suppression of this innate part of men that has caused a crisis of masculinity.

By the final scenes of the film, Nascimento and Matias are no longer with their female partners. With the purging of women from their lives, Matias and Nascimento become hyperfocused on completing their mission of avenging Neto's death. The narrative storyline in relation to female characters evokes Klaus Theweleit's discussion of representations of fascist masculinity among Freikorps soldiers in early twentieth-century Germany:

Relationships with women are dissolved and transformed into new male attitudes, into political stances, revelations of the true path, etc. As the woman fades out of sight, the contours of the male sharpen; that is the way in which the fascist mode of writing often proceeds. (35)

In *Tropa de Elite,* the disappearance of women allows Nascimento and Matias to increment their violent defense of dominant society and embodiment of neo-authoritarian masculinity.

Part of my argument in this book is that with the institution of an increasingly substantive democracy in Brazil,[24] traditional expressions of hegemonic masculinity came under threat as new social actors emerged. The changes can be attributed in part to the 2003 political success of Luiz Inácio Lula da Silva and the Partido dos Trabalhadores (PT) that he helped found in 1980. Lula's presidential campaign and the PT centralized an anticorruption political platform in the 2003 elections, which, at least on the surface, appeared threatening to the status quo of politics and corruption in Brazil.[25] In 2006 the *Americas* "Barometers" survey found that when Brazilians were asked to spontaneously name the single most serious issue affecting Brazilian society, the participants ranked corruption as number one (Power and Taylor 4). The perception that politicians and more generally government institutions are corrupt has grown since then, as scandals such as the one in 2014 involving the state oil company, Petrobrás, and the Lava Jato (Car Wash) scandal that affected the 2018 election cycle and beyond made headlines and dominated the news as inquiries expanded.

These corruption scandals ignited political animosities in the country as protesters, many of them from the middle and upper classes, took to the streets in 2015 and again in 2016 to call for the impeachment of President Dilma Rousseff. In the stories, interviews, and images that emerged from these protests, it was striking to note the lack of racial and socioeconomic diversity among the protesters. Even more remarkable was that some of these predominantly right-wing protests not only demanded the impeachment of the sitting president but also called for a return to authoritarian rule (Watts). This was the latest incarnation of a social nerve that *Tropa de Elite* sought to exploit. This social nerve is an authoritarian vein that runs through the Brazilian national body. It was responsible for the dictatorship that began in 1964 and lasted twenty-one years. It is revealed in discussions when people of a certain class and privilege lament the end of the dictatorship because at least they were not concerned with indiscriminate violence from the lower classes and felt safe on the streets. It can help us to understand segments of the public that responded to *Tropa de Elite* with a resounding "Yes, that is what we need" while calling for the return of a neo-authoritarian male figure to put the country on the right path.

Men on the Verge of a Nervous Breakdown

O Homem do Ano

On July 23, 1993, eight street children were murdered on the front steps of the Igreja da Candelária, a church in downtown Rio de Janeiro. One month later, twenty-one people were massacred in the favela of Vigário Geral, also in Rio de Janeiro. All twenty-nine deaths were attributed to vigilante police and were considered, in part, retaliation for the *arrastões* of 1992 and 1993 in Rio de Janeiro.[1] These disturbances of the middle- and upper-class beach enclaves of Rio's Zona Sul exacerbated already prevalent feelings of insecurity in the city's entrenched social sectors. The occurrences also led to more police brutality. As a consequence, the hope that the recent democratization of the country would usher in a new era of respect for citizens' rights was effectively undermined by the clash between marginalized and dominant social segments, epitomized by the *arrastões* and the vigilante police-led massacres (Caldeira).

The *arrastões*, the massacre in Vigário Geral, and the killing of the street children on the steps of the Candelária church were all taken up by the Brazilian media, which reinforced a culture of fear (Soares et al. *Criminalidade urbana*;[2] Ventura; Herschmann; Rotker and Goldman) that contaminated the Carioca imaginary in the 1990s. Susana Rotker and Katherine Goldman, in *Citizens of Fear*, contend that social practices are constructed around a generalized fear that shapes the truths of people's daily lives. The bodies that inhabit the cityscape understand fear as an instinctive survival mechanism they use to guide them in the urban space. A daily portrait of life in these urban centers as beyond control dominates how these individuals understand the urban arena. The city becomes a text, a work of fear, in which the mass public consumes daily images, stories, and other representations of violence.

Within these images there are few discernable narratives, but one that appears continually is that of the poor person as criminal. In this manner, violence rewrites the text of the city. Rotker and Goldman contend that this violence "makes victims of us all, this undeclared civil war obliterates spaces of difference and differentiation, making all of us experience injustice, insecurity, and inequality" (18). The fear is then only heightened by media outlets that repeatedly feed into sensationalistic constructions of the poor, immigrants, and others as the source of crime. The public conferred a heightened importance to these three incidents because they desecrated what previously were held to be safe territories within the Brazilian imaginary: the sacred ground of the church, the domestic space of the home, and the democratic terrain of the beach (Soares et al. *Criminalidade urbana*). The violation of these symbolically safe spaces cemented the culture of fear into the dominant public's imaginary. While at times misdirected, this fear did have some grounding in what was occurring in Brazilian society at the time. Homicide rates were on the rise, and democracy was not unassailable (Kingstone and Power *Democratic Brazil*). The long-term survival of Brazil's democratic experiment was far from certain.

Fast-forward to the initial decade of the twenty-first century. The rule and ideals of democracy were consolidated in Brazil in the political realm (Kingstone and Power *Democratic Brazil Revisited*). Brazil's political system had shed the baggage of the 1964–1985 authoritarian regime, moved beyond the intermediate transitional period of the later 1980s and early 1990s, and established stable substantive democratic governance. In theory, these political changes should usher in an epoch of democratic civil peace, which implies a reduction in violence within the country and, one would expect, a particularly prominent decrease in police violence (Hegre et al.).[3]

The consolidation of substantive democracy would supposedly challenge some of the traditional power structures of Brazil's patriarchal culture, such as authoritarian state security forces and vigilante groups that operated parallel to and yet frequently also in tandem with state security forces. Adjusting the figures for population rate increases, after two decades of rising homicide rates—1980 to 2000—homicide rates decreased in the first decade of the new millennium. The data fit with Havard Hegre and colleagues' ideas on democratic civil peace: rates of violence rise during transitional democratic periods, but once substantive democracy is established civil violence declines.

From 2003 to 2007, male and female homicide rates dropped most drastically in Brazil, particularly in the urban centers of the nation. This reduction in homicides correlates with the years that the films I am discussing in this book were released as well as the beginning of the Workers Party national government, growth in the economy, and the rooting of substantive democracy in the country. It is notable that during this same time span, narratives of violence and the marginal male exploded in the media and cultural production. Concurrently, extralegal violence by organized *milícias* (militias), paramilitary groups in Brazil, began to grow exponentially in the early to mid-2000s (Cano and Duarte; Zaluar and Siqueira Conceição). According to figures collected by Ignácio Cano and Thais Duarte, reported *milícia* crimes through the Disque Denúncia (Dial a Complaint) system in Rio went from just over 250 in 2006 to more than 13,000 in 2009. In light of the explosion of reports of *milícia* violence, the state created a special hotline, Disque Milícia (Dial Militia), in 2008 (Cano and Duarte 26–27). The Disque Milícia hotline is an anonymous call line to which individuals can phone in tips related to *milícia* activities in Rio de Janeiro.

Juxtaposed to the decline in homicide rates, the number of killings by police during this same time frame rose. The victims of state violence were and are, in their overwhelming majority, men of lower socioeconomic status between the ages of eleven and twenty-five (Vargas and Alves; Vigna; Alves). John Bailey and Lucía Dammert note that what both overall and police homicide rates do not reveal is how the perception of rising crime outpaced actual crime rates. The perception that crime was intensifying, especially in middle- and upper-class segments of society, created a culture of fear within dominant society that was not justified by the actual numbers of victims (Bailey and Dammert 8–9). Rather, the primary victims of violence have been young marginal men. Notably, state security forces and more recently *milícias*, many of them composed of off-duty officers, bear responsibility for a significant percentage of this body count.

Engaging with this culture of fear, José Henrique Fonseca's 2003 feature-length film, *O Homem do Ano*, brings under the purview of the camera questions of paralegal violence and its intersection with masculinity. The film asks what groups are responsible for societal violence, what the motivating factors are for that violence, and how masculinity is linked to acts of street and paralegal violence.[4] In contrast to *Cidade de Deus*, *Quase Dois Irmãos*, and *Tropa de Elite*, this film debunks the idea that the marginal male is the primary perpetrator of violence and questions the underlying premise that a neo-authoritarian masculine order would clean up society. *O Homem do Ano* demonstrates the consequences of neo-authoritarianism, as social relations tend to break down, reproducing an us/them mentality that is then reflected in the continuation and augmentation of the divided city. This breakdown challenges the mores of democratic civil society, such as the principles of majority rule, individual rights, and civic responsibility. Additionally, it undermines gains in the political realm of substantive democracy, such as guaranteeing the right to political participation and representation. *O Homem do Ano* exposes masculine neurosis, the individual and social malady that infuses neo-authoritarian masculine identity and social relations constructed through violence.

Neurosis, in Kenneth Paradis's estimation, is "the inability to understand, articulate, and therefore control one's own 'self'" (95). My use of the term "masculine neurosis" posits this inability to control oneself as a direct consequence of masculine subjective identity premised around violence. *O Homem do Ano* undermines traditional constructions of the neo-authoritarian male that centralize violence as a positive marker of self-assertion as embodied in the strong, aggressive man who controls a situation by dint of physical force. Fonseca's film suggests that violence in effect creates anxiety, paranoia, and neurosis and destabilizes this notion of masculinity.

During Brazil's 1985 transition to democracy, parts of the repressive governmental structure, the military and state security forces, were incorporated into the democratic regime. With their absorption, the authoritarian male was also subsumed into new expressions of hegemonic masculinity, claiming authority through "cultural consent, discursive centrality, institutionalization, and the marginalization of alternatives" (Connell and Messerschmidt 846). *O Homem do Ano* posits neo-authoritarian masculinity as occupying the apex of the hegemonic gendered social order. However, the film deconstructs this same hierarchy by revealing the neurosis caused by the reliance on violence to guarantee masculine domination to the neo-authoritarian male.

O Homem do Ano questions sociocultural discourses that posit the marginal male as the primary perpetrator of urban violence in contemporary Brazil. The film achieves this critique by revealing a link between the intensification of narratives of marginal-male violence and the veiled networks that promote the empowerment of the neo-authoritarian male. The film exposes how, within contemporary society, a de facto state of exception has been imposed that guarantees the immolation of the marginal male and buttresses predominant narratives that consecrate his erasure. Both processes have a social price in that they provoke a crisis in expressions of neo-authoritarian masculinity.

O Homem do Ano: A Brief Synopsis

O Homem do Ano takes place in the Baixada Fluminense, a peripheral area of Rio de Janeiro. The film narrates the story of Máiquel (Murilo Benício), who at the start of the movie is unemployed and says,

Before we are born, someone, maybe God, defines how your life will be fucked. That was my theory. God only thinks about man at the start. When he decides whether your life will be good or bad.

Antes da gente nascer, alguém, talvez Deus, define direitinho como vai foder a tua vida. Isso era minha teoria. Deus só pensa no homem na largada. Quando decide se sua vida vai ser boa ou ruim.

After losing a soccer bet with his friends, Máiquel makes good on a wager and dyes his hair blond. This transformation gives him newfound confidence and produces a shift in his self-definition, both in ontological and social terms. Returning to Gonzaga's, the neighborhood bar, Máiquel gets into an argument with Suel (Wagner Moura), the local drug dealer who runs their neighborhood. Suel insults Máiquel publicly, saying, "For me, the man who dyes his hair blond like you is very queer!" ("Para mim, homem que pinta o cabelinho loirinho assim como você é muito viado!"). The comment challenges Máiquel's self-definition as a heterosexual male and destabilizes his masculine identity.

Máiquel looks to violence to reaffirm his masculinity: he challenges Suel to a duel and ends up shooting him in the back. To Máiquel's surprise, the community, instead of punishing him as a murderer, praises his actions and showers him with gifts. Máiquel becomes infamous in his neighborhood as a *justiceiro*, a vigilante whose actions are bolstered by the community. His fame spreads and reaches the middle-class residents of the area including Dr. Carvalho (Jorge Dória), a local dentist. Carvalho hires Máiquel to shoot Ezequiel (Nill Marcondes) in a supposed honor killing to avenge Carvalho's familial pride.

The killings of Suel and Ezequiel set in motion a series of murders that establish Máiquel as the extralegal, neo-authoritarian enforcer of the community. Once Máiquel's fame is consolidated, he enters into a deal with Carvalho and his associates Zílmar (Agildo Ribeiro), Sílvio (José Wilker), and the local police inspector, Delegado Santana (Carlo Mossy). The dentist and his associates become the silent backers of the security firm SESPA that Máiquel operates under the auspices of the necessity to protect local companies.[5] After opening the firm, Máiquel is elected "O Homem do Ano" ("The Man of the Year") by local business leaders. As his role as a vigilante grows, the ensuing power spirals beyond his control. His personal life ruptures as the violence of the public sphere spills over into the private realm. Máiquel kills his wife, Cledir (Cláudia Abreu), and loses his lover, Érica (Natália Lage). As violence overtakes his life, his public and private worlds implode.

Spaces of Violence: The Baixada Fluminense

The film's setting in the Baixada Fluminense serves as a microcosm to engage issues of civil and state violence that have been particularly pronounced in Rio de Janeiro in recent decades.[6] Within dominant geopolitical mappings of Rio de Janeiro, the Baixada Fluminense has traditionally been considered a region plagued by a higher degree of violence than other areas of the city.[7] This violence has its roots in the 1950s, when the Baixada was an independent municipality and the terrain of Natalício Tenório Cavalcanti de Albuquerque, also known as the "Gunslinger Congressman" ("Deputado Pistoleiro"), a federal congressman representing the state of Rio de Janeiro. He ran the Baixada with an iron fist, regularly walking the streets with his infamous machine gun Lurdinha hidden beneath his black cape. From that practice he also became known as "The Man in the Black Cape" ("O Homem da Capa Preta"). Cavalcanti's violent masculine bravado gained national fame in 1953 after he killed Albino Imparato, a police commissioner who was investigating him for murder and influence peddling. When police forces surrounded his home, "The Fort" ("A Fortaleza"), to take him in, he vowed to resist, even claiming parliamentary immunity. Only after several high-ranking officials from the federal chamber intervened did the standoff end. Sérgio Rezende's *O Homem da Capa Preta* (*Man in the Black Cape,* 1986) pays homage to Cavalcanti and his brand of aggressive masculinity.

In the 1970s the Baixada Fluminense was annexed to metropolitan Rio de Janeiro. When it became part of the city of Rio, popular narratives of violence about the region increased (Souza Alves; Enne).[8] Many of these narratives blamed rogue groups, drug disputes, or marginal individuals for the violence that plagued the region (Souza Alves 24). This interpretation, however, belied the many violent actions by death squads and other forms of vigilante justice. José Cláudio Souza Alves notes, "State, justice system, economic sectors, and electoral processes are collapsed into the construction of this form of power that is extremely permeable to the use of violence and to those who employ it" ("Estado, sistema de justiça, setores econômicos e processos eleitorais associam-se na construção desta forma de poder extremamente permeável ao uso da violência e àqueles que a empregam") (25). The case of Cavalcanti in the 1950s and 1960s and accounts of death squads and popular lynchings in the 1960s, 1970s, and 1980s disprove these popular narratives and demonstrate that violence was an integral part of the sociopolitical system (Zaluar and Siqueira Conceição 91).

The history of extralegal and paramilitary violence in the Baixada foreshadows more recent problems that Rio de Janeiro has faced from *milícia* violence. According to data released in 2009 by the Núcleo de Pesquisa da Violência da Universidade do Estado do Rio de Janeiro (NUPEV-UERJ, Center for the Research of Violence at the State University of Rio de Janeiro), 41.5% of peripheral communities around Rio de Janeiro were controlled by *milícias*, surpassing the number of areas controlled by the Comando Vermelho. Alba Zaluar and Isabel Siqueira Conceição assert that the communities dominated by *milícias* generally have less drug use and trafficking, fewer conspicuous demonstrations of violence, fewer firearms, and less "visibly violent attitudes" ("atitudes visivelmente violentas") (95).

When a community is overtaken, the *milícia* imposes codes of conduct that, if violated, elicit reprisals as visible warnings to the community (Zaluar and Siqueira Conceição 95). Generally, while crime and acts of violence, particularly police violence, are reduced in the *milícia*'s territories, community members note that the *milícias*' actions do not demonstrate any type of solidarity with them. Many community members consider the *milícias*' primary motivators as economic, political, and power-related. For the community, the *milícia* "does not constitute a plausible alternative to democratic control of criminality and violence" ("não constitui absolutamente uma alternativa plausível para o controle democrático da criminalidade e da violência") (Zaluar and Siqueira Conceição 95–96). Rule under the *milícias* can be seen as a continuation of the 1964–1985 authoritarian regime, whose imposition of a state of exception is selectively applied within peripheral spaces of the city. For Giorgio Agamben, the state of exception defines the limits of the law through the suspension of the law to safeguard the application of the law. The state of exception is based on the concept of necessity, an eternally subjective notion that permits the suspension of the law and the rights of citizenship, an extrajuridical order that is decreed purportedly to guarantee juridical order.

O Homem do Ano places itself in dialogue with the turbulent history of the Baixada and Rio de Janeiro, engaging popular and official narratives of violence and the imposition of a state of exception in the region. Máiquel is a twenty-first-century version of Cavalcanti. He is the neo-authoritarian male who employs violence to achieve and retain masculine domination. Máiquel emblematizes the transfer of the state's prerogative of violence to the private sector that is characteristic of neoliberalism (Foucault *Birth of Biopolitics*).

Feeling the Colors of Masculinity

O Homem do Ano is narrated from within, presenting the perspective of Máiquel, who through a combination of firsthand narration and voiceover explains his initiation into the world of vigilante justice. His first-person narration inserts the viewers into the action, allowing them a direct experience of the protagonist's trials and tribulations. In conjunction with this perspective, *O Homem do Ano* employs a masculine aesthetic reminiscent of *Cidade de Deus* in its use of filming and editing techniques such as jump cuts, steady pans, and other stylistic practices that fragment the visual narrative. The use of these filming and editing techniques creates a fast-paced narrative that pulls the spectator in to experience the action.

The strategic employment of subjective shots shifts the focus between Máiquel as both subject and object of the camera. The cinematography positions Máiquel as the central figure who at once guides the narrative and is scrutinized by the camera. According to (Alfred) "Hitchcock's rule," the size of any in-frame element should correlate with its significance in the narrative (B. Brown 25, referencing François Truffaut). Framing continually returns to Máiquel, pulling the spectator beyond the protagonist's physical actions and into his mental state and his performance of masculinity.

The agitated visual style of *O Homem do Ano* augments the internal tension within the narrative and generates dramatic friction between the film and the spectator. This occurs through the continual rupturing of the visual narrative, which in turn undermines the narrative's stability, prompting the spectator to experience Máiquel's emotional anxieties, instability, and paranoia, particularly in regard to his masculine identity. As Máiquel slides into a state of masculine neurosis, the movements of the camera quicken, the pace of editing accelerates, and the visual space collapses.

Visual space is controlled and manipulated through the framing of the shots. The camera rarely pulls back to high, wide, bird's-eye-view framing that would allow the spectator to pull away from the action and establish a more open and controlled sense of the mise-en-scène. Rather, the film is composed primarily of straight-on medium, close-up, and extreme close-up shots. This framing draws the viewer into the protagonist's personal space and produces a feeling of claustrophobia that reflects how violence overtakes Máiquel.

Framing inserts the spectator into the scene and scrutinizes Máiquel's construction of masculinity. At Caju's (José Henrique Fonseca) bric-a-brac warehouse where Máiquel buys a handgun, the framing centralizes the relationship between Máiquel, the handgun, and masculine power. The mise-en-scène creates a chaotic setting, the background cast in blue and green hues against which Máiquel's platinum-blond hair glows. The camera registers Máiquel's nervousness through fast-paced edited cuts between Caju and Máiquel in close-up answering shots. The filming technique highlights the protagonist's growing anxiety. The camera's limited depth of field reflects the spatial confusion, creates a sense of claustrophobia, and amplifies the protagonist's mental disorientation. Between the two men, a stream of lethal weapons ruptures the space. In each instance, the camera cuts between the firearm and Caju and Máiquel, each in close-up shots. Finally, at the end of the sequence, Máiquel holds a 45 mm semiautomatic pistol in his hand. Caju inquires anxiously, "Are you feeling the power? It's like putting a crown on your head!" ("Está sentindo a força? É como colocar uma coroa na cabeça!"). Máiquel smirks slightly as he gazes along the barrel of the gun toward the camera, his platinum hair a visual crown. The

Figure 5.1. In Caju's warehouse, Máiquel first feels the power of the 45 mm semiautomatic pistol in his hand. Screen grab from *O Homem do Ano*.

Figure 5.2. A blue and green color palette predominates. Screen grab from *O Homem do Ano*.

nervousness and anxiety that Máiquel had projected until this point vanish. In the final shot, the camera gazes up the barrel of the 45 mm, the depth of field elongates, and Máiquel's elated face fills the background. Máiquel appears drunk with the prospect of neo-authoritarian power that the weapon implies. The framing of the scene gets tighter, moving from a cowboy framing when Máiquel first enters the space to a headshot, pulling the spectator into his mental space and the increasing feeling of diminishing alternatives to violence.

The handgun, as in other films I examine, has obvious phallic connotations. It is a metaphor for the manly status that Máiquel longs to attain; the gun reinforces masculine domination and proposes aggression as inherent to neo-authoritarian masculine authority. Within the scene there also is a subtle foreshadowing of the destructive nature of social relations and identities premised around violence and neo-authoritarian masculinity. Through a slight shift of the camera, an opening in the depth of field invites the spectator to peer into the dark nothingness that engulfs Máiquel as he is overcome with the power of the weapon. Just to the left of his head, a black vortex visually prefigures the neurosis that will accompany Máiquel as he ventures into a world of neo-authoritarian male violence. This blacked-out space symbolically points to the chaos and anxiety that violence breeds, juxtaposed to the myth of power and control the handgun elicits in Máiquel.

Beyond framing, masculine neurosis is also emphasized through the selection of a color palette marked by overly saturated color hues. Color visually engages and at the same time destabilizes the spectator's experience and expectations of the film at an aesthetic level. Rich colors garner the attention of the spectator, intensifying the scenes through the visceral responses they elicit while at the same time espousing or contradicting the emotional states of the protagonist. Fonseca manipulates the background of many scenes through the use of colored light. Saturated hues of blue, green, yellow, and red flood the setting, creating unnatural lighting situations that meld into the visual narrative. On a purely aesthetic level, these colors serve to control the scenes stylistically and psychologically.

Fonseca deploys and challenges standard psychological responses to warm and cool colors. A cool color palette (blue, green, violet) predominates in the background of most of the movie and is overwhelmingly linked to masculine relations and violence. While cool colors are typically considered to elicit a feeling of ease and relaxation, in the film, scenes in which the background is flooded in blues and greens challenge this psychological response. This disjuncture is a direct reflection of the schism in neo-authoritarian masculinity; such masculinity relies on violence to assert a hegemonic position sociopolitically, but violence destabilizes social relations. Dominant social narratives in Brazil assert that the neo-authoritarian male is able to impose order and guarantee safety through violence. This film, however, belies that argument because for Máiquel violence only breeds neurosis, anxiety, paranoia, and more violence. As the protagonist becomes more violent, he loses any sense of security and grounding. He reacts by committing more violent acts, in a downward irrational spiral.

Neno (Marcelo Biju), a rival mercenary and drug kingpin in the area, kills Robinson (Perfeito Fortuna), one of Máiquel's close friends. After news arrives of Robinson's death, Máiquel and his crew go back to Robinson and Marcão's (Lázaro Ramos) automobile chop shop. The background of the space is flooded in blue and green. The coolness of the hues creates an unnatural ease that contrasts directly with the tension of the action: Máiquel amped up on cocaine, the ambience charged with his desire to avenge Robinson's death, and then the killing of Neno and his associate Pereba (Guilherme Estevam).

The juxtaposition between the expected psychological response to the blue and green color palette and the action on screen emphasizes Máiquel's growing neurosis. His unstable mental condition is the result of both a desire to act violently and the unconscious rejection of this behavior, as he becomes increasingly aware of how violence affects his life. One can read the use of color as symbolic of neo-authoritarian violence, since over-saturated hues of blue and green prevail in many of the scenes that show intermale violence. The ambiguity that one witnesses in Máiquel's relation to violence finds parallels in how Brazilian society has reacted to rising rates of violence, although the growth has not to date necessarily spurred a rejection of said behavior.

The neo-authoritarian male, whether through state or paramilitary demonstrations of power, proposes to respond to violence with violence. His actions supposedly promise to eradicate criminal activity and (re)instill a sense of security in the public sphere. He embodies the myth that demonstrations of violence and power such as zero-tolerance policies, state or *milícia* killings will result in the suppression of crime and a secure public sphere. In the late 1990s and early 2000s in Brazil, dominant and often official discourse maintained that as criminal violence infected the cityscape, society and the state must respond with measures of equal force to quell the tide of criminal aggression. Zero-tolerance laws and punishment of criminal acts with longer mandatory jail sentences that were prevalent in the United States in the 1980s and 1990s were adopted, at least in part, in Brazil in the late 1990s and early 2000s.[9] In early 2006, the Copacabana military police chief, Colonel Celso Nogueira, introduced a zero-tolerance program in Copacabana. Half a year later, zero-tolerance initiatives were expanded in the city. Nogueira directly attributed these policies to New York City Mayor Rudy Giuliani's implementation of similar strategies to confront crime in the 1990s. In Rio, the crackdown was directed at urban disorder and street crime generally. The Rio military police chief contended that by targeting even relatively minor infractions with severity, the city would experience an overall reduction in crime (Khimm).

Loïc Wacquant contends that Brazil has overarchingly followed a US model of punitive containment. Contesting zero-tolerance policies, he maintains that the growth in criminal prosecutions was a direct result of the expansion of marginalized groups in the country and that their marginalization was exacerbated by policies that violated their social and civil rights throughout the 1980s and 1990s, such as ill-functioning justice and penal systems, as well as by high levels of police brutality. Wacquant states, "Residents of the declining *favelas* are treated as virtual enemies of the nation, tenuous trust in public institutions is undermined, and the spiral of violence accelerated" ("Militarization" 56). With this increase, one quantifiable result was the expansion of the penal system.

Besides Fonseca's deployment of cool colors in scenes of male-to-male violence, he infuses a limited number of scenes with warm hues (red, orange, yellow) normally associated with excitement and energy. Many of these scenes occur in Carvalho's home with his daughter Gabriela (Mariana Ximenes); other such scenes are shot in the home of Cledir's mother (Marilu Bueno) and when Máiquel visits Érica at Pastor Marlênio's (André Barros) evangelical church. This color scheme appears in scenes that take place in private spaces inhabited overwhelmingly by women who exert varying degrees of control over Máiquel. Within these areas, the protagonist finds himself unable to dominate the flow of events. He is pulled into situations that challenge his ideal of authority. Unwilling to accept the challenge to gender privilege and male authority, the protagonist slides into masculine neurosis. Following the paradigms of neo-authoritarian masculinity, he resorts to violence to reassert masculine power. Though his aggressive behavior initially occurs in the male-dominated public domain, it increasingly penetrates the private sphere as well, tainting his interactions with women.

The contamination of the domestic ambit by violence reaches its climax when Érica drops by Máiquel and Cledir's home to return the keys to Máiquel's old apartment, where she had been staying after Suel's death. After a tense exchange, Máiquel asks his wife, "Why can't she stay here? What did she do wrong?" ("Porque ela não pode ficar aqui? Que é que ela fez de errado?"). Cledir becomes enraged. As Érica leaves, she exchanges an accusatory glance with Máiquel. Cledir asks him, "Are you having a thing with her?" ("Está tendo uma coisa com ela?"). Their confrontation escalates. Máiquel, at first silent, meekly responds, "No" and walks out of the room. Cledir follows him yelling, "Are you two fucking, crazy bastard?" ("Estão trepando, pirado?"). Máiquel locks himself in the bedroom. Cledir repeatedly screams, "Sleazebag! Open this door!" ("Cafajeste! Abra essa porta!"). The handheld camera whirls around Máiquel in close-up. The salmon-toned walls that energized and dominated the scene are suddenly drowned in sunlight, blurring the image with overexposed hues of yellow and orange. A distorted soundtrack repeats Cledir's accusations. The camera lens slides in and out of focus as it pulls slightly back. Máiquel rocks to and fro. He throws open the door and slams Cledir against the wall, gripping her by the throat and killing her. Silence overtakes the scene in an extreme close-up of his face.

In this scene, color dramatizes Máiquel's slide into masculine neurosis and paranoia. He is poised between passivity and extreme aggression.

Figure 5.3. Overexposed hues of yellow and orange emphasize Máiquel's neurosis and paranoia. Screen grabs from *O Homem do Ano.*

Violence in this context is represented as a seemingly natural reaction to the challenge of masculine domination that Cledir's questioning represents. Nonetheless, the film emphasizes how male violence only begets further anxiety, destabilizing the male subject. Cledir's murder haunts Máiquel and exacerbates his neurosis. Though the murders he commits in the public sphere are sanctioned by his community, he fears the social consequences of having killed his wife.

This scene is particularly troubling because it evokes real-world issues of violence against women in Brazil. Although female homicide rates dipped in the early 2000s, they rose again since 2007. Much of the increase in violence against women has occurred in rural areas and smaller towns. Between 1980 and 2010, female homicides rose 230%, from 1,353 to 4,465 deaths, hitting a rate of 4.8 deaths per 100,000 in 2013, as reported in the *Mapa da violência 2015: Homicídio de mulheres* study by Júlio Jacobo Waiselfisz, and Brazil was in the top five countries in the world for female homicides.

The two female protagonists in *O Homem do Ano,* Cledir and Érica, suffer multiple forms of physical and mental abuse at the hands of Máiquel, yet the film only tangentially touches on femicides, with the death of Cledir. It is more generally focused on male aggression toward women and how violence against women is symptomatic of male anxieties in the construction and expression of masculinity. The film concentrates on violence enacted by men as the principal terrain of masculinities in dispute. It is as if the priority, even when violence toward women is depicted, remains the impact of violence on the perpetrators, the neurotic men who resort to violent acts.

Between Men

O Homem do Ano centralizes masculinity as a performance by and for men from the outset. Displays of virile masculinity depict men performing masculinity for other men. This is clear at the beginning of the film when Máiquel goes to Cledir's beauty salon. Completing his makeover, Cledir whirls Máiquel around so he can gaze upon his newly dyed platinum-blond hair. Máiquel's face loses the timidity that had dominated it moments earlier when he peered through the salon window from the street. He stares into the mirror and camera as a voiceover introduces us to his thoughts in retrospect:

> I always found myself an ugly man. I never liked to look in the mirror. That day was different. I looked at that guy who was and was not me, a blond man, a stranger. I spent the better part of my life wanting to be someone else. And then I saw that my time had come.

> Eu sempre me achei um homem feio. Nunca gostei de olhar no espelho. Naquele dia foi diferente. Olhei para aquele cara que não era eu mas era eu, um loiro, um estranho. Eu passei a melhor parte de minha vida querendo ser outra pessoa. E aí eu vi que tinha chegado a minha hora.

Empowered by his new look, he asks Cledir, "What are you doing tonight?" ("Que é o que vai fazer hoje à noite?").

When Máiquel looks into the mirror, the camera, the viewer sees a gesture that embodies the power of the male gaze. Laura Mulvey argues,

> As the spectator identifies with the main male protagonist, he projects his look onto that of his like, his screen surrogate, so that the power of the male protagonist as he controls events coincides with the active power of the erotic look, both giving a satisfying sense of omnipotence. (488)

The protagonist assumes the power of the male gaze. However, at the same time he becomes the object of his own "active power of the erotic look." Contrary to Mulvey's postulation of the power of the male gaze, in which

Figure 5.4. Máiquel with his newly dyed platinum-blond hair in Cledir's beauty salon. Screen grab from *O Homem do Ano*.

male authority is asserted through the objectification of the female body, the female is not the object of desire. Rather, Máiquel is the object of the erotic look, both the spectator's and his own, a classic case of mimetic desire (Girard). The scene embodies Stephen Neale's claim that very often the construction of the male as an object of desire is "stylized and fragmented by close-ups, but our look is not direct, it is heavily mediated by the looks of the characters involved" ("Prologue" 18). The objectification of Máiquel is mediated through his own gaze as well as the look of Cledir, who stares at him, in essence giving permission to the spectator to look at him as both subject and object of desire.

Máiquel's objectification, evidenced in his self-contemplation in the mirror and the camera's focus on him as the object of desire, emasculates and feminizes him through his makeover and focus on appearance. Neale has argued that in cinema, women have traditionally served as a source of anxiety, mystery, the unknown, whereas men are constructed as the norm, a stable "known" that might be tested but is rarely investigated by the camera ("Prologue" 19). These scenes open the door to an investigation of Máiquel's performance of masculinity, revealing his self-doubts and anxieties.

This same positioning is reiterated when, from the beauty parlor, the camera cuts to Máiquel and Cledir in the front seat of his 1970s Ford Maverick. He drives through darkness that is highlighted by exaggeratedly bright car-interior lighting. As he drives, Cledir sits beside him tossing her hair flirtatiously. Máiquel, however, scrutinizes his new look in the rear-view mirror.

The scene has a Tarantinesque playfulness that centralizes masculinity as a performance. This is emphasized in how the mise-en-scène calls attention to the performance and consumption of scripted gender roles, the female constantly primping her hair and staring at Máiquel while he focuses on himself over and above anyone else. The inclusion of the Ford Maverick in the scene emphasizes the performance of masculinity. The Maverick is an infamous 1970s Brazilian muscle car that symbolically foregrounds questions of manliness and a macho image. The importance of the car is dramatized through the use of tilt-up traveling shots that frame the front end of the automobile and amplify its symbolic power. The camera frames Máiquel and Cledir's exchange through the windshield, using the car as a projection of his masculine performance. Concurrently, exaggerated interior lighting focuses the spectator's attention on their body movements, further highlighting the performative nature of Máiquel's masculinity as seen through the spectator's gaze. Finally, masculinity is stressed through Máiquel recounting that he "wanted to take Cledir to a motel and fuck all night" ("queria levar a Cledir para um motel e foder a noite inteira"). The car, in conjunction with Máiquel's voiceover, emphasizes virility and sexual potency, dramatizes his enactment of manly ideals, and infuses his masculine performance with a sense of power. But instead of going to a

Figure 5.5. Máiquel and Cledir framed through the windshield of his 1970s Ford Maverick. Screen grab from *O Homem do Ano*.

Figure 5.6. Shot-countershot sequence of Máiquel in Gonzaga's bar when he challenges Suel to a fight in the plaza. Screen grabs from *O Homem do Ano*.

motel, Máiquel and Cledir go to Gonzaga's bar. The choice suggests the protagonist's desire to be seen and to perform for his male buddies.

As Máiquel and Cledir walk into the bar, he pulls his hand across his newly blond hair. Beyond Cledir, there are only men at Gonzaga's. Suddenly, a cackle breaks out. Suel, seated at a table playing cards, howls as Máiquel glances around nervously. The camera cuts in close-up answering shots between them. Tension overtakes the scene. Máiquel responds, "What, you think I'm a fag? The problem is that I'm not a fag nor a clown. I didn't like you laughing at me when I came in the bar, got it?" ("Qual é, está achando que eu sou viado? O problema é que eu não sou viado nem palhaço. Eu não gostei de ver você rindo de mim quando entrei no bar, viu"). Breaking a bottle over the bar, Máiquel continues, "You think I'm a fag, Suel? Let's go outside and resolve this shit like men" ("Pensa que sou viado, Suel? Vamos fora resolver essa merda como homens"). Instead, thanks to Gonzaga's intervention, Máiquel calms down, although he challenges Suel to a fight the following day at noon in the plaza.

The confrontation between the two men puts ideals of masculinity and their grounding in violence on display, a public spectacle for other men to witness and scrutinize. Máiquel interprets Suel's laughter as a questioning of his sexuality and directly links the idea of emasculation with the dyeing of his hair, as a preoccupation with bodily aesthetics. The anxiety that Máiquel feels is rooted in his fear of being emasculated or having his masculinity questioned by other men. Michael Kimmel in his article "Masculinity as Homophobia" argues,

> What we call masculinity is often a hedge against being revealed as a fraud, an exaggerated set of activities that keep others from seeing through us, and a frenzied effort to keep at bay those fears within ourselves. . . . We are afraid to let other men see that fear. Fear makes

us ashamed, because the recognition of fear in ourselves is proof to ourselves that we are not as manly as we pretend. . . . Violence is often the single most evident marker of manhood. . . . [I]t is the willingness to fight, the desire to fight. (103–4)

Kimmel's discussion of masculinity signals several paradigms that imbue Máiquel's construction of and anxieties around masculinity. Beyond anxiety about his masculinity, homophobia prompts Máiquel to act violently in an attempt to assert his newfound confidence in his masculinity. His internalized homophobia is particularly salient if we understand homophobia to be the fear of emasculation (Kimmel "Masculinity," 103). The performative repetition of violence is thus transformed into the chief marker of manhood. The male subject engages in violent activity to counteract being cast as a passive victim, to be emasculated. In the eyes of the other men, Suel, the neighborhood thug, embodies manliness because of his predisposition to use violence. Before killing Suel, Máiquel is seen as his opposite. He is passive, invisible in the universe of local male relations, a potential victim of aggressive masculinity. The antidote, or better said, the *pharmakon* to this condition is the performance of neo-authoritarian masculinity.

From the bar scene, the screen cuts to the protagonist seated on his bed, staring out the window, ruminating in voiceover:

I tossed and turned all night unable to sleep, thinking about Suel. . . . I shouldn't have done that. I was sorry. . . . Fuck, Suel is probably armed. I had never held a gun, fuck. I'll stay home, quiet, forget about it. Fuck him. I'm not going to set foot on the street.

Virei a noite sem conseguir dormir assim pensando no Suel. . . . Eu não devia ter feito aquilo. Estava arrependido. . . . Suel deve andar armado, caralho. Eu nunca tinha segurado uma arma, porra. Eu vou ficar em casa, quieto, esquecer aquele assunto. Foda-se ele. Não vou botar pé na rua.

Once out of the public's view, that is, the other men's gaze, Máiquel's male bravado vanishes. He is overwhelmed by fear and overcome by panic. The voiceover of Máiquel's stream of consciousness divulges his rational thoughts to not escalate the situation. The narrative shifts between Máiquel's paranoia and a more rational evaluation of the situation. The juxtaposition foregrounds the question of masculine neurosis evoked by the threat of violence. It also highlights how the performance of masculinity is

Figure 5.7. Images of Máiquel as he passes the day in the plaza waiting for Suel. Screen grabs from *O Homem do Ano*.

subject to indirect societal pressure through his feeling a need to perform, to act like a real man.

The following day, the camera tracks Máiquel walking down the subway platform with a cardboard fluorescent lightbulb box. He proceeds to the plaza to meet Suel at noon. The location, the plaza in front of Gonzaga's bar, at midday, evokes the setting of the Hollywood westerns in which two cowboys, one good and one bad, duel at high noon in the center of the town. Many Hollywood westerns and police thrillers reproduce the dynamic of the gunfighters' duel by replicating the tension inherent in the opposing values of law and civil obedience versus extralegal violence. However, the apparent opposites are mutually dependent, one needing the other to define itself against.

In the genre's standard, the gunfighter lawman often embodies heroic masculinity. Rewritings commemorate this manly icon by reimagining "a space for heroic male action" (Baker xii). *O Homem do Ano* reconstructs the scene of heroic male action, stripping it of heroic possibility. To begin with, both men represent extralegal violence. But the scene is truly deconstructed when we consider how the action progresses.

Once Máiquel reaches the plaza at noon, the camera accompanies him for the remainder of the day. The area is empty. Máiquel's masculine identity, symbolized in his challenge to a duel, is once again belittled by Suel, who completely ignores the confrontation. The community's lack of interest in the showdown adds to Máiquel's insecurity. The scene parodies the idea of performing violence for other men as a validation of masculinity that is inherent in the classic western. The day, shot over the course of a minute, cuts between close-up head-on shots of Máiquel and long shots of him alone, pacing, sitting, staring aimlessly. As time ticks by and darkness sets in, Máiquel's movements become more sporadic, nervous, and resigned. His body language contrasts with his demeanor the previous evening.

Finally, just after dusk, Suel appears. He is en route to another location and does not acknowledge Máiquel at first. Only as he walks by with his girlfriend, Érica, Suel smiles ironically at Máiquel, who is sitting on a bench staring at the ground, before continuing on. Máiquel retrieves a small-caliber rifle from the lightbulb box and runs to the center of the street, cocking the hammer and exclaiming, "Pick up your gun, Suel" ("Pega tua arma, Suel"). Suel spins around slowly and says, "You can shoot, blondie" ("Pode atirar loirinha"), echoing the verbal sparring of the previous evening. When he turns and begins to walk away, Máiquel shoots Suel in the back and kills him.

Máiquel reacts to the killing by becoming neurotic, recalling,

I wanted to get away, get out of town, but I stayed, frozen. Fear of revenge, fear of the police, fear of being arrested. The desire I had was to end the agony.

Eu queria fugir, sair da cidade, mas fiquei aí, parado. Medo da vingança, medo da polícia, medo de ser preso. A vontade que eu tinha era acabar com aquela agonia.

He doesn't know how to react and feels desperate to escape. However, his anxieties about the community's reaction are quickly dispelled.

Máiquel's killing of Suel does not elicit the community's scorn or reprisals. First, the local policemen thank him for cleaning the streets of "trash." "Thanks, man, for helping clean up trash from the streets" ("Valeu aí, ajuda a retirar lixo da rua"). Then community members begin to shower him with gifts to demonstrate their approval of his use of extralegal violence. This newfound status drastically transforms his life view. Before, he had a pessimistic outlook on life and felt isolated: "I always thought life sucked. I always did everything wrong" ("Eu sempre achei a vida uma merda.

Sempre fez tudo errado"). After people responded favorably, he felt like he was someone important and began to imagine a future for himself.

As we have already seen, gender is a sociocultural construct that materializes through the repeated enactment of gender codes within a group, community, society. Repetition establishes norms that then are imposed upon and delimit what individual material bodies may and may not do (Butler *Bodies*). As such, gender assumes meaning through the group and can be understood as a dialogical assemblage, in the Bakhtinian sense, between the perceiver, the community, and the perceived, the individual. In *O Homem do Ano*, Máiquel's understanding of his own masculine performance is filtered through the eyes of the community. Máiquel only becomes a man once the public sanctions his embodiment of masculinity performed through violence. By condoning his actions, they essentially delineate the social norm that sanctions his performance of masculine domination and endow him with a position of esteem and power.

Nonetheless, not all masculine expressions of violence meet the community's approval. In the case of men deemed marginal, they are reviled. Butler proposes that gender norms operate through a process of exclusion wherein boundaries are set that establish the limits of what and who is "human": "the human is not only produced over and against the inhuman, but through a set of foreclosures, radical erasures that are, strictly speaking, refused the possibility of cultural articulation" (*Bodies* 8). Fonseca's film places Suel and the marginal males whom Máiquel murders—Conan (Marcelo Portinari), Pedrão (Romeu Evaristo), Pereba (Guilherme Estevam)—outside the realm of the human. They are the constitutive outside of hegemonic masculinity. In contrast to the other films I have discussed in this book, *O Homem do Ano* does not spectacularize or even focalize on the marginal male. It centralizes the norms of neo-authoritarian masculinity that Máiquel embodies, society's role in the articulation of these paradigms, and their interface with the creation of male social outcasts. Through this shift, the film deconstructs dominant societal narratives that differentiate between Máiquel's masculine performance of violence and that of the marginal male. The film refuses this binary division to demonstrate that it is not who employs violence that society must question but rather the valuing of understandings of masculinity premised upon violence.

It's a Good Old Boys Club

Beyond the community's prototype of masculinity, Máiquel is also influenced by the paradigms that Zílmar, Sílvio, and Carvalho establish. These men occupy positions of social dominance and represent an elite male power structure in the community. R. W. Connell finds that social gender order is reflected in the institutions and power structures of society that reproduce the dominant gender paradigm. This gender configuration only reveals itself in instances in which the structure is challenged (73). Zílmar, Sílvio, and Carvalho represent the gendered power order. When they first meet Máiquel in Carvalho's home, the four men discuss the state of affairs in Brazil. They refer to the incompetence of state security forces, call for a more proactive, violent response to the male criminals who threaten the health and wealth of the dominant classes, and bemoan their status as citizens of fear. While the men's exchange reveals how they feel that their position of privilege is being challenged, their dialogue also references real-life events.

In their conversation they invoke the kidnapping of bus 174 in Rio de Janeiro by Sandro do Nascimento on June 12, 2000. The incident was televised live over a four-and-a-half-hour period to the Brazilian nation.[10] Referencing this tragic event, Carvalho characterizes Sandro do Nascimento as an "enraged black man" ("crioulo enfurecido") and claims that Nascimento screamed, "I am the son of the devil" ("Eu sou filho do demônio"). This story serves to reinforce their belief that marginal men are born with criminal impulses and, for this reason, they are ultimately not human. Carvalho explicitly forwards this argument when he states,

> Violence is transforming this city into a jungle. Banditry runs loose. I am in favor of the death penalty. Because that story about human rights is a joke. Because they are not humans: kidnappers, rapists. For me, they are born with those criminal impulses.

> A violência está transformando esta cidade em uma selva. A bandidagem corre solto. Eu sou a favor da pena de morte. Porque essa história de direitos humanos é uma piada. Porque eles não são humanos: os sequestradores, os estupradores. Para mim, o sujeito já nasce com esses impulsos criminosos.

The statements recall notions that were popular at the end of the nineteenth century, such as Francis Galton's theories on eugenics.[11] These same theories were later exploited by the 1964–1985 Brazilian military dictatorship to rationalize its actions against members of the opposition. Sérgio Paranhos Fleury, a police officer and torturer during the military dictatorship, stated in an interview, "The marginal is that little dog that is a bad actor, undisciplined, that it is useless to educate" ("O marginal é aquele cachorrinho que é mau caráter, indisciplinado, que não adianta educar") (qtd. in Coimbra 84). What one may find disturbing is that these same arguments continued to reappear well into the 1980s and beyond. Maurício Knobel, head of the Department of Psychiatry at the Universidade Estadual de Campinas, said in an interview with the newspaper *Estadão/Estado de São Paulo* in 1981, "Criminality has pathological origins, and the conditions that society offers facilitate people with pathological problems to externalize their violence" ("A criminalidade tem origens patológicas e as condições que a sociedade oferece facilitam os portadores de problemas patológicos a externarem sua violência") (qtd. in Coimbra 84). The socially undesirable have at different moments been posited within a medicalized discourse in which social sickness must be purged to allow for the advancement of the health of the national body. The words of Carvalho invoke these earlier treatises contending that "order and progress," the motto that adorns Brazil's national flag, are to be achieved through the "hygienic and patriotic" ("higiênico e patriótico") cleansing of society of those who are considered infectious.

The marginal male thus is cast as the limit or boundary of what is considered human, stripped of rights, and transformed into *homo sacer*. By calling for the cleansing of the marginal male from society, Carvalho and his buddies are fighting to maintain the masculine order that guarantees their dominance. The 1988 Constitution, the consolidation of formal rights by the end of the century, and the expansion of social and civil rights in the new millennium created a feeling of encroachment on terrains that were previously exclusive to the middle and upper classes. As peripheral communities began to expand and claim more rights, the marginal male became a flashpoint of these social and political changes. By reducing the marginal male to the position of criminal, thereby condoning his elimination, they are effectively negating his access to rights. Máiquel and SESPA become the guarantors of this traditional system of masculine domination that has privileged the middle- and upper-class male hegemonic order.

Máiquel and his associates at SESPA collect the newspaper clippings about their killings. They paste the articles into a binder. Headlines such as "Homem morto a tiros é encontrado na Baixada" ("Dead man found shot in the Baixada"), "Shootout and Death in Ramos" ("Tiroteio e morte em Ramos"), and "Violence Claims More Victims" ("Violência fez out-ras vítimas") declaim acts of violence in the Baixada Fluminense and by extension in the rest of the metropolis and Brazil more generally. These articles attribute the violence to *marginais, quadrilhas* (gangs), *bandidos, ladrões* (thieves), and the turf wars, drug trade, and *balas perdidas* (stray bullets) that the dominant media associate with these groups. The album of clippings can be read as a trophy that reminds the group of the actions they have committed. The mnemonic device serves to reaffirm (elite) male dominance. It also functions as a trigger for future performances of neo-authoritarian masculinity that will ensure the continuation of this power.

Paramilitary Violence

In his 1957 essay "The Authoritarian Personality," Erich Fromm concludes that the authoritarian character is not independent and "needs another person to fuse with because he cannot endure his own aloneness and fear." Zílmar, Sílvio, Carvalho, and Delegado Santana are the silent backers of the security firm SESPA. Máiquel fuses with these men because they form the traditional power structure in the community and give him access to that power. Initially, his relationship with them calms the guilt that he feels, which he expresses in the fears, anxieties, and paranoia that torment him. They represent the dominant social structure, validate his actions, and make him feel part of something larger.

Through SESPA, this group of men works toward the continuation of a neo-authoritarian masculine politics in the community. The firm protects local businesses. In essence, Máiquel and SESPA are a local *milícia* and are paid security fees to protect the community. Paradoxically, much of the crime in the area is committed by SESPA. The film showcases how vigilantism is tantamount to delinquency and how it generates a system that negates the humanity of those it deems objectionable. After having their security services turned down by several businesses, Máiquel and his accomplices break into their buildings to create an illusion of rampant criminality in the area. Next, Máiquel and SESPA take the law into their own hands as vigilantes, killing those they have marked as undesirables, negating to them the possibility of any legal process and generally imposing a state of exception. Not coincidentally, this state of exception is also profitable to SESPA and its associates.

O Homem do Ano foreshadows the dramatic shift in the power structure that controls peripheral communities in Rio de Janeiro. *Milícias* have become the largest faction that controls these communities. In the film, the deployment of paramilitary violence serves existing power structures, the male economic elites of the area. Máiquel becomes the neo-authoritarian leader of the community not only as the front man for Carvalho and the others but also as the authoritarian decision maker for the community. Máiquel and SESPA dominate the local institutional power system, assuming economic, political, and social control.

O Homem do Ano reveals the effects of masculine domination and paramilitary violence on society and social relations. The film reveals how neo-authoritarian masculine domination and its accompanying violence erode the possibility of a more democratic society. Øystein Gullvåg Holter has shown how the gender system is employed to negate societal and political developments aimed at equity not just between men and women but also between men of different socioeconomic strata (30–32). The deployment of this gendered system of control in the film negates social, civil, and formal rights to the marginal male, effectively guaranteeing the traditional configuration of institutions premised around a hegemonic masculine order. This is obvious when Máiquel is at Gonzaga's bar having his hand bandaged by the local pharmacist (Guil Silveira).

Pharmacist: I was robbed over ten times and was even shot. But after I associated myself with SESPA, they left me alone. I can keep the pharmacy open all night and no one would have the courage to do anything. I wanted to thank you, Máiquel. Thanks, you know. There is something that I wanted to talk to you about. You set curfew at ten p.m. here at the bar. This isn't very good. The night school has to let students out early.

Máiquel: I'll end the curfew today. Let everyone know.

Gonzaga: And the grass at the park? Would you be willing to open the grass areas for the kids to play soccer?

Máiquel: I prohibited the kids from playing on the grass at the park?

Gonzaga: You did prohibit it. Someone told you that they were messing up the grass at the park and you prohibited it.

Máiquel: I prohibited older punks from playing soccer. Young kids can play, kids that are ten or eleven years old. I even like young kids.

Pharmacist: Fui assaltado mais de dez vezes, até levei um tiro. Mas depois que me associei a SESPA, me deixam em paz. Posso deixar a farmácia aberta a noite inteira e ninguém tem coragem de fazer nada.

Queria agradecer o senhor, Máiquel. Muito obrigado, viu. Tem uma coisa que eu queria falar com o senhor. O senhor deu o toque de re-colher aqui no bar depois das dez horas. Não é bom. A escola noturna tem que dispensar os alunos mais cedo.

Máiquel: Vou acabar com o toque de recolher hoje mesmo, faz todo mundo saber.

Gonzaga: E o gramado do parque? Você bem podia liberar o gramado do parque para as crianças jogarem bola.

Máiquel: Eu proibi criança de jogar no gramado do parque?

Gonzaga: Proibiu. Alguém lhe disse que estavam estragando o gra-mado do parque e você proibiu.

Máiquel: Proibi marmanjo jogar bola. Criança pode, criança de dez, onze anos. Até eu gosto de criança.

As the neo-authoritarian leader of the community, Máiquel, assumes su-preme authority. The imposition of a neo-authoritarian masculine para-digm has direct consequences for the marginal male who is literally elimi-nated, and it implies tangible consequences in the lives of all community members who incrementally forgo their rights as citizens.

O Homem do Ano brings into the purview of the cinematic gaze ques-tions of violence as they relate to neo-authoritarian masculinity. Fonseca's cinematic work takes a critical stance toward the scapegoating of the mar-ginal male as the root cause of violence in contemporary Brazilian society. The work deconstructs masculine identity as it relates to violence, calling into question any definition of manhood premised upon aggression. Ul-timately, the film reveals the intimate relation between neo-authoritarian male violence and fear: fear of the other, fear of the unknown, fear of re-vealing one's own vulnerabilities, fear of not conforming to stereotypes of what it means to be a man.

A Superhero of Their Own

O Doutrinador and Neo-Authoritarian Masculinity

The world of superheroes, comic books, graphic novels, and, more broadly, science fiction have traditionally been framed, created, and consumed as the almost exclusive domain of male youth, particularly the white, middle-class, heterosexual, cisgender boy. This predominantly masculine narrative space has recently been cracked open, beyond smaller historical stress lines, in terms of racial diversity through cinematic works such as Ryan Coogler's 2018 international hit, *Black Panther*,[1] and gender diversity with *Wonder Woman* (Patty Jenkins, 2017), *Suicide Squad* (David Ayer, 2016), *Ant Man and the Wasp* (Peyton Reed, 2018), and *Birds of Prey* (Cathy Yan, 2020).[2] This being said, the world of superheroes remains steeped in masculine bravado,[3] violence, and many times sexist and racist tropes.[4]

Comics and Superheroes in Brazil

In Brazil, superheroes are a growing arena of cultural production and have been embraced, for example, as a space to reclaim Afro-Brazilian historical and mythological figures. Representative of this trend is João Daniel Tikhomiroff's 2009 *Besouro*. The film is based on the biography of real-life capoeira master Manuel Henrique Pereira. *Besouro* is a genre narrative that attributes virtual superhero status to this canonical figure. In the late 2010s, Hugo Canuto published a series of graphic texts that thematize the *orixás* of the *candomblé* religion. Superheroes and graphic narratives, however, are not new to Brazilian cultural production. David William Foster has noted that Brazil's tradition of visual storytelling stretches back to the late nineteenth century. Foster contends that this body of work has primarily focused on "internationalism, globalization, and cross-cultural identity" (*El Eternauta* xii).

The twenty-first century has brought with it a deluge of superhero narratives, many of which, to varying degrees, engage in a return to nationalist narratives that evoke nostalgia for the stories of yesteryear. Some of these narratives promote neo-authoritarian masculine figures who echo the characters of the films of this study. Among superhero narratives from Brazil, *Capitão 7* with Ayres Campos as the protagonist was one of the earliest Brazilian superheroes. *Capitão 7* first appeared as a television series that premiered on September 24, 1954, on Channel 7, Canal Record, and remained on the air until 1966. With the popularity of the television program, a homonymous comic book (*história em quadrinhos, gibi*) was launched in 1959 that ran until 1964, with a total of fifty-four issues. The publisher Catarse has revived *Capitão 7* with its series *Alfa-A Primeira Ordem* (2017–2019), and in 2019 Lancelott Martins began releasing *Réquiem para um herói* in installments through his Facebook account.

Comic books and graphic novels have grown in popularity and made inroads into cultural venues beyond their niche fandom markets nationally and internationally. One example in Brazil is *O Doutrinador*. In 2008 Carioca graphic artist Luciano Cunha published initial design plates on Facebook of what would eventually morph into *O Doutrinador*. Five years later, he self-published the first comic book of the *O Doutrinador* series. Cunha published the second installment, *O Doutrinador Dark Web*, in 2015. Guará Entretenimento and Redbox in 2017 published a special edition that brought together these first two editions with a third installment. And in October 2019, Cunha released the installment whose guiding narrative parallels the 2018 homonymous film.[5]

The world of cinema has taken notice of the expanding sphere of graphic narratives in Brazil. In March 2018, Vincente Amorim released his horror-thriller *Motorrad*. While the film is not based on any specific graphic novel, Amorim employed the talented hand of Brazilian comic artist Danilo Beyruth to create the concept art for the film. Beyruth's initial work infuses the movie with a comic book aura that is notable in the action sequences and narrative arc of the story. In an interview with Carol Prado for *G1*, the director stated,

> He [Beyruth] manages to bring not only language and characters that the viewing public of this type of film can identify with but also aspects of scripts that we are accustomed to seeing in Brazil. . . . The film will be able to communicate well with nerds but also with those

who like action movies, with all dramatic weight and subtleties that are generally not part of this universe.

Ele consegue trazer não só uma linguagem e personagens que se identificam com o público desse tipo de filme, mas também aspectos dos roteiros que a gente está acostumado a ver no Brasil. . . . O filme vai conseguir se comunicar bem com os nerds, mas também com quem gosta de filmes de ação, com um peso dramático e sutilezas que normalmente não estão nesse universo.

We can infer from Amorim that he was attempting to broaden his viewing public through Beyruth, a well-known and respected comic artist. This "nerd" world of superheroes and comic books in tandem with action films is emerging in entertainment markets in Brazil. Its growth reflects a turn toward national and nationalistic interests as well as the expanding presence internationally of Hollywood superhero narratives in the twenty-first century.[6]

In June 2018, Marcello Quintanilha's 2014 graphic novel *Tungstênio* premiered as a movie from Globo Films. *O Doutrinador*, directed by Gustavo Bonafé, was released in November 2018, following the certification of results of the presidential election. My primary interest here is in the cinematic production of *O Doutrinador*, Brazil's contribution to what seems an ever-expanding body of superhero movies that have become ubiquitous at the twenty-first-century cineplex.

O Doutrinador: A Study in Neo-Authoritarian Masculinity

O Doutrinador narrates the story of Miguel (Kiko Pissolato), a special agent of the state security forces Divisão Armada Especial (DAE), the equivalent to Rio de Janeiro's BOPE or São Paulo's ROTA in the fictional city of Santa Cruz. In the opening scenes of the film, Miguel and his daughter, Alice (Helena Luz), are en route to the local soccer stadium to watch the Seleção Brasileira (Brazilian national team) play. Stuck in a traffic jam, they decide to abandon their taxi and head to the stadium on foot. As they begin to walk, a stray bullet strikes Alice. Arriving at an overcrowded emergency ward, Alice dies from her wound due to medical negligence. Miguel faults pervasive budget cuts to health care implemented due to systemic corruption within Brazil's Sistema Único de Saúde (SUS) for her death. Following this traumatic event, Miguel, while out for a nighttime jog to clear his head, joins street protests against government corruption in front of the Santa

Cruz governor's palace. During the demonstrations, the *tropa de choque* (shock troop) responds violently to the protesters, attacking them with batons and tear gas. Caught in the chaos of the front lines, Miguel pulls on a gas mask to protect himself. It is in this moment that the *doutrinador* (indoctrinator) is born, giving expression to Miguel's rage at corrupt politicians and the corporate elite, particularly the governor, Sandro Correa (Eduardo Moscovis). First confronting the *tropa de choque* and eventually scaling the walls to the palace, Miguel breaks into the governor's office, kills his security detail, and pummels the governor to death. This incident initiates a series of murders of corrupt top-level executives and government officials until DAE officers finally catch Miguel. Following an interrogation session, Miguel manages to escape. The film closes as we witness Miguel, the Doutrinador, blowing up the National Congress.

O Doutrinador represents almost exclusively middle- and upper-class characters within its frames. In terms of form, Bonafé's work reflects mainstream aesthetic tastes, reminiscent of *Tropa de Elite* and the other cinematic works that I focus on in this study. *O Doutrinador* makes ample use of cutting-edge cinematic techniques, fast-paced action sequences, and the adoption of a high-gloss action-film aesthetic. Echoing the other cinematic works discussed, film form is deployed to designate the actors of sociopolitical dysfunction as corrupt politicians and business people, in turn obfuscating other underlying social issues. The film contends that if Brazilian society can rid itself of a corrupt state government, then society's unrest will largely dissipate. Form thus echoes the ideological position of the middle and upper classes and promotes their sociopolitical agenda of governmental change at the moment of the film's release.

Oh, Doutrinador Save Us: The Neo-Authoritarian Male Confronting Corruption

Sociopolitical critique of corruption within the government is not new in Brazilian cinema. We only need to think back to films such as Cacá Diegues's 1966 *A grande cidade* and 1970 *Os herdeiros,* Glauber Rocha's 1967 *Terra em transe,* or Sérgio Rezende's 1986 *O Homem da Capa Preta,* to name a few of the more salient titles. Yet there is a growing body of films that have been released in the twenty-first century that merit consideration as an expanding thematic cluster. The most obvious, from the chapters of this study, are the *Tropa de Elite* diptych as well as José Padilha's highly problematic foray into television with the Netflix series *O mecanismo.* While my primary interest in this book is not the representation of corruption, it is worth considering how the issue of corruption has been weaponized both in the real world of Brazilian politics and in the cultural arena to enrage and engage the Brazilian public. This leaves us to inquire into how cultural products such as *O Doutrinador* are deployed as ideological instruments. *O Doutrinador* uses corruption as its initial point of engagement, placing form and the embodiment of a "masculine aesthetic" (Bruzzi) at the service of neo-authoritarian masculinity in ways that parallel the films previously discussed in this study. *O Doutrinador* instrumentalizes its critique of corruption to resuscitate the neo-authoritarian male as an almost prophetic figure and embodied response to contemporary change and unrest.

O Doutrinador connects the dots between sociopolitical threats and the resurgence of neo-authoritarianism. The film was released during a moment of social unrest and political and economic instability, the kind of context that Bill Peterson and Emily Gerstein have called "periods of threat" in their work on North American comic books from the 1970s, 1980s, and 1990s. Their objective is to understand better the link between threat and authoritarianism and how it manifests at a societal rather than individual level in North American comics. The researchers have found that during times of high threat, authoritarianism appears in comics at far higher rates. Conventional storylines, moralizing messaging, reduced tolerance for ambiguity, and heightened representation of authoritarian aggression and binary hero-villain conflict serve as markers of authoritarianism in this context (Peterson and Gerstein 890–91). While I am not proposing a longitudinal study of comics and superhero narratives in Brazil, it is not a stretch to argue that Brazil since the 2010s has experienced increasing sociopolitical unrest. The perception, whether real or imagined, of greater "threat," to employ the terminology of Peterson and Gerstein, has culminated in the election of Jair Bolsonaro. *O Doutrinador*'s narrative comic panels and film frames project authoritarian discourse that I am terming "neo-authoritarian" to differentiate it from the dictatorial regime of 1964–1985 in Brazil. In *O Doutrinador*, the superhero genre lends itself to the promotion of a neo-authoritarian sociopolitical and ideological positioning.

Employing the superhero genre, *O Doutrinador* advances neo-authoritarian masculinity as the necessary response to social and political upheaval in Brazil, particularly after the 2013 protests. Luciano Cunha contends that *O Doutrinador* "does not carry an ideological flag, since there is not a single political party in our country that can raise the flag of honesty" ("não tem bandeira ideológica, já que não há um único partido político em nosso país que possa levantar uma bandeira de lisura") (qtd. in Lopes), the film (as well as the comic books and more recently the television series released by Space in October 2019) reflects the country's push to the right politically by positing the neo-authoritarian male as the potential savior of the nation in the implosion of a corrupt ostensibly democratic state governing system.

What's a Superhero, Anyway?

So how do we define a superhero? Should we consider *O Doutrinador* a superhero narrative, and if so, for whom? The primary defining characteristics of the superhero genre logically revolve around the story's protagonist, who, media scholar Peter Coogan finds, must have a mission and a unique power, and their identity must be secret—many times hidden behind a mask, special outfit, hideout, and/or code name.[7] *O Doutrinador* fulfills these requirements. Miguel protects his identity from the other characters. He dresses in black tactical gear, his face cloaked behind the glowing red eyes of a gas mask in an aesthetic reminiscent of Rio's BOPE officers, Padilha's *Tropa de Elite*, and the recent Antifa movement. The Doutrinador's hideout is an abandoned warehouse. However, the Doutrinador/Miguel is also markedly human, susceptible to bodily injury, lacking any ability to throw fire from his fingers, rays from his eyes, or anything of the sort. Much the same as Batman, he does not possess any superhuman powers. As Julia Round notes, "Batman stands out in the superhero ranks: he has no apparent superpowers and instead uses extensive martial arts training, detective skills, intellect, technology, and psychological warfare to combat crime" (54). The Doutrinador/Miguel is a large and imposing man with an athletic build and a masterful fighter reminiscent of Batman or in the context of Brazil, Besouro. The Doutrinador is a skilled warrior who faces off with countless opponents whom he soundly defeats or eliminates in hand-to-hand combat and shootouts through his superior marksmanship. In several scenes, we witness him scaling walls with superhuman ability, accessing the governor's second-story office, or jumping between levels in a parking garage with ease. Thus the Doutrinador falls within the ranks of superheroes and *O Doutrinador* as a Brazilian superhero narrative.

Nationalist Narratives: Neo-Authoritarian Masculinity against the State

The Doutrinador's mission is to expel corrupt politicians and federal agents from the city of Santa Cruz, which serves as a metonym for Brazil. *O Doutrinador* is a nationalist superhero narrative. In critic Jason Dittmer's description, "These are superhero narratives in which the hero . . . explicitly identifies himself . . . as a representative and defender of a specific nation-state, often through his . . . name, uniform, or mission" (7). *O Doutrinador* is an antistatist, nationalist superhero narrative insofar as it differentiates the nation of the people (represented through the explicit use of the Brazilian flag and national colors, visually linking it to everyday people within the film) from the state (embodied by Santa Cruz's black and white flag and the corrupt politicians that populate its halls of power).

The flag of the fictional state of Santa Cruz is a recurring symbol in the film. Its design is meant to evoke associations with the state flag of São Paulo. São Paulo's state flag is composed of thirteen alternating black and white horizontal stripes with a red rectangle in the upper left that is adorned with four gold stars in the corners and a central white circle inscribed with a blue relief map of Brazil. Santa Cruz's flag retains the thirteen black and white horizontal stripes but replaces the corner emblem with a black background and an eight-point compass rose that emphasizes the four cardinal points: north, south, east, and west. This is a telling choice since what has become known as the state flag of São Paulo was proposed by Júlio Ribeiro in 1888 as an alternative to Raimundo Teixeira Mendes's yellow and green Brazilian national flag. In 1932 Ribeiro's flag was taken up as a demonstration of resistance to the Vargas administration's outlawing of state symbols and in 1946 was adopted as the official state flag.[8]

The flag's symbolism would hardly be lost on a Brazilian audience. Since the early thirteenth century, the compass rose has been emblazoned upon maps to orient the user. Subsequently, it has taken on multiple meanings from sailors who adorned their bodies with tattoos of the compass rose, believing it would bring them luck and a safe return from their seafaring travels, to contemporary interpretations that emphasize focus and direction or orientation in life more generally. The film presents a state that has lost its direction and abandoned the very *povo* (people) that it serves. A political class has taken over the governing apparatus intending to augment their accumulation of wealth and power. In this way, the call for a reorientation of the state apparatus undergirds the film's aesthetics, but to what end? The black and white color choice emphasizes the film's postulation of a binary understanding of right and wrong as a black and white choice. Within this configuration, the Doutrinador imposes a clear division between right and wrong. He assumes the role of both judge and jury, doles out justice in the flash of pistol fire, and promises the nation that the neo-authoritarian male is the way back to *ordem e progresso* (order and progress), the motto on the Brazilian flag.

The visuals of the film reproduce the black and white color schematic of the flag. The film opens with an aerial long shot. Momentarily the camera descends upon a group of protesters in front of Santa Cruz's statehouse. Sirens, the whirl of helicopter blades, and the angry chants of demonstrators and the stomping of police forces provide the driving rhythm of the soundtrack. The camera descends into the crowd. The protesters are clad almost exclusively in black with face coverings and carry protest signs. As the camera cuts to the front of the group, the *tropa de choque* police cloaked in full riot gear prepare for confrontation. A protester throws a Molotov cocktail as the camera cuts to the halls of the government building. Bodyguards whisk Governor Correia away from the protests and into a meeting room. He glances around worriedly. Glass shatters in the background, and smoke begins to seep into the room from under the door. The governor crawls under a sprawling table that fills the middle of the room. From under the table we witness a figure dressed in black kick in the door, walk over to the table, and push the chairs to the side. This hooded figure, the Dourtrinador, donning a black gas mask with glowing red eyes, leans over and reaches for the governor. The screen cuts to black; the opening credits roll.

As spectators we equate the Doutrinador with the angry mob of protesters. He, like them, is dressed in black and has his face covered. The analogous relations between the demonstrators and the central government, on the one hand, and the Doutrinador and the governor, on the other, only becomes apparent when the scene is repeated in its entirety some twenty minutes into the film. These opening scenes project onto the viewer the rage that undergirds the protagonist's and the protesters' actions, creating a dialogue between them. Limiting the color palette of the protesters' wardrobe to black and stripping the protest of yellow, green, or red color schemes give the filmmaker cover to distance himself from the accusation of direct political commentary. Instead, at the time of the release of the film, December 2018, this opening scene pretends to harnesses the generalized frustration that Brazilian society felt toward politics and the political class on the eve of Jair Bolsonaro's inauguration. In this sense, the film mimics Cunha's claim that *O Doutrinador* does not assume an ideological position, a claim I believe to be quite disingenuous.

Bolsonaro was elected president in October 2018. He rode to victory on a wave of protests that had their roots in the 2013 Movimento Passe Livre

(Free Fare Movement). Transit fare hikes sparked massive demonstrations, first in São Paulo and then in the rest of Brazil, and triggered what has been referred to as the "Brazilian Spring." While these protests began as a demand for more rights and support from the leftist Partido dos Trabalhadores government of Dilma Rousseff, they were eventually co-opted by the political right and transformed into anti-PT, supposedly antiestablishment protests to root out crime. This took the form of Judge Sérgio Moro's campaign to eradicate corruption through his Lava Jato (Car Wash) investigations, which now are known to have been infused with political divisiveness. The original PT red and anarchist red and black color scheme that predominated during the early days of the Movimento Passe Livre protests became dotted with and eventually subsumed by yellow and green protesters who lauded a nationalistic spirit and viscerally reacted to the red of the PT.[9] A bird's-eye view shows the Eixo Monumental (Monumental Axis) in Brasília where police had established barricades and a purportedly neutral police zone down the center of the esplanade with the pro-PT protesters on one side in red and the pro-impeachment group in yellow and green on the other. At this same moment, friends anecdotally recounted stories of being semi-accosted on the street in Porto Alegre, Brasília, Rio de Janeiro, and São Paulo if they donned anything red that could be read as pro-PT. These narratives are given heightened credence in media such as when journalists Sabrina Valle and David Biller recount similar situations in their article in *Bloomberg*, "Dare to Wear Red in Brazil as Crisis Widens Public Fury."

Returning to the opening scenes of *O Doutrinador*, while the film initially feigns an absence of direct political commentary, it very quickly inserts itself into these political events. The establishing shots transition to the opening credits sequence through an extreme close-up of the red eyes and black relief of the Doutrinador gas mask. The camera zooms in and out on the mask as a series of scenes of corruption embedded within the glowing red of the mask's eyes stream across the screen. The video footage is displayed through a red filter: politicians celebrating with alcohol-infused toasts, money being counted, congressional chambers empty.

In December 2018, it was nearly impossible not to read the screening of these scenes of corruption as a direct commentary on the Partido dos Trabalhadores. The red-filtered presentation of rolls of money being stuffed into trousers, pockets, and socks, boxes of cash piled on floors, and large bills being counted by rows of workers very clearly serves to implicate the PT. At a moment of political tension, these images bathed in red seemed almost intuitively constructed to correlate with the accusations leveled

Figure 6.1. Boxes and suitcases overflowing with cash in the opening scenes. Screen grab from *O Doutrinador.*

against the PT: the 2005 *mensalão* (big salary) vote-buying corruption scandal that was tried by the Supreme Court in 2012–2013, the impeachment of Rousseff in August 2016 for fiscal maneuvering known as *pedalada* (although she was never personally charged with any sort of corruption), the Lava Jato corruption inquiry, and the arrest of ex-president Lula Inácio da Silva in April 2018 as part of this inquiry (dispelled in large part with the revelation of coordination between presiding judge Sérgio Moro and prosecutor general Deltan Dallagnol).[10]

These scenes of government excess and abuse are intercut with clips from what appear to be the 2013 street manifestations in Brazil. The footage from the street protests infuses the establishing shots of the street protesters in Santa Cruz with meaning and places them into direct dialogue with contemporary politics and events in Brazil. At the same time, it is interesting to read these scenes of corruption and the not-so-veiled references to the PT in the credits in conjunction with the soundtrack of Brazilian rapper GOG (Genival Oliveira Gonçalves), who lays down the lyrics of "Brasil com 'P.'"[11]

GOG's lyrical composition infuses the scenes with a sense of social consciousness and political denouncement, which then reframe the visual imagery as he raps:

> Pesquisa publicada prova / Preferencialmente preto / Pobre prostituta pra polícia prender / Pare pense por quê? / Prossigo pelas periferias praticam perversidades / PM's / Pelos palanques políticos prometem / Pura palhaçada / Proveito próprio / Praias programas piscinas palmas

/ Pra periferia / Pânico pólvora pa, pa, pa / Primeira página / Político privilegiado preso / Parecia piada / Pagou propina pro plantão policial / Passou pela porta principal / Posso parecer psicopata / Pivô pra perseguição / Prevejo populares portando pistolas / Pronunciando palavrões / Palavras pronunciadas / Pelo poeta irmão.[12]

Research published proves / Preferably black / Poor prostitute for the police to arrest / Stop think why? / I proceed through the peripheries practice perversities / PM's / Make promises by political platforms / Pure clowning / Personal profit / Beach programs pools palms / On the periphery / Panic powder pa, pa, pa / First page / Privileged politician arrested / Looked like a joke / Paid bribes for police duty / Passed through the principal door / I can look like a psychopath / Pivot for persecution / I predict popular people porting pistols / Pronouncing profanities / Pronounced words / By the poet brother.

The music flows in direct dialogue with the images on screen. The lyrics of GOG's rap juxtapose the differentiated treatment of Afro-Brazilians from the periphery to the almost untouchable status of politicians and the wealthy who game the system through bribes. The opening credits create a visual narrative that links corruption to the Workers Party through the use of the red filter, then generalizes these images as representative of a corrupt upper class. In counterposition, the intercalated images of working-class youth frustrated with their situation and rebelling against the system are associated with marginalized Afro-Brazilians through the lyrics of the song. The deployment of GOG's rap takes this conjecture and posits it within an intersectional racist system where the state security forces support the privileged classes. This framing of the film from the opening scenes appropriates the discourse of denunciation, much in the same way that the 2013 Movimiento Passe Livre protests were appropriated by the middle and upper classes in Brazil.

This appropriation, while not initially apparent, is made explicit by the casting of almost exclusively white actors except for Edu (Samuel de Assis), Miguel's partner and the one good cop, and the exclusive representation of white middle and upper classes in the frames of the film. There is a glaring absence of socioeconomic as well as gender and racial diversity.[13] The opening credits of the film would have viewers believe that, as with many superhero narratives, the Doutrinador fights for the underclass against the abusive power of Brazil's corrupt elite. However, once this binary is established, the rich and powerful are associated with the Workers Party, and the

Figure 6.2. City streets and people cloaked in the yellow and green of the Brazilian flag. Screen grabs from *O Doutrinador*.

marginalized classes are transformed into a middle-class white family, that of Miguel. In the opening credits, the only scene that moves beyond this binary, intercalated view is a giant Brazilian flag waving in the wind. The flag presents this fight as a struggle for the soul of the nation. As the film progresses, the Doutrinador becomes a nationalist hero who battles to set the country on the right path and defend the working middle class. This working class is pulled from the grip of the red hand, the filter of the credits early on in the film, when the nation becomes a surrogate for his daughter, Alice, whom he must defend and avenge.

Let's consider the scene when the yellow and green of the national flag figure most prominently. It is fifteen minutes into the film when Alice is struck by a stray bullet en route to a national soccer game. The scene is marked by high-key lighting and a broad color palette, in part because it is one of the few scenes that occur during the day in an outdoor setting.[14] As Miguel announces that they will get out of the taxi and just walk because it will be faster, the noise of the street floods the soundtrack. The scene cuts to the camera tracking forward between automobiles. Yellow and green streamers adorn the cars and apartment buildings and are strung high above, crisscrossing the street. A man carrying a cardboard box on his shoulder steps in front of the camera from off-screen right; a giant tattoo of the Brazilian flag adorns his entire dorsal region. As he moves off screen, the mise-en-scène is flooded in yellow and green. The camera frames father and daughter as they walk together, the soundtrack fades, and we hear the sound of a bullet cutting through the air. In slow motion, we witness Alice's body go limp. She falls backward as blood overtakes the yellow of her number 10 national soccer jersey. Miguel cries out for help. The screen cuts, and the camera follows him through the green emergency-room doors and into an empty, faded yellow and green waiting room. Two nurses immediately roll out a gurney and rush Alice through the swinging doors to the emergency department, telling Miguel he cannot go with them. Although at first he respects their directive, he is quickly overcome with a sense of panic and rushes through the swinging doors. A child on a respirator and a plethora of sickly individuals crowd the worn yellow corridor waiting for medical attention. Among the sick, Miguel finds the nurse sopping up blood from Alice's corpse with cotton gauze. The nurse walks away with a "Sinto muito" ("I'm very sorry"), as Miguel interrogates him as to where the doctor is and why his daughter had not been taken to surgery as promised.

The hospital and Alice can be read as a metaphor of the *povo* of Brazil, projected as both the innocent victims of a political system that has sidelined them and the sacrifice that ignites change. In this context, her death initiates Miguel's search for vigilante justice and revenge that within the narrative plot structure promises to reinvigorate the fading yellow and green of Brazil by igniting political change through the elimination of politicians.

Sacrificial violence to ignite political change has a long and at times sordid social and political history. In the specific case of *O Doutrinador*, Alice is constructed as the sacrifice that incites Miguel's entrance into vigilante violence in search of political change. Alice's death provokes Miguel's revolutionary exploits to achieve the wholesale elimination of corrupt politicians and eventual implosion of the National Congress. This final act implies a direct challenge to the democratic political system, which is an underlying rationale for his actions. These acts, in a sense, build upon the myth of making possible political change by way of sacrificial violence. In this area, Georges Bataille's critique of sacrifice and sacrificial violence is illuminating. Jesse Goldhammer, in his seminal work *The Headless Republic*, discusses sacrifice in Bataille:

> Bataille develops a theory of sacrifice that leads to the rupture of the historical relationship between sacrificial violence and political foundation. In seeking a revolutionary role for sacrifice, Bataille theoretically unmasks the great danger in using sacrificial violence to found new regimes: it generates authoritarian politics whose stability requires further bloody sacrifices. This realization breaks the continuity of the discourse on sacrificial violence by severing the historical relationship between violent revolutionary acts and political foundation.[15] . . . Any attempt to use sacrifice in order to constitute or reconstitute founding authority risks fascism. (153)[16]

In *O Doutrinador,* while the opening scenes present what appears to be an intersectional approach that foregrounds questions of systemic racism and class struggle, these themes quickly fade into the background. Any critical engagement of systemic racism is jettisoned with the soundtrack and video clips in the opening credits. Class consciousness follows close behind, although the film does give a cursory nod to it without offering any significant critique by revealing the detrimental effects of the economic starving of the government's SUS program. Instead, the sacrifice of Alice as a founding political gesture signals the leitmotif of the film, the positioning of the neo-authoritarian male figurehead as the savior to the nation.

Within the superhero narrative of *O Doutrinador,* the film posits the hypervirile masculinity and bravado of the protagonist, the Doutrinador, as a metonymic device to represent a change in the state's political structure through the ascension of a strong neo-authoritarian masculine leader. His rise occurs within a symbolic space that necessitates the imposition of a literal and figurative "state of exception," to borrow Agamben's formula, which denotes the paradoxical annulment of the law in the interest of "public good." The film presents the assassination of political figures as this public good. *O Doutrinador* constructs these political personages as cliched villainous archetypes: the big man bureaucrat drinking scotch and smoking his cigar at the office while boisterously fraternizing with friends, the greedy politician in his dressing robe counting money into the wee hours of the night, the sexually exploitive older man with the younger woman, and so forth.

The extermination of these despicable political caricatures by the Doutrinador ideologically endorses the state of exception and its attendant social and political violence as guarantors of the continued predominance of a neo-authoritarian masculine paradigm. Thus, masculinity expresses an ideology that links to social and political structures of power (Reeser). Neo-authoritarian masculinity is promoted in the film as society's savior in the face of unrest. The neo-authoritarian male superhero of *O Doutrinador* embodies an antistatist paradigm and transforms the corrupt system of bureaucrats into his antithesis.

The Doutrinador: We Need a Hero

Tony Spanakos argues concerning North American superhero narratives, "The superhero genre has taught us to believe our liberty is more likely to be protected by heroes, who are above and beyond the state, than by the bureaucrats who comprise it. Of course, that is usually because those heroes are, well, heroic" (37). While Spanakos's focus is not Brazil, with the predominance of superhero narratives at the box office worldwide, we would be hard-pressed to say that this ideological stance is not applicable to the Brazilian context. Many heroes whom Brazilian film puts forward are projected as idealized hyperviolent, authoritarian, male saviors. These neo-authoritarian figures embody the authoritarian personality that Juremir Machado da Silva, Lilia Moritz Schwarcz, and Marilena Chauí, among others, argue undergirds the Brazilian nation.

The closing ten minutes of the film are revelatory. Freeing himself from DAE custody after killing a corrupt agent, the Doutrinador gathers an arsenal of artillery, and then we accompany him on his drive to the National Congress. In a shot-countershot sequence, Miguel glances in the car's rearview mirror. His daughter is listening to her headphones; we cut back to him driving as the solemn notes of a piano play. He glances back again and she asks, "Pai, falta muito?" ("Dad, is it a long way?") Miguel responds, "Não filha, agora falta pouco" ("No, daughter, we're almost there"). As the words fall off his tongue, he glances down and then at the mirror again. We see him reach up to readjust the mirror. When the camera cuts back, what we see is not his daughter but rather several rapid-firing long-barrel firearms. The camera registers his face as he takes another double-take and then looks toward the front passenger seat and the Doutrinador's gas mask. The soundtrack drones menacingly. The visual cues are meant to remind us that what we are about to witness is not senseless violence but rather the rage of a grieving father in a fight to change an indelibly corrupt system.

What the film delivers is exactly that. A crane shot swoops down from behind Miguel, who stands on an overpass bridge with the Brazilian Congress in the background. The camera cuts to a low-angle shot of Miguel's

Figure 6.3. Miguel on an overpass with the Brazilian National Congress in the background and in Antero Gomes's office with members of Congress celebrating on television in the background. Screen grabs from *O Doutrinador*.

Figure 6.4. The fireball that engulfs the National Congress building repeating across news media platforms. Screen grabs from *O Doutrinador*.

face as the rhythmic pulse of grunge music amplifies the scene. The lyrics declaim, "I'm gonna lose control / There's a gun on my back / I'm on track this time / Alone / Feels like powerless control / Hit my soul / Heal my soul" as we follow the bloody trail of the Doutrinador as he makes his way through the halls and to presidential candidate Antero Gomes's (Carlos Betão) office.[17] Gomes is smoking a cigar, watching the Congress members give speeches before they vote. The scene on television necessarily recalls the impeachment of Rousseff. Arriving at the office, the Doutrinador kills Antero, only to be surrounded by security details. At that moment, he pulls a detonator from his pocket and implodes the Brazilian Congress in a glowing fireball that rises like a phoenix above the Eixo Monumental. Agile camera work and fight sequences animate these final scenes, once again inserting the spectator into the action and a masculine aesthetics that relies on violence. The film's hero is on his final mission.

From the fireball of destruction that engulfs the Doutrinador along with the National Congress building, we cut to images of this scene of the destruction repeating across the news media platforms. In a voiceover monologue, Nina (Tainá Medina), the Doutrinador's hacker accomplice, closes the film:

> When it all started, I didn't even care, maybe because in a way I was like them, like those corrupt people who were killed, the same motherfuckers who are part of this shitty mess that is our country. Our country, can you not be corrupt here? A country where everything is difficult, shitty bureaucracy: vouchers, certificates, notaries. Everything to force you to find a *jeito,* our *jeito, jeitinho.* You can even play the victim, but in the end we'll sink together. It's a cycle. And everything is wrong, everything is wrong. Miguel thought that too. But he did it his way. He killed the guys. He killed a fuckload. And for what? If corruption is ingrained in us, in the population's DNA. It's only that this DNA is not permanent. Nothing is permanent. We can evolve, we must evolve. When that day comes, we no longer need a revolution. But until then, what are you going to do?

> Quando isso tudo começou, eu nem me liguei, talvez porque de certa forma fizesse que nem eles, que nem esses corruptos que foram mortos, os mesmos filhos de puta que fazem parte de essa maranhada de merda que está nosso país. Nosso país, tem como não ser corrupto aqui? Um país onde tudo é difícil, essa burocracia escrota: comprovante, atestado, certidão. Tudo para te obrigar a dar um jeito, nosso jeito, o jeitinho. Dá até para pagar de vítima, mas ao final a gente vai fundar junto. É um ciclo. E está tudo errado, tudo errado. O Miguel também achava isso. Mas foi lá fez do jeito dele. Matou os caras. Matou uma porrada. E para que? Se a corrupção está entranhada na gente, no DNA da população. Só que esse DNA não é permanente. Nada é permanente. A gente pode evoluir, deve evoluir. Quando esse dia chegar, a gente não mais precisar de uma revolução. Mas até lá, o que você vai fazer?

The voiceover ends with a scene of workers finding the Doutrinador's gas mask in the rubble of the congressional building. It is interesting that the closing sequence is framed by the ghost of the daughter and the final disembodied voiceover offered by the Doutrinador's female sidekick. Throughout the film, women are relegated to secondary roles, but these final words use women as a voice of reason to back the idea that society must embrace neo-authoritarian masculinity because until Brazilian society does, change is not possible. The film, just as each volume of Luciano Cunha's *O Doutrinador* comic series, eliminates the lead character at the end, only to revive the hero in the next, another iteration of the same man. In specific ways, this tactic implies an approximation with the reader, if we see him as a common everyday man, implying all the gendered, racial, sexual, and socioeconomic stereotypes that accompany this trope. Within the frames of the film, this serves to point to the viewer as potentially taking up this role at the same time that it also embraces the ideal of following the leader. Nina's closing words only amplify this message.

The film promotes the idea that revolution is the answer to Brazil's current sociopolitical issues. The problem is that the film does not actually promote a revolutionary agenda. Rather, as in other films discussed in this book, neo-authoritarian masculinity is only the latest iteration of Brazil's authoritarian character. We might say that *O Doutrinador* promotes a status quo politics cloaked in revolutionary clothing. Ultimately, as Henry Giroux has argued, "Each country will develop its own form of authoritarianism rooted in the historical, pedagogical, and cultural traditions best suited for it to reproduce itself" (*Dangerous Thinking* 194). *O Doutrinador* and the films that I have considered in this volume participate in the reproduction of the neo-authoritarian male in Brazil. One must ask what role culture plays in setting the stage for the reemergence of neo-authoritarian masculine leaders, the most recent iteration being Jair Bolsonaro.

Conclusion

The Rise of the Neo-Authoritarian Masculine Paradigm

In this study I have probed into the constructed nature of masculinity and have attempted to reveal how the repetition of social scripts naturalize masculinity. We perform these scripts daily through our enactment of gender. This is expressed in our clothes, our walk, how we carry ourselves, what others expect of us, and how society polices our actions as gendered subjects. We impose these social codes between us: men, women, intersex, trans, +. Two male strangers nod at one another on the street as their gazes cross. They might be picking one another up or acknowledging each other as if saying, "I recognize you as a man . . . so we don't have any beef between us." The line between these looks can be thin and tenuous and the results very different if they are not enacted following expected social norms. These masculine scripts are many times repeated "as if" they were a natural part of being a man. Everyone is subject to them because they infuse the core of society and the institutions that have been constructed. And, as Jack Halberstam has said, they are hell to pry apart (2).

It is precisely the display of these gendered codes that permits us to begin to recognize their inherent violence. Identifying these conventions starts the process of breaking the repetition of the scripts, denaturalizing their falsely naturalized performance. In this process, as the screen has become increasingly central in our lives, cinema functions as a mirror onto society. Representations of masculinity, violence, and crime on screen enable us to gain perspective on the social and institutional mechanisms of power that envelop us (Hansen-Miller).

The representation of masculinity in film is an area that deserves attention and reflection. Films about men, or as Brett Martin has put it, men behaving badly, have proliferated in cinema. This is true historically, but there has been a surge of the genre in the twenty-first century. This trend is particularly troubling if film and culture, as Michel de Certeau contends, "'go in a procession' ahead of social practices in order to open a field for them. Decisions and juridical combinations themselves come only afterwards, like statements . . . arbitrating the areas of action granted . . ." (125).

In my discussion of contemporary Brazilian crime film, I have argued that a neo-authoritarian masculine paradigm is axiomatic to contemporary constructions of hegemonic masculinity. The neo-authoritarian male characters on whom I have focused are yet another iteration in a long history of the authoritarian character that Machado da Silva, Moritz Schwarcz, Chauí, and da Matta argue is part of Brazil's social fabric. Gender is central to the maintenance of power structures and ideological frameworks that continue to propagate this authoritarian thread, particularly the dominant position of men and masculinities. Revealing these networks of power by deconstructing gender, sex, and sexuality opens the possibility of dismantling these naturalized scripts and the nefarious results of these frames of power: masculine domination of women, domestic violence, sexism, homophobia, and racism, to mention only a few ways that bodies are policed and at times sacrificed to the preservation of status quo power relations. It is here that we find echoes of these films in real-world social and political events.

Between 2000 and 2016, there was a rise from 10% to 27% of women holding legislative seats in the region (K. Funk et al. 400), as part of the "pink tide" including a surge of female presidents in Latin America.[1] In 2016, media proclaimed the end of the pink tide in Latin America. As I have worked on this book, much has changed as retrograde politics and policies have taken hold and hope has faded into the background. If Brazil is emblematic of this shift sociopolitically, then events since 2016 are very telling.

On May 12, 2016, Dilma Rousseff's presidential powers were rescinded, and she was forced to step down while impeachment proceedings ensued, culminating in her impeachment on August 31, 2016. With the suspension of her tenure, Vice President Michel Temer assumed office and imposed a wave of abrupt changes. First on this list was the naming of his cabinet, which initially did not include a single female and was stacked with representatives of the BBB coalition, the Bancada da Bala, da Bíblia e do Boi (Bullet, Bible, and Bull bloc).[2] *Bloomberg*'s May 12 headline touted, "Brazil's New Club Is All Boys and They're Running the Show" (Leite and Biller). This was the first time since Ernesto Geisel's 1974 administration that an all-male cabinet had been appointed. Temer also eliminated the ministries of women and racial equality, clearly indicating that women and the challenging of racial privilege were not part of his administration's priorities.

As part of his cabinet, Temer in 2016 selected Alexandre de Moraes as the minister of justice. This was a very telling appointment and revealed the degree to which a neo-authoritarian stance infuses men, masculinity, and Brazilian society. Moraes is a constitutional lawyer who was the secretary of public security of São Paulo in 2015.[3] During his brief tenure in that state position, Moraes oversaw the violent repression of students denouncing school reorganization and organizing demonstrations against raising bus and metro fares in the city. He also deployed militarized antidemonstration weapons such as bulletproof Israeli water-cannon vehicles against protestors. He opposed the passing of the state legislative assembly's prohibition of the use of rubber bullets at protests. Most striking is that during Moraes's year in office, the number of killings by police rose to 25% of all homicides, the highest percentage registered to that time. Also during his tenure, the number of killings by state forces attributed to inmates' attempting escapes rose 61% ("Alexandre de Moraes (PSDB)"). His actions as São Paulo state's secretary of public security led one to wonder how justice would be defined in future administrations.

At the same time, social violence was not limited to state security forces. On June 17, 2016, thirty members of an extremist right-wing group invaded the campus of the Universidade de Brasília. The group aligned with the politician Jair Bolsonaro, a member of the Bullet Coalition who later became president of Brazil. During the group's occupation of the university's Instituto Central das Ciências (Central Institute of the Sciences), the members verbally attacked students, calling them "parasites," "pot smokers," and "gay perverts" ("Pelo menos 30 pessoas"). The group was in possession of homemade bombs but did not deploy them. Police discovered that in the group's planning through social media exchanges, members spoke of killing people and using extreme violence against students (Cieglinski).

It is telling that this group decided to attack the university, a center of cultural production and the first federal university to integrate racial quotas into its admissions process. The attack on the Universidade de Brasília was an assault on the power of culture and the democratization of education. This incident echoed then-president Temer's actions such as the elimination of the Ministry of Culture as one of his first decrees in office and Congress's decision to eliminate references to gender from the 2014 Plano Nacional de Educação (National Education Plan).[4] They took those actions despite Brazil having some of the highest indicators of violence against women and sexual minorities in the world.

On March 14, 2018, gender violence was on full display. Marielle Franco, a Carioca from the favela Maré, a human rights and LGBTQIA+ activist, Rio city council member, and vocal critic of police violence, had just finished participating in the roundtable "Jovens negras movendo estruturas" ("Young Black Women Moving Structures"). She concluded her contribution to the panel with words from Audre Lorde's 1981 essay "The Uses of Anger: Women Responding to Racism": "I am not free while any woman is unfree, even when her shackles are very different from my own." After leaving the roundtable, Marielle and Anderson Pedro Gomes, her driver, were gunned down in cold blood in their vehicle (Mesquita). Marielle's assassination set off a wave of protests across the country, and Marielle has remained a powerful voice and icon of resistance for Brazil.

That year the #EleNão (#NotHim) campaign spearheaded by the Mulheres Unidas contra Bolsonaro (Women United against Bolsonaro) Facebook group had almost four million members. Across the country protests once again broke out as women and their allies denounced the sexist and homophobic language of presidential candidate Bolsonaro. The protests focused on abominable statements by Bolsonaro, from his affirmation to the *gaúcho* newspaper *Zero Hora* in 2014 that women should earn less because they give birth to children (qtd. in Resende), to his rape comments in 2003 and repeated in 2014 to Congresswoman Maria do Rosário (Kaiser), to his claim in an interview with *Playboy* magazine published in the June 2011 issue that if he had a son who was gay, the son would be "dead" to him. The violence and hatred embedded in these perturbing comments were an omen of the presidency of Bolsonaro and the rise of the extreme right in Brazil.

Following the 2018 election and inauguration of Bolsonaro, the country experienced an imposition of retrograde policies that target women's reproductive rights and an all-out assault on the LGBTQIA+ community and gay rights by declaiming the supposed leftist promotion of gender ideology (*ideologia de gênero*). This political move was not born out of the Bolsonaro regime but rather has its roots in the political bantering over the 2104 Plano Nacional de Educação (National Education Plan) and the 2017 Base Nacional Comum Curricular (National Common Core Curriculum) legislation, but Bolsonaro escalated the vitriol of the battle. Conservative factions, predominantly from the BBB congressional coalition, spearheaded resistance to any mention of gender in basic education.[5] The Bolsonaro regime has only pushed this agenda further. In lockstep with Bolsonaro's vision, Vice President Hamilton Mourão, a retired army general, has claimed that households that lack a male patriarch are "fábricas de desajustados" ("factories of misfits"), squarely blaming the families for the drug trade in poor areas of cities (Gielow). Again, women, and in many cases women of color, are employed as scapegoats for this macho regime and the neo-authoritarian models they embrace.

Taking this compendium of deplorable statements and actions by the Bolsonaro regime alongside the machinations of the BBB and other conservative factions in Brazil, a clearer vision emerges of how Brazil has arrived at ever-worsening social indicators. Citing data from the Instituto de Segurança Pública (Institute for Public Security) and Human Rights Watch, César Muñoz Acebes reports that in April 2019 killings by police rose by 43% compared to April 2018. Data compiled by the World Bank show that March and April 2020 saw a 22% increase in lethal violence against women in Brazil and a 27% surge in reports to the Violence against Women hotline compared to the same time frame in 2019 (Bastos et al.).[6] The LGBTQIA+ community has suffered a similar spike in violence. Brazil ranked highest in the world for killings of trans people in 2020, according to the *Dossiê assassinatos e violência contra travestis e transexuais brasileiras em 2020* (Benevides and Bonfim Nogueira). The year 2020 saw numbers that were 43.5% higher than the median of the previous twelve years. The staggering numbers reveal a rise of almost 30% in killings compared to 2019. These are only a few examples of the very real consequences of the embrace of neo-authoritarian masculine models by the Bolsonaro government and Brazil's extreme right.

That being said, I refuse to end this book with a further enumeration of what seems to be an ever-expanding black hole of retrograde actions. Instead, as I finalize this book, I find hope in and embrace the many nodes of resistance that have surged across Brazil and the world. In 2017 Peter Kingstone and Timothy J. Power's *Democratic Brazil Divided* was published, the third edited volume of their study of Brazilian democracy. In their introduction they contend, in agreement with the contributors to the volume, that while there are many challenges facing Brazilian democracy, the challenges are consistent with those of a mature democracy. This is obviated, Kingstone and Power assert, through high levels of citizen participation, new and steadfast institutions of civil society, a strong judiciary, and developing demand for increased accountability. Datafolha polls from June

28, 2020, appear to back Kingstone and Power's claims. These surveys from the *Folha de São Paulo* reveal that 75% of Brazilians supported democracy, while only 10% favored dictatorship. This is the highest level of democratic support in the previous thirty years. In the midterm elections of November 2020, trans candidates were able to run under their elected names for the first time and had a strong showing, with 294 candidates winning 30 seats nationally. This number represents an almost 300% increase in comparison with 2016 (Benevides).

In tandem with these wins, Mônica Benício, widow of the late Marielle Franco, was elected to the city council in Rio de Janeiro. On July 14, 2020, a coalition of social movements filed an impeachment request against President Bolsonaro with the Brazilian Congress. While their claim centered around the Covid-19 pandemic and the government's incompetent response, it also delineated a host of other offenses, from malpractice and negligence to infringement on the rights of workers, Afro-Brazilians, Indigenous populations, the environment, and culture. In January 2021, these calls intensified. While the coalition's hope of an impeachment is fleeting, what it does signal is an organized resistance to the extreme right, retrograde politics, and the continuation of neo-authoritarian masculinity as a driving force within society.

May we stand in solidarity with the continued resistance of social movements, academic studies, artistic expressions, and the everyday existence and practices of those who align against the hatred and toxicity of neo-authoritarian masculinity. May we continue to pull apart, question, and understand the power of culture in both the maintenance of frames of power and the possibility of dismantling them as the screen becomes ubiquitous in our daily lives and the space between the reel and real more tenuous. MARIELLE PRESENTE!

NOTES

Introduction: Neo-Authoritarian Masculinity in the New Millennium

1. Dilma was impeached by the Senate on August 31, 2016.

2. For a critical analysis of media representations of this mega pride event, please consult Steve Butterman's *Invisibilidade vigilante.*

3. The term "pink tide" was deployed in Rohter's 2005 *New York Times* article "With New Chief, Uruguay Veers Left, in a Latin Pattern," referring to the left-leaning shift in Latin American politics that he marks as beginning in 1999 with the election of Uruguayan President Tabaré Vázquez. Please also consult the work of Geraldine Lievesley and Steve Ludlam.

4. Some critics such as Renato Rosaldo and Toby Miller also include cultural citizenship within this schema.

5. I employ the English term "marginal" in this text in the sense of the Brazilian Portuguese usage, particularly when I refer to "marginal male."

6. In his canonical 1979 discussion of Brazilian culture and society, da Matta unearths the authoritarian specters that resonate in the saying "Sabe com quem está falando?" that individuals have deployed to impose authority and reinstate social hierarchy. It is not an equalizing gesture like the English question "Who do you think you are?" The Brazilian phrase is employed to question or destabilize power hierarchies by those who occupy the lower rungs of the social order, revealing an authoritarian streak that pervades Brazilian society.

7. Pierre Bourdieu developed the ideas of cultural capital and habitus. Loïc Wacquant, discussing the origins of the concept of habitus in Bourdieu, asserts that habitus means "the ways in which the sociosymbolic structures of society become deposited inside persons in the form of lasting dispositions, or trained capacities and patterned propensities to think, feel and act in determinate ways, which in turn guide them in their creative responses to the constraints and solicitations of their extant milieu" ("Concise" 65). Habitus is thus an embodied knowledge into which people are socialized through the passing of cultural capital in spaces such as the family, friend networks, and workplace. Cultural capital is not material capital in the Marxian sense, but rather symbolic, cultural, and social in nature. Bourdieu, in *Distinction*, describes cultural capital as knowledge that infuses how people consume cultural objects (literature, art, film, theater), how they embody culture (the way they speak and walk and a host of other mannerisms), and institutionalized cultural capital (education, titles, credentials, qualifications).

8. For a succinct discussion of how these groups advanced an extreme-right agenda in the Brazilian Congress, please consult Roxana Pessoa Cavalcanti's article "How Brazil's Far Right Became a Dominant Political Force."

9. The ABCDE social class definitions of the Instituto Brasileiro de Geografia e Estatística (IBGE, Brazilian Institute of Geography and Statistics) are as follows:

- "A" refers to the upper class who hold higher managerial, administrative, and professional positions. The A class earns above 20 times the minimum salary.
- "B" refers to the middle class who hold higher-education degrees and occupy intermediate managerial, administrative, and professional positions. The B class earns between 10 and 20 times the minimum salary.
- "C" refers to the lower middle class and skilled working class, which is composed of laborers who have completed a high school degree and possibly hold a technical or higher-education degree. In terms of income, the C class earns between 4 and 10 times the minimum salary.
- "D" refers to the lower working class of semiskilled and unskilled labor who provide services and hold low-paid jobs. The D class earns between 2 and 4 times the minimum salary.
- "E" is the lowest level of income earners, normally referring to the intermittently employed, unemployed, pensioners, and those at the lowest levels of subsistence. The E class earns below 2 times the minimum salary.

10. Sacolinha's poem appeared as part of the Literatura e Paisagismo–Revitalizando a Quebrada public art project he initiated in 2017. The poem was written as graffiti on a cement-block wall in São Paulo next to the image of a green military tank. All translations in this book should be understood as my translations unless otherwise noted.

11. Film ticket sales information comes from Box Office Mojo by IMDbPro.

12. Please consult Gramsci's *Prison Notebooks* as well as Steven Lukes's discussion of Gramsci's concept in *Power: A Radical View*, page 27.

13. I would like to note that the leftist movements in Brazil were culpable of much of the same machismo toward women that the regime purveyed. Please consult Sonia Álvarez.

14. During the *anos de chumbo*, James Green points out in *Beyond Carnival*, homosexual activity was curtailed by the military's objective to "stamp out 'subversion'" (246), creating a culture of fear that had direct repercussions in homosexual subculture and more generally expressions of masculinity, especially until 1972.

15. By 1967 Vidal had risen through the ranks of the armed forces and attained the rank of colonel of artillery. In 1972 he was transferred to the reserve units. He was a member of the Instituto de Geografia e História Militar do Brasil (Institute of Geography and Military History of Brazil) and emeritus faculty of the Academia de História Militar Terrestre do Brasil (Academy of Terrestrial Military History of Brazil).

16. Please consult Avelar's "Revisões da masculinidade sob ditadura" about masculinity at the end of the dictatorship; Green's *Beyond Carnival*; Green and Renan Quinalha's *Ditadura e homosexualidades*; and Benjamin Cowan's *Securing Sex*.

Chapter 1. Being a Man in Brazil: Masculinity in Brazilian Crime Film since Cinema Novo

1. I would like to call attention to Cinema Novo's beginnings in 1960, before the installation of the military dictatorship in 1964. The film movement cannot be read as simply responding to the regime but rather as underscoring the reiterative quality of authoritarian masculinity in Brazil.

2. For more information please consult the work of Randal Johnson, for example in *Cinema Novo x 5* and with Robert Stam in *Brazilian Cinema*; the many studies of Ismail Xavier, such as *Allegories of Underdevelopment*; Lúcia Nagib's *Brazil on Screen*, to reference only one of her many contributions to the field; and Humberto Pereira da Silva's *Glauber Rocha*.

3. The *anos de chumbo* were the most repressive years of the Brazilian authoritarian regime. It was during this period, beginning in 1968, that Ato Institucional no. 5 was enacted. AI-5, as it is known, took a hard line of censorship and repression and imposed harsh restrictions on political and social dissent. These were the darkest years of the dictatorship, when many artists lived in exile and people were disappeared, imprisoned, and tortured.

4. I would recommend consulting Fernando Beleza's "Sustainability at the Margins," a 2020 rereading of Sganzerla's work through the lens of ecocriticism.

5. No formal charges were brought against Acácio for rape. During the 1960s, sexual assault was gravely underreported due to the stigma associated with rape in Brazil's highly patriarchal society.

6. The final installment of Marins's compendium, *Encarnação do demônio*, was not released until 2008.

7. Please consult Charles St-Georges's excellent article "Brazilian Horrors Past and Present" as well as Gustavo Subero's second chapter, "Zé do Caixão and the Queering of Monstrosity in Brazil," in *Gender and Sexuality in Latin American Horror Cinema* for two discussions of Marins's works analyzed in 2016 through a gender/sexuality lens.

8. For a more complete compendium of films from this period, please consult Alfredo Sternheim's *Cinema da boca*.

9. In the twenty-first century, critics generally argue that pornographic material has become more rudimentary with a wave of "gonzo" films that dispense with narrative altogether. They are part of a change that makes film material heavier, with directors competing through the use of aggressive sexual acts and explicitly humiliating language. Thus, while pornography is becoming ubiquitous in society, the industry is simultaneously becoming more brutal in how it depicts sex.

10. Amanda Rossi, Julia Dias Carneiro, and Juliana Gragnani wrote "#EleNão."

11. It is nearly impossible to calculate exact revenue totals of the international pornographic movie industry. Following the 2008 economic crisis, the industry saw its revenues fall, but subsequently porn films came streaming back and experienced a surge, particularly with the Covid-19 crisis worldwide. Pornography revenues are difficult to calculate because many porn producers are privately held companies, with estimates veering from $6 billion to $90 billion annually. To put this into context, Netflix's annual

revenue is between $20 billion and $25 billion and Hollywood's approximately $40 billion. The pornography industry releases an estimated 10,000 to 11,000 films per year, and Hollywood produces 400 to 500 films annually. In Brazil pornography saw considerable growth in the 2010s. Frenesi Filmes do Brasil is one of the most important adult-entertainment companies in the world, and the country has become a destination for production due to lower costs, exotic appeal, and a more intense international interest in Brazil stimulated in part by the 2016 World Cup and Olympics. Concrete data on the finances of the pornography industry are difficult to survey, but Brazil reportedly is one of the fastest-growing markets in the world and has the second-largest pornography industry in the West, after the United States (Clendenning).

12. Please consult Randal Johnson's *Film Industry in Brazil* for a discussion of the industry in the 1980s and Melina Izar Marson's *Cinema e políticas de estado* for analyses through the end of Embrafilme in 1990 and the founding of Ancine in 2001.

13. Additional crime films released from 1979 to the turn of the century include *Paula: A história de uma subversiva* (*Paula: The Story of a Subversive*, F. Ramalho Jr., 1979), *O bom burguês* (*The Good Bourgeois*, Oswaldo Caldeira, 1983), *Eles não usam black tie* (*They Don't Wear Black Tie*, Leon Hirszman, 1981), *Pra frente, Brasil* (*Go Ahead, Brazil*, Roberto Faria, 1982), *Nunca fomos tão felizes* (*Happier Than Ever*, Murilo Salles, 1984), *Kuarup* (Ruy Guerra, 1989), *Corpo em delito* (*The Body of the Crime*, Nuno César Abreu, 1990), *ABC da greve* (*ABC of a Strike*, Leon Hirszman, 1990), *Lamarca* (Rezende, 1994), *O que é isso, companheiro?* (Bruno Barreto, 1997), *Dois córregos: Verdades submersas no tempo* (*Two Streams*, Carlos Reichenbach, 1999).

14. The *coroa de Cristo* was a circular metal band that had screws at the height of the individual's temples. These screws were tightened down on the individual's skull, causing unfathomable pain and at times resulting in bursting the victim's cranium.

15. The rural, backlands setting in Brazil is a well-established trope in Brazilian cinema. In the reels of Cinema Novo, backland banditry and the men who propagate these exploits loom large. A few of the films that thematize this trope are *Vidas secas* (*Barren Lives*, Nelson Pereira dos Santos, 1963), Rocha's *Deus e o diabo na terra do sol* and Guerra's *Os fuzis* in 1964, *O dragão da maldade contra o santo guerreiro* (*Antônio dos Mortes*, Glauber Rocha, 1968), and *Os deuses e os mortos* (*Of Gods and the Undead*, Ruy Guerra, 1970).

16. Vladimir Herzog was a professor of journalism at the University of São Paulo as well as an editor for the public television station TV Cultura. On October 24, 1975, he was called to the local DOI-CODI (Destacamento de Operações de Informações–Centro de Operações de Defesa Interna, Department of Information and Operations–Center of Internal Defense Operations) offices for questioning about his involvement with the outlawed Partido Comunista Brasileiro (Brazilian Communist Party). He was beaten and tortured during the interrogation session and ultimately died. The state agents attempted to stage his death as a suicide by hanging, but photographic evidence disproved that claim.

Chapter 2. Spectacular Men and the Violence They Perform: *Cidade de Deus*

1. Meirelles directed the television series *Rá-tim-bum* (1989) and *O que você vai ser quando crescer?* (1997).

2. Though Meirelles codirected *Cidade de Deus* with Kátia Lund, in many of the reviews she is either not mentioned or following an initial mention is cast in a secondary role at best to Meirelles.

3. Ticket sales information comes from Box Office Mojo by IMDbPro.

4. *Ônibus 174 (Bus 174*, José Padilha, 2002), *O invasor (The Trespasser*, Beto Brant, 2002), *Carandiru (Carandiru*, Héctor Babenco, 2003), *Cidade baixa (Lower City*, Sérgio Machado, 2005), *Antônia (Antônia*, Tata Amaral, 2006), *Querô (Querô: A Damned Report*, Carlos Cortez, 2007), *Os 12 trabalhos (The 12 Labors*, Ricardo Elias, 2007), *Era uma vez (Once upon a Time*, Breno Silveira, 2008), *Linha de Passe (Linha de passe*, Daniela Thomas and Walter Salles, 2008), *Última parada 174 (Last Stop 174*, Bruno Barreto, 2008), *Verônica (Verônica*, Maurício Farias, 2009), *O contador de histórias (The Story of Me*, Luiz Villaça, 2009), *Salve geral (Time of Fear*, Sérgio Rezende, 2009), *Os inquilinos (The Tenants: Don't Like It, Leave*, Sergio Bianchi, 2009), *5x favela: Agora por nós mesmos (5x Favela: Now by Ourselves*, Manaíra Carneiro, Wagner Novais, Rodrigo Felha, Cacau Amaral, Luciano Vidigal, Cadu Barcellos, and Luciana Bezerra, 2010), *Bróder (Brother*, Jeferson De, 2010).

5. *O rap do Pequeno Príncipe contra as Almas Sebosas (The Little Prince's Rap against the Wicked Souls*, Paulo Caldas and Marcelo Luna, 2000), *O prisioneiro da grade de ferro (Prisoner of the Iron Bars*, Paulo Sacramento, 2003), *Justiça (Justice*, Maria Augusta Ramos, 2004), *Violência (Violence*, Eduardo Benaim, 2005), *Atos dos homens (Acts of Men*, Kiko Goifman, 2006), *Juízo (Judge*, Maria Augusta Ramos, 2008), *Território e violência (Territory and Violence*, Rute Imanashi Rodrigues and Patrícia S. Riviero, 2008), *Entre e luz e a sombra (Between the Light and the Shade*, Luciana Burlamaqui, 2009), *A casa dos mortos (The House of the Dead*, Débora Diniz, 2009), *Cortina de fumaça (Smoke Screen*, Rodrigo Mac Niven, 2010).

6. MV Bill made his public comments on the website *Vivafavela.com* on January 22, 2003. On December 31, 2004, at the request of Else Ribeiro Pires Vieira, he contributed a piece to her edited volume that was subsequently published in 2005 and is cited here.

7. Celso Athayde, MV Bill, and Luiz Eduardo Soares wrote *Cabeça de porco*. Athayde and Bill wrote *Falcão: Os meninos do tráfico* and *Falcão: Mulheres e o tráfico* and directed the film *Falcão: Os meninos do tráfico*.

8. The Nós do Cinema theatrical troupe from the Vidigal favela in Rio's Zona Sul was directed by Guti Fraga, a well-known actor in Rio. The acting project, in preparation for the filming of *Cidade de Deus*, kept the script as a work in progress. Working from the students' reactions to the scenes and the subsequent improvisation of them, Mantovani further adapted the script.

9. Ed Guerrero has used the term "hood-homeboy action formula" (76) to refer to films that thematize the urban ghetto and focus on the poor, black, marginal subject who is involved with drugs, gangs, and urban violence. Stephen Neale refers to this genre as "ghetto film" (*Genre*).

10. Representative films from this genre are *Boyz n the Hood, Menace II Society, La Haine* (Mathieu Kassovitz, 1995), *Bones* (Ernest R. Dickerson, 2001), *Get Rich or Die Tryin'* (Ernest R. Dickerson, 2001).

11. For an in-depth discussion of these debates and an informed reading of the politics that surround the hood-film cycle, please read Norman K. Denzin's *Reading Race*, especially part 3 on racial allegories.

12. David Bordwell has been a central figure in neoformalist film criticism, which eschews more psychoanalytical approaches and instead opts to concentrate on more formal elements of film form such as shot composition and framing, mise-en-scène, lighting, sound, and editing.

13. The *pai de santo*'s warning will later mark the beginning of the end of Zé Pequeno when he rapes Mané Galinha's girlfriend while wearing the amulet. The audience doesn't see the rape, but the camera focuses in on the swaying of the necklace. Zé Pequeno's failure to heed the warning of the *pai de santo* and respect Exu brings his downfall.

14. The *Jornal do Brasil* is the third-oldest newspaper in Brazil and one of the principal daily newspapers in circulation in Rio de Janeiro.

15. Joseph Murray, Daniel Ricardo de Castro Cerqueira, and Tulio Kahn are the authors of "Crime and Violence in Brazil."

16. For an in-depth analysis of the role of violence perpetrated by both the state and criminal factions in marginal communities in São Paulo, please consult Graham Denyer Willis's excellent book *The Killing Consensus*.

17. "Playboy" in Brazil is used to refer to a well-off youth who likes to show off with the latest fashions and be seen; they are often considered to be players or gigolos. It is a play on the *Playboy* style, referring to the men's magazine and the usage of the word in English that came out of the 1950s.

18. "A hen" here is slang for a good-looking woman who calls attention to herself.

19. It is interesting to read this scene in conjunction with a similar transformation of Máiquel in O *Homem do Ano*.

20. In Brazil the statistics on violence against women are disturbing. In *Mapa da violência 2015: Homicídio de mulheres no Brasil*, Júlio Jacobo Waiselfisz reports that the homicide rate of females in Brazil was 4.8 per 100,000 inhabitants in 2013 and hovered around that number for the previous decade. In 2013 Brazil had the fifth-highest rate of femicide in the world. Of these murders, approximately half were perpetrated by family members. All indications are that during the 2020–2021 Covid-19 epidemic, these numbers only got worse and violence against women, particularly by family members, intensified.

21. Buscapé's friend was also with him on the bus where they met Mané Galinha.

Chapter 3. Brotherhoods of Exception: Power, Politics, and Masculinity in *Quase Dois Irmãos*

1. The Comando Vermelho is the oldest organized criminal gang in Brazil. It was founded in the 1970s when common street criminals and leftist political dissidents banded together to resist the abusive conditions at the Instituto Penal Cândido Mendes on Ilha Grande off the coast of Rio de Janeiro. By the late 1970s, the gang had moved

beyond the walls of the prison, participating in bank robberies and other criminal activities to help finance the escape of prisoners. In the 1980s the gang began to control larger territories in Rio de Janeiro as it expanded operations to include the large-scale distribution of cocaine from Colombian drug cartels. As the gang gained a stronger foothold in Rio de Janeiro, it also began to expand to other areas of the country, including São Paulo. Rifts within the group's command structure caused splinter factions such as the Primeiro Comando da Capital who were responsible for the attacks in São Paulo, the Terceiro Comando (Third Command), and the Amigos dos Amigos (Friends of Friends) to break away and form rival factions. At the turn of the twenty-first century, the Comando Vermelho controlled more than 50% of Rio's drug territories. Subsequently, the group lost terrain to both the official occupation by Unidades de Polícia Pacificadora (Peacemaking Police Units) and the extralegal police militias that increasingly have occupied the various gangs' territories.

2. Lúcia Murat has a very intense biography that has parallels with her cinematic production. During the 1964–1985 dictatorship she was imprisoned and tortured by the military regime for being a leftist militant. In 1989 she released *Que bom te ver viva* (*How Nice to See You Alive*), a testimonial-style film that intermixes fiction and documentary cinema. That film confronts the regime's legacy of sexual violence and torture inflicted on female political prisoners. Subsequently, *Doces poderes* (*Sweet Power*, 1996) and *Quase Dois Irmãos* broach the violent political history of the dictatorship from other vantage points. Specific to *Quase Dois Irmãos*, Murat wrote the screenplay with Paulo Lins, creating a direct link to *Cidade de Deus*. From my research, it appears that neither Murat's nor Lins's personal history nor those of the actors were directly deployed as forms of propaganda to make claims of authenticity when the film was released, unlike Meirelles's assertions on the release of *Cidade de Deus*.

3. Agamben cites as concrete examples of the state of exception and *homo sacer* Nazi Germany and its concentration camps. He draws a parallel between these and measures such as the US Patriot Act enacted on October 26, 2001, by George W. Bush, and the Guantanamo Bay detention camp.

4. *Elite da tropa*, written by Luiz Eduardo Soares with André Batista and Rodrigo Pimentel, also signals toward this legacy of violence and has direct ties to the works I am considering.

5. Galeria LSN was also known as the Fundão and o Coletivo (the Collective) throughout much of the 1970s. The designation o Coletivo was bestowed on the wing for the leftist politics of the political prisoners who were housed there.

6. Freyre would not formally use the term "racial democracy" until the 1940s. Emanuelle Oliveira notes in *Writing Identity*, "Although the 'myth of racial democracy' was indelibly connected to Gilberto Freyre, it should be noted that he did not coin the term. In *Classes, raças e democracia*, Antônio Sérgio Alfredo Guimarães demonstrates that Roger Bastide was the first to use the term in 1944. In 'A meta mitológica da democracia racial' Hermano Vianna observes that the term 'racial democracy' was never present in Freyre's *Casa grande e senzala* (trans. *The Masters and the Slaves*). I thank Christopher Dunn for these references" (226n9).

7. In these scenes, samba is present as part of the musical score and an organizing marker of the relationship between Miguel's and Jorginho's fathers. While I won't touch on samba directly in this chapter, it is interesting to consider how the scenes of the 1950s engage with the Vargas administration's use of samba in the consolidation of Brazil's national identity by this time.

8. The red and white colors evoke the first iteration of the modern samba school Deixa Falar that was formed in the neighborhood of Estácio in Rio de Janeiro in 1928.

9. Cartola (1908–1980), born Angenor de Oliveira in Rio de Janeiro, was one of the foundational figures of samba music in Brazil in the 1930s. He is credited with writing and cowriting more than five hundred sambas.

10. The denial of political detentions was clearly delineated in letters exchanged between the International Affairs Committee of the Latin American Bureau of the National Council of Churches, the Inter-American Commission on Human Rights, and the Brazilian government. In this series of letters written in 1970 and 1971, the Council of Churches contests the Brazilian government's claim that "there are no political prisoners in Brazil." In a December 6, 1971, letter the council summarily contests the claims of the government that no extraordinary or secret tribunals were held, no individuals were imprisoned based on the free expression of opinion, no individuals were denied judicial process and legal defense, nor were political opposition members being imprisoned in specific penitentiaries such as at Ilha Grande.

11. From the coup on March 31, 1964, through 1966, the military government targeted employees who previously formed part of the oppositional government of João Goulart for removal from their positions. From this point, the authoritarian regime expanded from government offices to target civil society through censorship, removal of professors from their positions at universities, and more general persecution of activists on the left.

12. AI-5 effectively suspended the legislative bodies of the government by decree of the president, limited the protections of the 1967 Constitution, adjourned the judiciary's review of the institutional act, and granted supreme authority to the president during the recess of the legislative bodies that he ordered. AI-5 formed part of a shift toward an increasingly restrictive authoritarian regime in Brazil.

13. AI-17 permitted the transfer of military soldiers who were found to have committed acts against the "cohesion of the armed forces" to reserve units.

14. As a point of clarification, I am referencing Agamben's ideas on *homo sacer. Homines sacri* is the plural in Latin.

15. The regime's denial of the existence of political detainees preemptively voids the tenets of the 1976 United Nations International Covenant on Civil and Political Rights (both pre- and post-incarceration). This covenant is meant to guarantee political and social rights, such as the right to legal recourse, to be recognized as a person before the law, and the right of opinion and expression. Significantly, Brazil did not sign this document at this point. Instead, the military government kept in effect previously instituted laws that directly or indirectly countered the 1976 treaty. Examples include the aforementioned Lei de Segurança Nacional, the AI-1, and the AI-5 that were employed to effectively implement and maintain a state of exception. Within this state, suspects

were detained under the pretext of national security, however, they were not necessarily charged with specific crimes. Since prisoners were not charged with any specific crime, or since they were processed as common criminals, the government could deny the allegations of political detentions. Thus, the regime effectively transformed them into *homines sacri*.

16. Michel Foucault introduced the concept of biopolitics in "Society Must Be Defended," his 1975–1976 lecture series at the College of France. He subsequently incorporated these ideas into the final chapter of the first volume of *The History of Sexuality* (published in French in 1976). He also broaches the concepts of biopolitics and biopower in his 1976–1977 and 1977–1978 lecture series. Foucault takes a genealogical approach to modern power and argues that biopolitical power shifted in modernity from thanatopolitics to incorporate a more productive model. Power shifted from a paradigm constructed around death and the disciplining of the individual body to incorporate the promotion and control of life through the assessment of and intervention upon the social body. Thus, the sovereign's right, which previously emanated from a legal code, was integrated within a normative logic founded upon the power to measure, qualify, assess, and establish collective norms. These norms are enforced through regulatory apparatuses (medicine, education, governmental administration). Thus, Foucault centered on the development, management, and discipline of the biopolitical existence of the collective social body as well as the adaptation of the individual body to diverse norms.

17. Documentation of authorities' concern comes from Informação no. S-084/77/ JSPDN 04/NOV/77, Divisão de Normas e Controle de Insegurança (DOI-CODI). Peixoto's pronouncement is recorded as "Pronunciamento de Amaral Peixoto," 8 Nov. 1977, Atividade Legislativa, Senado Federal.

18. I would like to recognize that inserting the sexed body into a binary understanding is problematic. I will not enter into this discussion here, but I would recommend Anne Fausto-Sterling's *Sexing the Body* for an informed problematization of the sex binary through the lens of the hard sciences.

19. For a very informative discussion of the postwar crisis of masculinity, please consult Stéphane Audoin-Rouzeau's "Exércitos e guerras."

20. In 1998, Human Rights Watch estimated that women made up approximately 4% of the total inmate population ("Behind Bars"). That number rose to 4.3% by 2001, 5.6% in 2005, 7.0% in 2010, 6.1% in 2013, 5.9% in 2014, and 4.9% in 2019 ("Brazil" *World Prison Brief*). Carla Ruas and Silvia Lisboa report in *The Intercept* an almost 700% increase in the number of women incarcerated in the country between 2000 and 2016.

21. Don Sabo, Terry A. Kupers, and Willie London edited *Prison Masculinities* and wrote the introduction to it.

22. The word *filha* (daughter) is used in reference to Ana rather than *filho* (son) in the colloquial expression; literally, *filha da puta* means "daughter of a prostitute."

23. Zuenir Ventura, in *Cidade partida*, argues that division governs the geosocial organization of many Brazilian cities. In metropolitan areas such as São Paulo, Rio de Janeiro, Recife, and Belo Horizonte, social tensions are amplified under the strain of cohabitation, as the margins become more visible and impinge upon the privileged spaces of the social elites.

24. The only exception is the repetition of the opening scene at Bangu prison when, just as Miguel sits down, Jorginho receives a call from Deley to discuss the purchase of firearms and confer about the problems that Duda is causing in the *morro*. This scene is later repeated; chronologically, however, it is out of order. The brief cut to a short clip from the opening Bangu scene is reintegrated when Deley is making an arms deal in the favela with the local police officers. While the first time we only hear Jorginho speaking, the scene repetition cuts between the two men on the telephone.

25. One of the few exceptions is the funk artist Mr. Catra, who has a cameo appearance, first at a *baile funk* and then in the final scenes warning Juliana to leave the favela. Mr. Catra attained national recognition when his polyandrous lifestyle was exposed in 2014 on *Programa Altas Horas* (*Primetime Program*), a variety program on the Globo network. The program aired an interview with him and his three female partners to discuss their lifestyle together as well as his thirty children and three adopted kids.

Chapter 4. It's a Man's World: Neo-Authoritarian Masculinity in *Tropa de Elite*

1. For an in-depth discussion of film form in documentary filmmaking, I would highly recommend Louise Spence and Vinicius Navarro's *Crafting Truth*.

2. While Amy Villarejo argues in "Cities of Walls" that the film relies on video-game aesthetics, I would note that authenticity does play a part in first-person shooter video games to help suture the player into the mediated space of the gaming experience.

3. I intentionally use the masculine "himself" because I would argue that the intended spectator of the film is a male viewership either literally or ideologically.

4. While my interest here is with the most recent authoritarian regime, Benjamin Cowan argues in his article "Rules of Disengagement" that the beginnings of these operatives can be located in the period post–World War II. Wellington Fontes Menezes tacitly signals the authoritarian specters that underlie BOPE's actions in Rio de Janeiro in his article "A carnavalização da barbárie."

5. The authors of the index's 2014 *Relatório* (*Report*) are Luciana Gross Cunha, Rodrigo de Losso da Silveira Bueno, Fabiana Luci de Oliveira, Joelson Oliveira Sampaio, Luciana de Oliveira Ramos, and Gabriel Hideo Sakai de Macedo.

6. Please consult the chapter "Uses of Repression" in Thomas Skidmore's *The Politics of Military Rule* for more information.

7. Many of the other military police special-forces units have emblems that are derivations of these same themes.

8. I use the term "extraordinary measures" to invoke yet another wrinkle in the reassertion of the authoritarian male figure post-9/11 in the world when special-forces operatives worldwide have been given unilateral power to pursue terrorists.

9. Canavarro Pereira was a central figure in the development and implementation of Operação Bandeirante (OBAN) in 1969. OBAN was a center for the armed forces information and investigative center that organized and coordinated responses to alleged leftist threats during the authoritarian regime. In a confidential telegram sent from the US embassy in Rio to Washington in July 1969, the general called for "immediate all-out war [to] be declared on terrorists and subversives" (US Department of State, telegram

Rio de Janeiro to Washington, DC, Subject: Military Coordination of Security Agencies, received July 25, 1969, declassified April 14, 2014).

10. We should remember the hypocrisy in that stance since torturers were promoted within the regime to an almost untouchable status (Starling 258–59; Gaspari 12). There was limited accountability for their actions, allowing for the abuse of their power and positions. In many reported cases, women who were accused of subversive actions suffered rape by agents of the regime.

11. "The dichotomy masculine/feminine is linked to other dichotomous pairs, which operate in a similar fashion. Thus such pairs as hard/soft, rational/irrational, strong/weak, tough/tender, culture/nature, mind/body, dominant/submissive, science/art, active/passive, inside/outside, competitive/caring, objective/subjective, public/private, abstract/concrete, independent/dependent, aggressor/victim, Self/Other, order/anarchy, war/peace, and prudence/impulsiveness are either used to define masculinity and femininity, respectively, or are otherwise associated with them, with the former term always constructed in relation to its opposite, and generally privileged over it. Often what counts as active and therefore masculine is a question of semantics, so that for example while passivity is a devalued feminine trait, restraint is a valued masculine one" (Hooper 43–44).

12. It is interesting to note that Rodrigo Nogueira in *Como nascem os monstros* describes a parallel scene in relation to his protagonist Rafael.

13. An example is found in the US Marines' institutionalization of the "Rifleman's Creed," written during World War II, that has since formed part of basic training in the United States: "This is my rifle. There are many like it, but this one is mine. My rifle is my best friend. It is my life. I must master it as I must master my life. My rifle, without me, is useless. Without my rifle, I am useless. I must fire my rifle true." These words connect the soldier with his rifle as inextricable from himself.

14. While it might be a bit of an overreach, one also could interpret the BOPE insignia covering the Brazilian flag as emblematizing the film's argument that to save the country from its state of social, political, and cultural decadence, the imposition of a more authoritarian masculine force is required.

15. Cinema: *Pixote: A lei do mais fraco* (Babenco, 1980), *Última parada 174* (Barreto, 2008), *Alemão* (Belmonte, 2014), *O invasor* (Brant, 2002), *Manda bala* (Kohn, 2007), *Domésticas* (Meirelles, 2001), *Maré: Nossa história de amor* (Murat, 2008), *Ônibus 174* (Padilha, 2002), *Disparos* (Reis, 2012), *Era uma vez* (Silveira, 2008), *Sonhos roubados* (Werneck, 2010).

Literature: *Subúrbio* (Bonassi, 1994), *Feliz ano novo* (Fonseca, 1975), *Angu de sangue* (Freire, 2000), *Inferno* (Melo, 2000), *Graduado em marginalidade* (Alves, 2009), *Capão Pecado* (Ferréz, 2005), *Cidade de Deus* (Lins, 1997).

16. Connell and Messerschmidt respond to and modify the theoretical construction of hegemonic masculinity to incorporate elements of Demetriou's critique.

17. A *fogueteiro* is the individual, typically a young kid, who shoots off fireworks to alert dealers in the favela that police have arrived.

18. For more specific information on the legal aspects of the dead, please consult Jean-Marie Henckaerts, Louise Doswald-Beck, and Carolin Alvermann's "The Dead."

19. This is evidenced in the comedy troupe Porta dos Fundos's June 17, 2013, short *Reunião de traficante* (*Drug Trafficker Meeting*), which in 2021 had more than thirteen million views on YouTube. In the video, a drug lord prohibits the burning of individuals in tires because of the detrimental effects it has on the environment.

20. Violence has been a focal point of many of the studies that have been written on *Tropa de Elite* such as Silvia Beatriz Adoue's "*Tropa de Elite*," Simone Rocha and Ângela Salgueiro Marque's "'Bandido bom é bandido morto,'" and Rafael Araújo and Priscilla Alves Teixeira Branco's "A polêmica sobre a violência." While violence is central, masculinity has been overwhelmingly overlooked in these studies.

21. I am using the term "zone of exception" rather than Giorgio Agamben's "state of exception" to emphasize the spatial component of the favela as a state of exception.

22. Here I am referencing specifically the underlying socioeconomic disparities that drive poor youth into the drug trade as well as the prison industrial complex that jails so many drug offenders.

23. Lilia Blima Schraiber, Ana Flávia P. L. d'Oliveira, Ivan França-Junior, Simone Diniz, Ana Paula Portella, Ana Bernarda Ludermir, Otávio Valença, and Márcia Thereza Couto are the authors of "Prevalência da violência."

24. On this point, see Peter R. Kingstone and Timothy J. Power's first two edited volumes, *Democratic Brazil* and *Democratic Brazil Revisited*.

25. For a more nuanced discussion of corruption in Brazil, please consult Timothy J. Power and Matthew M. Taylor's *Corruption and Democracy in Brazil*.

Chapter 5. Men on the Verge of a Nervous Breakdown: *O Homem do Ano*

1. An *arrastão* typically refers to the use of fishing nets, but in this case it is when a group of youth run across the beach causing havoc.

2. Luiz Eduardo Soares, João T. S. Sé, José A. S. Rodrigues, and Leandro P. Carneiro are the authors of *Criminalidade urbana e violência*.

3. Havard Hegre, Tanja Ellingsen, Scott Gates, and Nils Petter Gleditsch are the authors of "Toward a Democratic Civil Peace?"

4. José Henrique Fonseca is the son of Rubem Fonseca, an author well known for his crime novels. Beyond this, Rubem Fonseca and fellow writer Patrícia Melo cowrote the screenplay of the movie. Melo wrote the novel *O matador*, published in 1995, upon which the screenplay is based. Due to the length and focus of this chapter, I will not compare the film to the novel *O matador*. This being said, I would like to signal that the visual narrative that Fonseca creates engages the development of the internal monologues of the protagonist in the novel. For an incisive discussion of the adaptation of the novel to film, please consult Luciano Rodolfo's "Criação, recriação."

5. Both Santana and Carvalho are from the upper middle class. This is demonstrated by their ability to install home security systems, own businesses, and take vacations as well as by the general décor of their homes.

6. In a discussion during a radio interview on August 30, 1993, a representative of the federal government incorrectly located the August 29 massacre at Vigário Geral as having occurred in the Baixada Fluminense (Souza Alves 14). The geographic relocation of this event from Vigário Geral, to the south nearer central Rio, to the peripheral

Baixada Fluminense signals a geo-epistemological issue: "This mistake, in turn, reveals the problem of the limits of this region. The geographical is collapsed into the political and the social, which results in the construction of imprecise borders." ("Este equívoco, por sua vez, revela o problema dos limites dessa região. O aspecto geográfico acaba se relacionando com o político e com o social na construção de fronteiras não muito precisas" [Souza Alves 14].) This rewriting of the geographical boundaries of Rio de Janeiro by the media and state representative signals an understanding of the urban space that collapses the different regions of the city into one homogeneous mass understood as socioeconomic divisionary lines. The remapping of Rio de Janeiro by the state representative transformed the Baixada Fluminense into a microcosm that epitomizes urban violence. Additionally, this rewriting of the urban space negates a differentiation of individual *comunidades* and *bairros* and illustrates how the Baixada Fluminense occupies a privileged position in the imaginary of Rio de Janeiro's elites as an epicenter of violence.

7. Historical developments of the Baixada Fluminense during the latter half of the twentieth century delineate its relation to the metropolitan center of Rio de Janeiro. Before 1975 the Baixada Fluminense was part of the state of Rio de Janeiro, separate from the Federal District (1889–1960) and the state of Guanabara (1960–1975). It was only in the 1970s, when the states of Guanabara and Rio de Janeiro merged, that the Baixada Fluminense officially became a peripheral community of the metropolis, the Região Metropolitana do Rio de Janeiro.

8. The proliferating narrative about the Baixada was made clear in articles such as "Câncer vizinho" ("Neighboring Cancer"), an editorial from 1977 in *O Jornal do Brasil* (Souza Alves).

9. William Bratton, founder of the Bratton Group and former police chief of New York City, was largely responsible for the development of zero-tolerance laws in that city. Bratton was hired in 1997 for a three-year contract to consult with the city of Fortaleza and the state of Ceará in Brazil to respond to the state's rising insecurity issues (Lifsher 2001). In 1999 Joaquim Roriz was inaugurated as governor of the federal district of Brasília. He implemented "tolerância zero" laws at the same time that he hired eight hundred new civil and military police officers to crack down on a crime spree that had plagued the capital. This occurred after the January visit of two high-ranking police officers from the New York City Police Department (Wacquant *Prisons*, 20).

10. The events of this day are thematized in José Padilha's documentary *Ônibus 174* (*Bus 174*, 2002) as well as Bruno Barreto's feature film *Última parada 174* (*Last Stop 174*, 2008).

11. Medicalizing discourses in the treatises and studies of nineteenth-century Europe traversed the Atlantic and had a profound effect in Brazil. The "criminal," the "homosexual," and other social "deviants" became the location of perversion, bodies in need of study that were placed within the purview of science, quantifying and categorizing the "other's" material and symbolic body. At this same historical moment, Brazil was undergoing significant social transformations. In 1888, the Lei Áurea (Golden Law) abolished slavery. The same medical discourses that studied those who were considered social deviants were also employed to "understand" race. Darwinian ideas and Francis Galton's theories on eugenics were exploited by intellectuals of the epoch to promote the

"whitening" of Brazil and attest to the detrimental influences and consequences of Afro-Brazilian elements in the society (Stam).

Chapter 6. A Superhero of Their Own: *O Doutrinador* and Neo-Authoritarian Masculinity

1. In the United States, the first African American superhero to appear on screen was Abar (Tobar Mayo), protagonist of Frank Packard's 1977 blacksploitation film *Abar: Black Superman.* In 1993 Robert Townsend directed and starred in *Meteor Man,* and in 1997 Mark Dippé released *Spawn.* Wesley Snipes fought his way onto the big and small screens with the *Blade* triptych (*Blade,* Stephen Norrington, 1998; *Blade II,* Guillermo del Toro, 2002; *Blade: Trinity,* David Goyer, 2004). According to announcements at San Diego Comic-Con in 2019, Marvel Studios planned to reboot the Blade character, casting Mahershala Ali in the lead role. Will Smith appeared in *Hancock* (Peter Berg, 2008), Michael B. Jordan costarred in *Fantastic Four* (Josh Trank, 2015), and Mike Colter starred as Luke Cage in Cheo Hodari Coker's homonymous 2016 and 2018 two-season Netflix series.

2. While these are more recent, if we look historically, there are *Supergirl* (Jeannot Szwarc, 1984), *Tank Girl* (Rachel Talalay, 1995), *Catwoman* (Pitof, 2004), and *Elektra* (Rob Bowman, 2005), as well as a host of characters from the X-Men films that integrate controlled degrees of gender diversity with Storm (Halle Berry), Jean Grey (Desiree Zurowski/Sophie Turner), Mystique (Jennifer Lawrence), Rogue (Anna Paquin), Polaris (Emma Dumont), and Kitty Pryde (Ellen Page), to name a few.

3. There has been new light shed on the space of superhero narratives with recent inquiries into questions of ableism that underlie these narratives, either attributing disability to villains or curing superheroes via their super powers (Ratto).

4. I would like to call attention to Gene Luen Yang's *Superman Smashes the Klan* (DC Comics 2020), a comic that takes racism head-on.

5. The 2019 installment is essentially a storyboard of the film with a "making of" section added.

6. While I am not going to get into a discussion of the growth of the superhero genre within the United States post-9/11 (see, for example, Marc DiPaolo's 2011 *War, Politics, and Superheroes*), it is worth considering to what degree the surge in superhero narratives coming out of Hollywood since 2001 in combination with the policies and politics of US film distribution at the multiplex may be working in tandem with national trends and traditions of graphic novel and comic book consumption.

7. Please consult chapter 3, "The Definition of the Superhero," in Coogan's *Superhero.*

8. According to São Paulo's state website (saopaulo.sp.gov.br), between 1888 and 1932 the flag had been adopted as São Paulo's de facto state flag although it was not consecrated into law until November 27, 1946, under federal decree law 16.349.

9. Maria Augusta Ramos's 2018 documentary *O processo* visually captures the deep division between these two groups when they came to a head during Rousseff's impeachment proceedings.

10. For more information, please refer to Glenn Greenwald, Leandro Demori, and Betsy Reed's "Secret Brazil Archive."

11. In a 2010 interview with Luiz Maklouf Carvalho of the cultural publication *Piauí*, GOG explained the origin of the song. Selling his CDs on the street in front of the Secretaria Municipal de Cultura de União dos Palmares building in the state of Alagoas, he promised a rap with only words that begin with "P" to a potential buyer of one of his CDs.

12. GOG's lyricism is not done justice in translation. Please listen to the rhythm and the rhyme of the original text.

13. While women do populate the frames of the film, they are relegated to supporting roles, the most salient of which are Alice, the sacrificial daughter; Nina (Tainá Medina), Miguel's sidekick hacker; and the minister Marta Regina (Marília Gabriela), who is presented as the gray eminence of corruption.

14. These scenes can be read in contrast to the opening scenes, when the DAE invade Governor Correa's home to arrest him. These scenes are also filmed during the day with high-key lighting, but a muted gray and white color palette prevails.

15. Here Goldhammer continues, "Bataille becomes increasingly disillusioned with the political effects of sacrificial violence. At first, following Sorel, he seeks a role for sacrifice in the class struggle. Yet this effort occurs at precisely the time that fascism emerges in Europe. Fascism's overtly sacrificial motifs laid bare both the revolutionary possibility as well as the terrible risks of violent sacrifice in the service of founding politics. When Bataille turns his attention to fascism in an attempt to comprehend its significance for the working class, he discovers that fascism itself illustrates the frightful political outcome of vigilantly pursuing the French discourse's sacrificial logic" (153).

16. Please also consult Illan rua Wall's *Human Rights and Constituent Power*, pages 70–72.

17. The song itself is not listed in the film credits. The musical score seems based on the 2009 song "Lose Your Soul" released by the band Dead Man's Bones, but the lyrics are very different and demonstrate a shift in perspective from Dead Man's Bones, chorus, "You're gonna lose your soul tonight . . . You're gonna lose control tonight," to the film's emphasis on the first-person narrative voice. The music also features prominently in the trailer and closing credits of the French film *La Bataille de Solférino* (*The Age of Panic*, Justine Triet, 2013).

Conclusion: The Rise of the Neo-Authoritarian Masculine Paradigm

1. Kendall D. Funk, Magda Hinojosa, and Jennifer M. Piscopo are the authors of "Still Left Behind."

2. The resignation of several cabinet members under the shadow of corruption and a heightened degree of public scrutiny forced Temer to appoint several women to his cabinet subsequently.

3. Moraes also represented Eduardo Cunha, a conservative right-leaning politician who, as president of the Chamber of Deputies, spearheaded the impeachment of Dilma. Cunha was suspended on charges related to the Lava Jato (Car Wash) scandal as well as accusations of bribery, intimidation, and obstruction of justice.

4. The National Education Plan determines what subject areas must be taught in primary and secondary schools.

5. Elder Luan dos Santos Silva, in his article "'A ideologia de gênero' no Brasil," offers a thorough engagement with and refuting of the conservative deployment of *ideologia de gênero* (gender ideology).

6. Gabriela Bastos, Flávia Carbonari, and Paula Tavares are the authors of "Addressing Violence against Women," published by the World Bank Group.

WORKS CITED

À meia noite levarei sua alma. Directed by José Mojica Marins, Indústria Cinematográfica Apolo, 1964.

Ação entre amigos. Directed by Beto Brant, Dezenove Som e Imagem / TV Cultura, 1998.

Adorno, Sérgio, and Fernando Salla. "Criminalidade organizada nas prisões e os ataques do PCC." *Estudos Avançados,* vol. 21, no. 61, 2007, pp. 7–29.

Adoue, Silvia Beatriz. "*Tropa de Elite*: E as narrativas da violência." *Passages de Paris,* no. 7, 2012, pp. 213–22.

Agamben, Giorgio. *Homo Sacer: Sovereign Power and Bare Life.* Translated by Daniel Heller-Roazen, Stanford UP, 1998.

———. *State of Exception.* Translated by Kevin Attel, U of Chicago P, 2005.

Alcântara, Ana Alice, and Cecilia Sardenberg. "Brazil: 'State Feminism' at Work." *50.50 Inclusive Democracy,* 18 Apr. 2012.

"Alexandre de Moraes (PSDB), ministro da justiça do governo de Temer." *G1 São Paulo,* 12 May 2016.

Álvarez, Sonia E. *Engendering Democracy in Brazil: Women's Movements in Transition Politics.* Princeton UP, 1990.

Alves, Jaime A. "Police Terror in Brazil." *Open Democracy: Free Thinking for the World,* 10 Oct. 2015.

Anderson, Craig A., and Brad J. Bushman. "Effects of Violent Video Games on Aggressive Behavior, Aggressive Cognition, Aggressive Affect, Physiological Arousal, and Prosocial Behavior: A Meta-Analytic Review of the Scientific Literature." *Psychological Science,* vol. 12, no. 5, 2001, pp. 353–59.

Araújo, Rafael, and Priscilla Alves Teixeira Branco. "A polêmica sobre a violência em *Cidade de Deus* e *Tropa de Elite.*" *Aurora: Revista de Arte, Mídia e Política,* no. 5, 2009, pp. 59–75.

Athayde, Celso, and MV Bill. *Falcão: Mulheres e o tráfico.* Objetiva, 2007.

———. *Falcão: Os meninos do tráfico.* Objetiva, 2006.

Athayde, Celso, et al. *Cabeça de porco.* Objetiva, 2005.

Audoin-Rouzeau, Stéphane. "Exércitos e guerras: Uma brecha no coração do modelo viril?" *História da virilidade,* vol. 3, *A virilidade em crise? Séculos XX–XXI,* edited by Alain Corbin et al., Vozes, 2013, pp. 239–68.

Avelar, Idelber. "Revisões da masculinidade sob ditadura: Gabeira, Caio e Noll." *Estudos de Literatura Brasileira Contemporânea,* no. 43, Jan./June 2014, pp. 49–68.

———. "*Tropa de Elite*, de José Padilha." *O biscoito fino e a massa*, 10 Oct. 2007.

———. *The Untimely Present: Postdictatorial Latin American Fiction and the Task of Mourning*. Duke UP, 1999.

Bailey, John, and Lucía Dammert. *Public Security and Police Reform in the Americas*. U of Pittsburgh P, 2005.

Baker, Brian. *Masculinity in Fiction and Film: Representing Men in Popular Genres, 1945–2000*. Continuum, 2006.

O Bandido da Luz Vermelha. Directed by Rogério Sganzerla, Urano Filmes, 1968.

Barrett, Frank J. "The Organizational Construction of Hegemonic Masculinity: The Case of the US Navy." *The Masculinities Reader*, edited by Stephen Whitehead and Frank J. Barrett, Polity, 2001, pp. 75–99.

Barros, Sandro. "Cidade de Deus entre o testemunho e a ficção." *Estudos de Literatura Brasileira Contemporânea*, no. 40, July/Dec. 2012, pp. 135–49.

Barthes, Roland. *Mythologies*. Translated by Annette Lavers, Hill and Wang, 1972.

Bastos, Elide Rugai. *Gilberto Freyre e o pensamento hispânico: Entre Dom Quixote e Alonso El Bueno*. Editora da Universidade do Sagrado Coração, 2003.

Bastos, Gabriela, et al. "Addressing Violence against Women (VAW) under COVID-19 in Brazil." World Bank Group, 25 June 2020.

Baudrillard, Jean. *Simulations*. Translated by Paul Foss, Paul Patton, and Philip Beitchman, Semiotext(e), 1983.

Beato, Cláudio. "A mídia define as prioridades da segurança pública." *Mídia e violência: Novas tendências na cobertura de criminalidade e segurança no Brasil*, edited by Anabela and Sílvia Ramos Paiva, IUPERJ, 2007, pp. 33–36.

"Behind Bars in Brazil: Women Prisoners." Human Rights Watch, 1998.

Beleza, Fernando. "Sustainability at the Margins: Avant-Garde Cinema and Environment in Rogério Sganzerla's *Cinema do Lixo*." *A Contracorriente: Una Revista de Estudios Latinoamericanos*, vol. 17, no. 2, winter 2020, pp. 182–98.

Benevides, Bruna G. *Candidaturas trans foram eleitas em 2020 direitos e política*. Associação Nacional de Travestis e Transexuais, 2021.

Benevides, Bruna G., and Sayonara Naider Bonfim Nogueira. *Dossiê assassinatos e violência contra travestis e transexuais brasileiras em 2020*. Expressão Popular / Associação Nacional de Travestis e Transexuais / IBTE, 2021.

Bentes, Ivana. "'Cosmética da fome' marca cinema do país." *Jornal do Brasil*, 8 July 2001.

Bill, MV. "Cidade de Deus: History's Silent Protagonist." *City of God in Several Voices: Brazilian Social Cinema as Action*, edited by Else Ribeiro Pires Vieira, Critical, Cultural, and Communications P, 2005, pp. 121–26.

Bordwell, David. *Making Meaning: Inference and Rhetoric in the Interpretation of Cinema*. Harvard UP, 1989.

Bourdieu, Pierre. *Distinction: A Social Critique of the Judgement of Taste*. Harvard UP, 1984.

———. *Masculine Domination*. Stanford UP, 2001.

Brasil: Nunca mais. Edited by Paulo Evaristo, tenth edition, Vozes, 1985.

"Brasil: Reformas foram insuficientes para coibir tortura." Human Rights Watch, 2014.

"Brazil." *World Prison Brief*, Institute for Crime and Justice Policy Research, Birbeck University of London, annual.

Brown, Blain. *Cinematography: Theory and Practice.* Focal, 2011.

Brown, Claude. "The Family and the Subculture of Violence." *Violence in the Family,* edited by Suzanne K. Steinmetz and Murray A. Straus, Harper and Row, 1974, pp. 262–68.

Brum, Elaine. "Os novos 'vândalos' do Brasil." Opinion, *El País,* 23 Dec. 2013.

Bruzzi, Stella. *Men's Cinema: Masculinity and Mise-en-Scène in Hollywood.* Edinburgh UP, 2013.

Buarque de Hollanda, Heloisa. "A Short Sketch on Some Signs of Transformation." *Brazil and the Americas: Convergences and Perspectives,* edited by Peter Birle, Sérgio Costa, and Horst Nitschack, Iberoamericana-Vervuert, 2008, pp. 171–83.

Butler, Judith. *Bodies That Matter: On the Discursive Limits of Sex.* Routledge, 1993.

———. *Gender Trouble: Feminism and the Subversion of Identity.* Routledge, 1990.

———. "Performative Acts and Gender Constitution: An Essay in Phenomenology and Feminist Theory." *Theatre Journal,* vol. 40, no. 4, 1988, pp. 519–31.

Butterman, Steve. *Invisibilidade vigilante: Representações midiáticas da maior parada gay do planeta.* nVersos, 2012.

Caldeira, Teresa Pires do Rio. *City of Walls: Crime, Segregation, and Citizenship in São Paulo.* U of California P, 2000.

Caldeira, Teresa Pires do Rio, and James Holston. "Democracy and Violence in Brazil." *Comparative Studies in Society and History,* vol. 41, no. 4, 1999, pp. 691–729.

Cano, Ignácio, and Thais Duarte. *No sapatinho: A evolução das milícias no Rio de Janeiro [2008-2011].* Fundação Heinrich Böll, 2012.

Certeau, Michel de. *The Practice of Everyday Life.* Berkeley: U of California P, 1984.

Chauí, Marilena de Souza. *Brasil: Mito fundador e sociedade autoritária.* Fundação Perseu Abramo, 2000.

Cidade de Deus. Directed by Fernando Meirelles and Kátia Lund, O2 Filmes, 2003.

Cieglinski, Thais. "Ativistas de direita articularam detalhes da invasão à UnB." *Metrópoles,* 22 June 2016.

Clendenning, Alan. "HIV Cases Put a Kink in Two Film Industries." Chron.com, 13 Aug. 2011.

Coimbra, Cecília. *Operação Rio: O mito das classes perigosas; um estudo sobre a violência urbana, a mídia impressa e os discursos de segurança pública.* Oficina do Autor e Intertexto, 2001.

Comissão Nacional da Verdade. *Relatório,* vol. I. Dec. 2014.

———. *Relatório,* vol. II, *Textos temáticos.* Dec. 2014.

———. *Relatório,* vol. III, *Mortos e desaparecidos políticos.* Dec. 2014.

Comissão Nacional da Verdade do Rio. *Relatório,* Dec. 2015.

Connell, Raewyn. *Masculinities.* Second edition, U of California P, 2005.

Connell, Raewyn, and James Messerschmidt. "Hegemonic Masculinity: Rethinking the Concept." *Gender and Society,* vol. 19, no. 6, 2005, pp. 829–59.

Coogan, Peter. *Superhero: The Secret Origin of a Genre.* Monkey Brain, 2006.

Couto, Adolpho João de Paula. *O que é subversão?* Ministério da Educação, Comissão Nacional de Moral e Civismo, 1984, pp. 18–19.

Cowan, Benjamin A. "Rules of Disengagement: Masculinity, Violence, and the Cold War

Remakings of Counterinsurgency in Brazil." *American Quarterly*, vol. 66, no. 3, 2014, pp. 691–714.

———. *Securing Sex: Morality and Repression in the Making of Cold War Brazil.* U of North Carolina P, 2016.

———. "Sex and the Security State: Gender, Sexuality, and 'Subversion' at Brazil's Escola Superior de Guerra, 1964–1985." *Journal of the History of Sexuality*, vol. 16, no. 3, 2007, pp. 459–81.

Cunha, Luciana Gross, et al. *Relatório: Índice de confiança na justiça brasileira, ano 6.* Escola de Direito de São Paulo / Fundação Getúlio Vargas, 2014.

Dagnino, Evelina. "Citizenship: A Perverse Confluence." *Development in Practice*, vol. 17, no. 4–5, 2007, pp. 549–56.

Da Matta, Roberto. *Carnavais, malandros e heróis: Para uma sociologia do dilema brasileiro.* Zahar, 1979.

Dassin, Joan. "Testimonial Literature and the Armed Struggle in Brazil." *Fear at the Edge: State Terror and Resistance in Latin America*, edited by Manuel A. Garretón Merino et al., U of California P, 1992, pp. 161–83.

Demetriou, Demetrakis Z. "Connell's Concept of Hegemonic Masculinity: A Critique." *Theory and Society: Renewal and Critique in Social Theory*, vol. 30, no. 3, 2001, pp. 337–61.

Denzin, Norman K. *Reading Race: Hollywood and the Cinema of Racial Violence.* Sage, 2002.

Diken, Bülent, and Carsten Bagge Lausten. *Sociology through the Projector.* Routledge, 2007.

DiPaolo, Marc. *War, Politics and Superheroes: Ethics and Propaganda in Comics and Film.* McFarland, 2011.

Dittmer, Jason. *Captain America and the Nationalist Superhero: Metaphors, Narratives, and Geopolitics.* Temple UP, 2013.

Divisão de Normas e Controle de Insegurança. Informação no. S-084/77/JSPDN, 4 Nov. 1977.

O Doutrinador. Directed by Gustavo Bonafé, Guará Entretenimento / Paris Entretenimento, 2018.

Enne, Ana Lúcia. "Imprensa e Baixada Fluminense: Múltiplas representações." *Ciber-legenda*, no. 14, 2004.

Esta noite encarnarei no teu cadáver. Directed by José Mojica Marins, Ibérica Filmes, 1967.

Falcão: Os meninos do tráfico. Directed by MV Bill and Celso Athayde, Central Única das Favelas, 2006.

"'Fantástico' revela os bastidores do filme 'Tropa de elite.'" *G1 Cinema*, 23 Sep. 2007.

Fausto-Sterling, Anne. *Sexing the Body: Gender Politics and the Construction of Sexuality.* Basic, 2000.

Feldman, Allen. *Formations of Violence: The Narrative of the Body and Political Terror in Northern Ireland.* U of Chicago P, 1991.

Ferréz, Reginaldo Ferreira da Silva. *Capão pecado.* Labortexto Editorial, 2000.

———. *Literatura marginal: A cultura da periferia, ato I.* Special issue of *Caros Amigos*, Aug. 2001.

———. *Literatura marginal: A cultura da periferia, ato II.* Special issue of *Caros Amigos,* Aug. 2002.

———. *Literatura marginal: A cultura da periferia, ato III.* Special issue of *Caros Amigos,* Aug. 2004.

Flood, Michael. "Men, Sex, and Homosociality: How Bonds between Men Shape Their Sexual Relations with Women." *Men and Masculinities,* vol. 10, no. 3, 2008, pp. 339–59.

Fontes Menezes, Wellington. "A carnavalização da barbárie: Uma análise da endêmica 'guerra civil' no Rio de Janeiro." *Revista do Laboratório de Estudos da Violência,* UN-ESP-Marília, no. 6 2010, pp. 28–42.

Fórum Brasileiro de Segurança Pública. *Anuário brasileiro de segurança pública,* year 14, 2020.

Foster, David William. *El Eternauta, Daytripper, and Beyond: Graphic Narrative in Argentina and Brazil.* U of Texas P, 2016.

———. *Gender and Society in Contemporary Brazilian Cinema.* U of Texas P, 1999.

Foucault, Michel. *The Birth of Biopolitics: Lectures at the Collège de France, 1978–79.* Palgrave Macmillan, 2010.

———. *Discipline and Punish: The Birth of the Prison.* Second edition, Vintage, 1995.

———. *The History of Sexuality.* Pantheon, 1978.

———. *Society Must Be Defended: Lectures at the Collège de France, 1975–76.* Picador, 2003.

Freyre, Gilberto. *Casa-grande e senzala, edição crítica.* Edited by Guillermo Giucci et al., Allca XX, 2002.

Friedberg, Anne. *The Virtual Window: From Alberti to Microsoft.* MIT P, 2006.

Fromm, Erich. "The Authoritarian Personality." Translated by Florian Nadge, *Deutsche Universitätszeitung,* no. 9, 1957, pp. 3–4, Marxists.org, 2011.

———. *Escape from Freedom.* Farrar and Rinehart, 1941.

Full Metal Jacket. Directed by Stanley Kubrick, Warner Bros. Entertainment, remastered 2007.

Funk, Jeanne B., et al. "Violence Exposure in Real-Life, Video Games, Television, Movies, and the Internet: Is There Desensitization?" *Journal of Adolescence,* vol. 27, no. 1, 2004, pp. 23–39.

Funk, Kendall, et al. "Still Left Behind: Gender, Political Parties, and Latin America's Pink Tide." *Social Politics,* vol. 24, no. 4, 2017, pp. 399–424.

Os fuzis. Directed by Ruy Guerra, Copacabana Filmes, 1964.

Gaspari, Elio. *A ditadura escancarada.* Companhia das Letras, 2002.

Gielow, Igor. "Casa só com 'mãe e avó' é 'fábrica de desajustados' para tráfico, diz Mourão." *Folha de São Paulo,* 17 Sep. 2018.

Girard, René. *Deceit, Desire, and the Novel.* Johns Hopkins UP, 1976.

Giroux, Henry A. *Dangerous Thinking in the Age of the New Authoritarianism.* Routledge, 2015.

———. *Fugitive Cultures: Race, Violence, and Youth.* Routledge, 1996.

———. "Racism and the Aesthetic of Hyper-Real Violence: Pulp Fiction and Other Visual Tragedies." *Social Identities,* vol. 1, no. 2, 2010, pp. 333–54.

GOG (Genival Oliveira Gonçalves). "Brasil com 'P.'" *CPI da favela,* Zámbia, 2000.

Goldhammer, Jesse. *The Headless Republic: Sacrificial Violence in Modern French Thought.* Cornell UP, 2005.

Gonçalves, Danyelle Nilin. *O preço do passado: Anistia e reparação de perseguidos políticos no Brasil.* Expressão Popular, 2009.

Gormley, Paul. *The New-Brutality Film: Race and Affect in Contemporary Hollywood Cinema.* Intellect, 2005.

Gramsci, Antonio. *Prison Notebooks.* Edited by Joseph A. Buttigieg, Columbia UP, 1992.

Green, James. *Beyond Carnival: Male Homosexuality in Twentieth-Century Brazil.* U of Chicago P, 1999.

Green, James, and Renan Quinalha. *Ditadura e homossexualidades: Repressão, resistência e a busca da verdade.* EDUFSCAR, 2014.

Greenwald, Glenn, et al. "Secret Brazil Archive." Special edition, *The Intercept*, 9 June 2019.

Guerrero, Ed. "The Spectacle of Black Violence as Cinema." *Cinematic Sociology.* Sage, 2012, pp. 69–108.

Halberstam, Jack. *Female Masculinity.* Duke UP, 1998.

Hammarén, Nils, and Thomas Johansson. "Homosociality: In between Power and Intimacy." *SAGE Open*, vol. 4, no. 1, 2014, pp. 604–20.

Hansen-Miller, David. *Civilized Violence: Subjectivity, Gender and Popular Cinema.* Ashgate, 2011.

Haroche, Claudine. "Anthropology of Virility: The Fear of Powerlessness." *A History of Virility*, edited by Alain Corbin et al., Columbia UP, 2016, pp. 403–15.

Heard, Kevin. "To Live and Die in Rio." *Call and Post*, 10–16 June 2004.

Heath, Stephen. *Questions of Cinema.* Indiana UP, 1981.

Hegre, Havard, et al. "Toward a Democratic Civil Peace? Democracy, Political Change, and Civil War, 1816–1992." *The American Political Science Review*, vol. 95, no. 1, 2001, pp. 33–48.

Henckaerts, Jean-Marie, et al. "The Dead." *Customary International Humanitarian Law*, vol. 1, *Rules, International Committee of the Red Cross.* Cambridge UP, 2005, pp. 406–21.

Herschmann, Micael. *Abalando os anos 90: Funk e hip-hop: Globalização, violência e estilo cultural.* Rocco, 1997.

Hill Collins, Patricia. *Black Feminist Thought: Knowledge, Consciousness, and the Politics of Empowerment.* Routledge, 2000.

Holston, James. "Citizenship in Disjunctive Democracies." *Citizenship in Latin America*, edited by Joseph S. Tulchin and Meg Ruthenburg, Lynne Rienner, 2007, pp. 75–94.

———. *Insurgent Citizenship: Disjunctions of Democracy and Modernity in Brazil.* Princeton UP, 2008.

Holter, Øystein Gullvåg. "Social Theories for Researching Men and Masculinities: Direct Gender Hierarchy and Structural Inequality." *Handbook of Studies on Men and Masculinities*, edited by Michael S. Kimmel et al., Sage, 2005, pp. 15–34.

O Homem da Capa Preta. Directed by Sérgio Rezende, Embrafilme and Morena Film, 1986.

O Homem do Ano. Directed by José Henrique Fonseca, Film Movement, 2003.

hooks, bell. *Reel to Real: Race, Sex, and Class at the Movies.* Routledge, 1996.

———. *Teaching to Transgress: Education as the Practice of Freedom.* Routledge, 1994.

Hooper, Charlotte. *Manly States: Masculinities, International Relations, and Gender Politics.* Columbia UP, 2001.

"Ibope: Bolsonaro volta a crescer e vai a 31% enquanto Haddad vê rejeição disparar." *El País, Brasil,* 2 Oct. 2018.

Informe 2018. Latinobarómetro: Opinión Pública Latinoamericana, 2018.

O invasor. Directed by Beto Brant, Drama Filmes, 2001.

Johnson, Randal. *Cinema Novo x 5 : Masters of Contemporary Brazilian Film.* U of Texas P, 1984.

———. *The Film Industry in Brazil: Culture and the State.* U of Pittsburgh P, 1987.

Johnson, Randal, and Robert Stam. *Brazilian Cinema.* Columbia UP, 1995.

Kaiser, Anna Jean. "Woman Who Bolsonaro Insulted: 'Our President-Elect Encourages Rape.'" *The Guardian,* 23 Dec. 2018.

Khimm, Suzy. "'Zero Tolerance' Comes to Brazil: Rio Authorities Are Rolling Out a Crime-Fighting Plan That Mirrors Policies Rudy Giuliani Used in New York and Mexico City." *Christian Science Monitor,* 4 May 2006.

Kimmel, Michael S. *The Gendered Society.* Fourth edition, Oxford UP, 2011.

———. *Manhood in America: A Cultural History.* Third edition, Oxford UP, 2012.

———. "Masculinity as Homophobia." *Reconstructing Gender: A Multicultural Anthology,* edited by Estelle Disch, third edition, McGraw-Hill Education, 2004, pp. 103–9.

Kingstone, Peter R., and Timothy J. Power. "Introduction: Still Standing or Standing Still? The Brazilian Democratic Regime Since 1985." *Democratic Brazil: Actors, Institutions, and Processes,* edited by Kingstone and Power, U of Pittsburgh P, 2000, pp. 3–16.

———. "Introduction: A Fourth Decade of Brazilian Democracy/Achievements, Challenges, and Polarization." *Democratic Brazil Divided,* edited by Kingstone and Power, U of Pittsburgh P, 2017, pp. 3–30.

———. Introduction. *Democratic Brazil Revisited,* edited by Kingstone and Power, U of Pittsburgh P, 2008, pp. 1–14.

Koonings, Kees, and Dirk Kruijt. *Fractured Cities: Social Exclusion, Urban Violence, and Contested Spaces in Latin America.* Zed, 2007.

Kronsell, Annica. *Gender, Sex, and the Postnational Defense: Militarism and Peacekeeping.* Oxford UP, 2012.

Kruttschnitt, Candace. "Gender and Interpersonal Violence." *Understanding and Preventing Violence,* vol. 3, *Social Influences,* edited by Albert J. Reiss and Jeffrey A. Roth, National Academy, 1994, pp. 293–376.

Lally, Kevin. "Cruel City: Fernando Meirelles Directs Dazzling Tale of Rio's Slum Kids." *Film Journal International,* vol. 106, no. 1, 2003, pp. 22–24.

Leite, Julia, and David Biller. "Brazil's New Club Is All Boys and They're Running the Show." *Bloomberg,* 12 May 2016.

Lievesley, Geraldine, and Steve Ludlam. *Reclaiming Latin America: Experiments in Radical Social Democracy.* Zed, 2009.

Lifsher, Marc. "If He Can Fight Crime There, He'll Fight It . . . Anywhere: Bratton, of New York Cleanup, Works in South America." *Wall Street Journal,* 8 Mar. 2001.

Linha Direta Justiça. "O Bandido da Luz Vermelha." *Memória Globo,* 7 Dec. 2006.

Lins, Paulo. *Cidade de Deus: Romance.* Companhia das Letras, 1997.

"Listagem dos filmes brasileiros lançados comercialmente em salas de exibição 1995 a 2019." Observatório Brasileiro do Cinema e do Audiovisual / Agência Nacional do Cinema, 2021.

Lopes, Larissa. 'O Doutrinador': Anti-herói que luta contra a corrupção chega aos cinemas." *Galileu*, 1 Nov. 2018.

Lovell, Peggy A. "Gender, Race, and the Struggle for Social Justice in Brazil." *Latin American Perspectives*, vol. 27, no. 6, 2000, pp. 85–102.

Lúcio Flávio: O passageiro da agonia. Directed by Héctor Babenco, Embrafilme, 1977.

Lukes, Steven. *Power: A Radical View*. Second edition, Palgrave Macmillan, 2005.

Machado da Silva, Juremir. *Raízes do conservadorismo brasileiro: A abolição na imprensa e no imaginário social*. Civilização Brasileira, 2017.

Marshall, T. H. *Citizenship and Social Class: And Other Essays*. Cambridge UP, 1950.

Marson, Melina Izar. *Cinema e políticas de estado: Da Embrafilme à Ancine*. Escrituras, 2010.

Martin, Brett. *Difficult Men: Behind the Scenes of a Creative Revolution; from The Sopranos and The Wire to Mad Men and Breaking Bad*. Penguin, 2014.

Martín-Barbero, Jesús. *Communication, Culture and Hegemony: From the Media to Mediations*. Sage, 1993.

Martins Villaça, Mariana. "'América nuestra': Glauber Rocha e o cinema cubano." *Revista Brasileira de História*, vol. 22, no. 44, 2002, pp. 489–510.

Os matadores. Directed by Beto Brant, Istoé Novo Cinema, 1997.

Médici, Emílio Garrastazu. "Aula inaugural do Presidente Emílio G. Médici." Escola Superior de Guerra, Biblioteca General Cordeiro de Farias, document C1-123-70, 10 Mar. 1970, pp. 20–21.

Meirelles, Fernando. "Writing the Script, Finding and Preparing the Cast." *City of God in Several Voices: Brazilian Social Cinema as Action*, edited by Else Ribeiro Pires Vieira, Critical, Cultural, and Communications P, 2005, pp. 13–25.

Mesquita, Lígia. "Os últimos momentos de Marielle Franco antes de ser morta com quatro tiros na cabeça." BBC News Brasil, 15 Mar. 2018.

Messerschmidt, James W. *Crime as Structured Action: Doing Masculinities, Race, Class, Sexuality, and Crime*. Second edition, Roman and Littlefield, 2014.

———. *Masculinities and Crime: Critique and Reconceptualizaton of Theory*. Roman and Littlefield, 1993.

Miller, Toby. *Cultural Citizenship: Cosmopolitanism, Consumerism, and Television in a Neoliberal Age*. Temple UP, 2007.

Moritz Schwarcz, Lilia. *Sobre o autoritarismo brasileiro*. Companhia das Letras, 2019.

Mulvey, Laura. "Visual Pleasure and Narrative Cinema." *Film and Theory: An Anthology*, edited by Robert Stam and Toby Miller, Blackwell, 2000, pp. 483–94.

Muñoz Acebes, César. "Brazil Suffers Its Own Scourge of Police Brutality: Police Killings of Black Men Have Added to Suffering and Anger in the Middle of a Pandemic." *America Quarterly: Politics, Business, and Culture in the Americas*, 3 June 2020.

Murray, Joseph, et al. "Crime and Violence in Brazil: Systematic Review of Time Trends, Prevalence Rates, and Risk Factors." *Aggression and Violent Behavior*, vol. 18, no. 5, 2013, pp. 471–83.

Nagib, Lúcia. *Brazil on Screen: Cinema Novo, New Cinema, Utopia*. I. B. Tauris, 2007.

———. *The New Brazilian Cinema*. I. B. Tauris with U of Oxford Centre for Brazilian Studies, 2003.

———. "Talking Bullets: The Language of Violence in 'City of God.'" *Third Text*, vol. 18, no. 3, 2004, pp. 239–50.

Neale, Stephen. *Genre and Contemporary Hollywood*. British Film Institute, 2002.

———. "Prologue: Masculinity as Spectacle: Reflections on Men and Mainstream Cinema." *Screening the Male: Exploring Masculinities in Hollywood Cinema*, edited by Steve Cohen and Ina Rae Hark, Routledge, 1994, pp. 9–19.

Oliveira, Emanuelle. "An Ethic of the Esthetic? Racial Representation in Brazilian Cinema Today." *Vanderbilt e-Journal of Luso-Hispanic Studies*, vol. 4, 2008.

———. *Writing Identity: The Politics of Contemporary Afro-Brazilian Literature*. Purdue UP, 2008.

Oppenheimer, Jean. "Shooting the Real: Boys from Brazil." *City of God in Several Voices: Brazilian Social Cinema as Action*, edited by Else Ribeiro Pires Vieira, Critical, Cultural, and Communications P, 2005, pp. 26–31.

Paradis, Kenneth. *Sex, Paranoia, and Modern Masculinity*. State U of New York P, 2007.

Parker, Richard G. *Bodies, Pleasures, and Passions: Sexual Culture in Contemporary Brazil*. Second edition, Vanderbilt UP, 2009.

"Pelo menos 30 pessoas participaram de invasão à UnB, aponta investigação." *Congresso em Foco*, 24 June 2016.

Pessoa Cavalcanti, Roxana. "How Brazil's Far Right Became a Dominant Political Force." *The Conversation*, 25 Jan. 2017.

Peterson, Bill E., and Emily D. Gerstein. "Fighting and Flying: Archival Analysis of Threat, Authoritarianism, and the North American Comic Book." *Political Psychology*, vol. 26, no. 6, Dec. 2005, pp. 887–904.

"Polícia usa bombas de gás e balas de borracha em ação contra 'rolezinho.'" *G1 São Paulo*, 11 Jan. 2014.

Power, Timothy J., and Matthew M. Taylor. *Corruption and Democracy in Brazil: The Struggle for Accountability*. U of Notre Dame P, 2011.

Prado, Carol. "Mania das adaptações de HQs chega ao cinema brasileiro; conheça projetos." *G1 São Paulo*, 26 Oct. 2016.

Preto, Marcus. "Os 100 maiores discos da música brasileira." *Rolling Stone Brasil*, 9 Nov. 2007.

Quase Dois Irmãos. Directed by Lúcia Murat, First Run Features, 2004.

Rafter, Nicole Hahn. *Shots in the Mirror: Crime Films and Society*. Oxford UP, 2000.

Ratto, Casey. "Not Superhero Accessible: The Temporal Stickiness of Disability in Superhero Comics." *Disability Studies Quarterly*, vol. 37, no. 2, 2017.

Ray, Larry J. *Violence and Society*. Sage, 2011.

Reeser, Todd W. *Masculinities in Theory: An Introduction*. Wiley-Blackwell, 2010.

Reiter, Bernd, and Gladys L. Mitchell. "The New Politics of Race in Brazil." *Brazil's New Racial Politics*, edited by Bernd Reiter and Gladys L. Mitchell, Lynne Rienner, 2010.

Repo, Jemima. *The Biopolitics of Gender*. Oxford UP, 2015.

A república dos assassinos. Directed by Miguel Faria Jr., Roma Filmes do Brasil, 1979.

Resende, Leandro. "No Datena, Bolsonaro volta a falar sobre salário de mulheres e homens." *Folha de São Paulo*, 23 Apr. 2018.

Rocha, Simone Maria, and Ângela Salgueiro Marque. "'Bandido bom é bandido morto': Violência policial, tortura e execuções em *Tropa de Elite*." *Galáxia: Revista do Programa de Pós-Graduação em Comunicação e Semiótica*, no. 19, 2010, pp. 90–104.

Rodolfo, Luciano. "Criação, recriação e violência armada: Do romance 'O Matador' ao filme 'O Homem do Ano.'" *Conexão Letras*, vol. 5, no. 5, 2010, pp. 103–12.

Rodríguez, René. "The Gangs of Brazil's *Favelas*." *Hispanic*, vol. 16, no. 1/2, 2003, 66.

Rohter, Larry. "With New Chief, Uruguay Veers Left, in a Latin Pattern." *New York Times*, 1 Mar. 2005.

Rosaldo, Renato. "Citizenship and Educational Democracy." *Cultural Anthropology*, vol. 9, no. 3, 1994, pp. 402–11.

Rossi, Amanda, et al. "#EleNão: A manifestação histórica liderada por mulheres no Brasil vista por quatro ângulos." BBC Brasil and Época Negócios, 30 Sep. 2018.

Rotker, Susana, and Katherine Goldman. *Citizens of Fear: Urban Violence in Latin America*. Rutgers UP, 2002.

Round, Julia. "Naturalizing the Fantastic: Comics Archtypes." *Investigating Heroes: Essays on Truth, Justice, and Quality TV*, edited by David Simmons, McFarland, 2012, pp. 51–65.

Ruas, Carla, and Silvia Lisboa. "As Female Imprisonment in Brazil Skyrockets, a Heavy Burden Falls on the Women Left at Home." *The Intercept*, 8 Mar. 2018.

Sabo, Don. "Doing Time, Doing Masculinity: Sports and Prison." *Prison Masculinities*, edited by Sabo et al., Temple UP, 2001, pp. 61–66.

Sabo, Don, et al. Introduction. *Prison Masculinities*, edited by Sabo et al., Temple UP, 2001, pp. 3–18.

Santos, José Vicente Tavares dos. "Microfísica da violência, uma questão social mundial." *Ciência e Cultura*, vol. 54, no. 1, 2002, pp. 22–24.

Santos Silva, Elder Luan dos. "A ideologia de gênero' no Brasil: Conflitos, tensões e confusões terminológicas." *Periódicus: Revista de Estudos Interdisciplinares em Gêneros e Sexualidades*, vol. 1, no. 10, 2018, pp. 269–96.

Sartori, Giovanni. *Homo videns: La sociedad teledirigida*. Taurus, 1998.

Schraiber, L. B., et al. "Prevalência da violência contra a mulher por parceiro íntimo em regiões do Brasil." *Revista de Saúde Pública*, vol. 41, no. 5, 2007, pp. 797–807.

Sedgwick, Eve Kosofsky. *Between Men: English Literature and Male Homosocial Desire*. Columbia UP, 1985.

Segal, Lynne. *Slow Motion: Changing Masculinities, Changing Men*. Rutgers UP, 1990.

"Seguridad, justicia y paz: 50 Most Violent Cities 2015." Consejo Ciudadano para la Seguridad Pública y Justicia, 2015.

Senado Federal. "Pronunciamento de Amaral Peixoto." *Catálogo: Segurança pública, direitos humanos*, Publicação no. DCN2, 11 Sep. 1977, p. 6422.

Shaviro, Steven. *The Cinematic Body*. U of Minnesota P, 1993.

Shaw, Miranda. "The Brazilian *Goodfellas*: *City of God* as a Gangster Film?" *City of God in Several Voices: Brazilian Social Cinema as Action*, edited by Else Ribeiro Pires Vieira, Critical, Cultural, and Communications P, 2005, pp. 59–69.

Silva, Humberto Pereira da. *Glauber Rocha: Cinema, estética e revolução*. Paco, 2016.

Silverman, Kaja. *Male Subjectivity at the Margins*. Routledge, 1992.

———. *The Subject of Semiotics*. Oxford UP, 1983.

Siwi, Marcio. "City of God, City of Man." *SAIS Review*, vol. 23, no. 2, 2003, pp. 233–38.

Skidmore, Thomas E. *The Politics of Military Rule in Brazil, 1964–1985*. Oxford UP, 1988.

Soares, Danielle. "Poucos presos provisórios exercem o direito de voto." *Agência Brasil*, 4 Sep. 2014.

Soares, Luiz Eduardo, et al. *Criminalidade urbana e violência: O Rio de Janeiro no contexto internacional*. Third edition, Núcleo de Pesquisa, ISER, 1993.

Soares, Luiz Eduardo, et al. *Elite da tropa*. Objetiva, 2006.

Sobchack, Vivian Carol. *Carnal Thoughts: Embodiment and Moving Image Culture*. U of California P, 2004.

Souza Alves, José Cláudio. "Baixada Fluminense: A violência na construção do poder." Dissertation, Universidade de São Paulo, 1998.

Spanakos, Tony. "Super-Vigilantes and the Keene Act." *Watchmen and Philosophy: A Rorschach Test*, edited by Mark D. White, John Wiley and Sons, 2009, pp. 33–46.

Spence, Louise, and Vinicius Navarro. *Crafting Truth: Documentary Form and Meaning*. Rutgers UP, 2011.

Stam, Robert. *Tropical Multiculturalism: A Comparative History of Race in Brazilian Cinema and Culture*. Duke UP, 1997.

Starling, Heloísa Maria Murgel. "Ditadura militar." *Corrupção: Ensaios e críticas*, edited by Leonardo Avritzer, Editora UFMG, 2008, pp. 251–62.

Sternheim, Alfredo. *Cinema da boca: Dicionário de diretores*. Imprensa Oficial do Estado de São Paulo, Cultura, and Fundação Padre, 2005.

St-Georges, Charles. "Brazilian Horrors Past and Present: José Mojica Marins and Politics as Reproductive Futurism." *Journal of Latin American Cultural Studies*, vol. 25, 2016, pp. 555–70.

Subero, Gustavo. *Gender and Sexuality in Latin American Horror Cinema: Embodiments of Evil*. Palgrave Macmillan, 2016.

Theweleit, Klaus. *Male Fantasies*. U of Minnesota P, 1987.

Tiburi, Marcia. *Como conversar com um fascista: Reflexões sobre o cotidiano autoritário brasileiro*. Record, 2015.

———. *Como derrotar o turbotechnomachonazifascismo*. Record, 2020.

Tropa de Elite. Directed by José Padilha, Weinstein Home Entertainment, 2008.

Tropa de Elite II: O inimigo agora é outro. Directed by José Padilha, Globo Filmes / Feijão Filmes / Riofilme, 2011.

Truffaut, François. *Hitchcock*. With collaboration of Helen G. Scott, Simon and Schuster, 1967.

Valle, Sabrina, and David Biller. "Dare to Wear Red in Brazil as Crisis Widens Public Fury." *Bloomberg*, 30 Mar. 2016.

Vargas, João Costa, and Jaime Amparo Alves. "Geographies of Death: An Intersectional Analysis of Police Lethality and the Racialized Regimes of Citizenship in São Paulo." *Ethnic and Racial Studies*, vol. 33, no. 4, 2009, pp. 611–36.

Ventura, Zuenir. *Cidade partida*. Companhia das Letras, 1994.

Vidal, Germano Seidl. "Projeção dos valores espirituais e morais na atuação das forças armadas brasileiras." *Leitura selecionada*, 6 Dec. 1967, Escola Superior de Guerra, 1971, 11, Biblioteca General Cordeiro de Farias, LS7-123-71, pp. 28–31.

Vigna, Anne. "Violência legalizada." Pública: Agência de Reportagem e Jornalismo Investigativo, 10 Dec. 2014.

Villarejo, Amy. "Cities of Walls: Mediated Urbanity, Viral Circulation, and *Elite Squad*." *Literatur Inter- und Transmedial / Inter- and Transmedial Literature*, edited by David Bathrick and Heinz-Peter Preußer, Brill / Rodopi, 2012, pp. 419–30.

Viñas, Silvia. "Latin Women Take the Helm." *World Policy Journal*, vol. 31, no. 1, 2014, pp. 39–47.

Wacquant, Loïc. *Body and Soul: Notebooks of an Apprentice Boxer.* Oxford UP, 2004.

———. "A Concise Genealogy and Anatomy of Habitus." *The Sociological Review*, vol. 64, 2016, pp. 64–72.

———. "The Militarization of Urban Marginality: Lessons from the Brazilian Metropolis." *International Political Sociology*, vol. 2, no. 1, 2008, pp. 56–74.

———. *Prisons of Poverty.* Expanded edition, U of Minnesota P, 2009.

———. "Toward a Dictatorship over the Poor? Notes on the Penalization of Poverty in Brazil." *Punishment and Society*, vol. 5, no. 2, 2003, pp. 197–205.

Waiselfisz, Júlio Jacobo. *Mapa da violência 2013: Homicídios e juventude no Brasil.* Centro Brasileiro de Estudos Latino-Americanos (CEBELA) / Faculdade Latino-Americana de Ciências Sociais (FLACSO), 2013.

———. *Mapa da violência 2015: Homicídio de mulheres no Brasil.* Faculdade Latino-Americana de Ciências Sociais (FLACSO), 2015.

———. *Mapa da violência 2015: Mortes matadas por armas de fogo.* Secretaria-Geral da Presidência da República, Secretaria Nacional de Juventude, Secretaria de Políticas de Promoção da Igualdade Racial, 2015.

Wall, Illan rua. *Human Rights and Constituent Power: Without Model or Warranty.* Routledge, 2013.

Watts, Jonathan. "Brazil: Hundreds of Thousands of Protesters Call for Rousseff Impeachment." *The Guardian*, 15 Mar. 2015.

Weintraub, Bernard. "Twins' Movie-Making Vision: Fighting Violence with Violence." *New York Times*, 11 Nov. 1993.

Whitehead, Stephen. *Men and Masculinities: Key Themes and New Directions.* Polity, 2002.

Wieland, Christina. *The Fascist State of Mind and the Manufacturing of Masculinity: A Psychoanalytic Approach.* Routledge, 2015.

Willis, Graham Denyer. *The Killing Consensus: Police, Organized Crime, and the Regulation of Life and Crime in Urban Brazil.* U of California P, 2015.

"Women in National Parliaments." Inter-Parliamentary Union, 1 Feb. 2019.

"World Report 2020." Human Rights Watch, 2020.

Xavier, Ismail. *Allegories of Underdevelopment: Aesthetics and Politics in Modern Brazilian Cinema.* U of Minnesota P, 1997.

Zaluar, Alba, and Isabel Siqueira Conceição. "Favelas sob o controle das milícias no Rio de Janeiro: Que paz?" *São Paulo em Perspectiva*, vol. 21, no. 2, 2007, pp. 89–101.

INDEX

JEREMY LEHNEN is director of the Center for Language Studies, director of the Brazil Initiative, and senior lecturer in Portuguese and Brazilian studies and in language studies at Brown University.

Digital Satire in Latin America: Online Video Humor as Hybrid Alternative Media, by
    Paul Alonso (2024)
Periodicals in Latin America: Interdisciplinary Approaches to Serialized Print Culture,
    edited by Maria Chiara D'Argenio and Claire Lindsay (2025)